Welcome to Thailand

Thailand is blessed: exotic and mysterious yet approachable and hospitable, it has the looks and personality to entice the world to its shores.

Bangkok, the kingdom's capital, is an adrenalin rush. The pace is fast, the spaces cramped and the sights and smells dizzying. It is disorienting but addictive for urban junkies. In contrast, the tranquil southern coast will soothe modern nerves. The waters are clear, the diving is spectacular and the pace is oh-so sleepy. Thailand's famous islands and beaches specialise in fun, from beach parties to casual dining. Along the Andaman Coast dramatic limestone mountains cluster like prehistoric monuments.

Beyond the beach scene, Thailand's culture trail educates and enlightens. Intense displays of religious devotion and tangible history unfold in Bangkok, the seat of religion and monarchy. Further north, the ancient capitals of Ayuthaya and Sukhothai are peppered with gravity-ravaged ruins and serene Buddha figures. Northern Thailand is lush mountains, historic cities and border intrigue. The gateway to the region, Chiang Mai, has a well-preserved old city and university atmosphere. In higher altitudes, minority hill tribes cling to a distinct cultural identity.

In every corner of the kingdom, Thais concoct flavourful feasts from simple ingredients. Travelling from region to region becomes an edible buffet, from fresh coconut curries in southern Thailand to steamy bowls of noodles in Bangkok and hearty stews in Chiang Mai.

Beyond the beach scene, Thailand's culture trail educates and enlightens.

Traditional Thai dancers
ATLANTIDE PHOTOTRAVEL/GETTY IMAGES ©

Plan Your Trip
Thailand's Top 12

PRACHANART/GETTY IMAGES ©

Bangkok
Bangkok has it all in super-sized portions

This high-energy city (p35) loves neon and noise, chaos and concrete, fashion and the future. But look beyond the modern behemoth and you'll find an old-fashioned village napping in the shade of a narrow soi (lane). Zip around town in the sleek, elevated BTS; watch the sun sink into the muddy Chao Phraya River on a commuter ferry; or get stuck in one of the city's famous traffic jams. Then reward your adventurousness with top-notch pampering.

Wat Phra Kaew (p38), Bangkok

NUKORN PLANPAN/GETTY IMAGES ©

Ayuthaya

Once great capital packed with temples

Ayuthaya (p81) was once Siam's vibrant, glittering capital packed with temples. It has been ravaged by war and gravity but the brick-and-stucco ruins, which form a Unesco World Heritage site, can be visited on a cycling tour that evokes their history and artistic legacy. Ayuthaya is an easy day trip from Bangkok or an alternative landing pad for city phobics. Wat Chai Wattanaram (p85)

Sukhothai

Crumbling temple ruins and picturesque countryside

Step back in time about 800 years at Thailand's most impressive historical park (p95). Explore the ruins by bicycle, winding past crumbling temples, graceful Buddha statues and fish-filled ponds. Worthwhile museums and good-value accommodation round out the package. Despite its popularity, Sukhothai rarely feels crowded, and nearby Si Satchanalai-Chaliang Historical Park attracts only a few history adventurers willing to scale ancient stairways. Wat Si Chum (p101)

Chiang Mai
The cultural capital of the north

Chiang Mai (p111) is a cultural darling wearing its Lanna heritage with pride. Its old walled city is crowded with temples dating to the days of the teak boom. Bookshops and ethnic-chic shops outnumber glitzy shopping centres. The dining scene celebrates the fresh and local produce of the region and flirts only casually with flashy trends. Great country escapes are just an hour's journey outside the city. Nowhere else in Thailand has such a delightful mixture of big city attractions with a provincial pace. Wat Chedi Luang (p115)

Chiang Rai
Ethnic diversity and dramatic mountain scenery

Thailand, Laos and Myanmar converge in what was formerly a remote and lawless area known as the Golden Triangle, the centre of opium poppy cultivation. Little border intrigue persists, now that there are roads, and modern farming has replaced the illicit trade. The tidy provincial capital of Chiang Rai (p143) serves as a logical base for visits to minority tribes. Chiang Rai's hill-tribe treks often have a social justice mission to help villages meet the demands of cultural autonomy.

GLEN ALLISON/GETTY IMAGES ©

Nong Khai

Riverside border town with friendly, laid-back charms

Representing the hardworking northeast, Nong Khai (p157) is not
a usual stop on a quick country tour. But it is worth the effort for
its pretty Mekong River setting and laid-back provincial charms. A
curious sculpture garden shelters an astounding collection of avant
garde art. The riverside market displays its Lao heritage and visitors
spend the rest of their visit cycling around town, past chickens,
school children and tropical fruit gardens. Statues at Sala Kaew Ku (p160)

Hua Hin

City and sea escape fit for royalty

The king's choice, Hua Hin (p167) is a fine fit for city and sea creatures within striking distance of Bangkok. The beaches are long and wide, the market meals are fantastic and there's even Thai culture. Explore the quiet beaches south of the city for a more secluded feel, hike to the top of a headland shrine or master the sea and wind with a kiteboarding lesson. In between seaside frolicking you can feast like Thai royalty from morning to night.

7

Ko Samui

Synonymous with sun, fun and comfort

Eager to please, Ko Samui (p181) is a civilised resort island for the vacationing masses, many of whom fly in and out without much cultural exchange. Chaweng is a luxurious stretch of sand where sun-worshippers come to see and be seen; but beyond the brassy beaches are reminders of Samui's old moniker, 'Coconut Island,' and a few gentle coves for families. Samui also boasts a thriving health scene with yoga, massage, detoxing and other yins to the island's partying yang. Right: Lamai beach (p184)

STRIEL/GETTY IMAGES ©

JOHN HARPER/GETTY IMAGES ©

KIMBERLEY COOLE/GETTY IMAGES ©

9

Ko Pha-Ngan

Party hard, or take it easy

Famous for its sloppy Full Moon parties, Ko Pha-Ngan (p197) has graduated from a sleepy bohemian island to a stop on the party-people circuit. In between the lunar festivities, it still excels in laid-back island life accessible to everybody. Backpackers can still find rustic, kick-back spots, just like the old days. And comfort seekers are attracted by Ko Pha-Ngan as an alternative to too-comfortable Ko Samui. Divers will be rewarded with easy access to some of the Gulf of Thailand's best dives sites. Far left: Chalok Lam (p206); left: vendors at a Full Moon party, Hat Rin (p200)

JOHN HARPER/GETTY IMAGES ©

Phuket

The ultimate laid-back beach escape

An international resort, Phuket (p211) is an easy-peasy destination. You can fly in from Bangkok, cutting out the long land journey, and retreat into a five-star resort or arty boutique hotel for a trouble-free tropical vacation. There are slinky stretches of sand, hedonistic party pits and all the mod cons needed for 21st-century rest and recreation. Mix it up with day trips to mangrove forests, water sports and monkey-rescue centres. Hat Kata (p215)

JAMES MORGAN/GETTY IMAGES ©

Railay

Dramatic karst towers are the main event

You'd never know that you were still on the mainland when you wade from a long-tail boat to the shore of this limestone-studded peninsula (p237). Towering karst peaks hem in all sides, creating the illusion of a rocky fortress. Rock-climbers have transformed the cliffs into vertical challenges, while kayakers and snorkellers take to the sea to explore low-tide caves and peek at the marine life sheltered by these hulking missile-shaped islands.

VIJKR69J/GETTY IMAGES ©

Ko Phi-Phi

The darling of the Andaman coast

The prettiest island in all of Thailand, Ko Phi-Phi (p245) has gorgeous blonde-sand beaches, scenic limestone cliffs and jewel-toned waters. It's a car-free and carefree island where the parties last all night and sound systems serenade the stars. Don't come looking for serenity. Its sister island Ko Phi-Phi Leh is an uninhabited park with coral reefs and interior lagoons. And, of late, party boats sail among the scenery, tipple in hand. Ao Maya (p251)

Plan Your Trip
Need to Know

When to Go

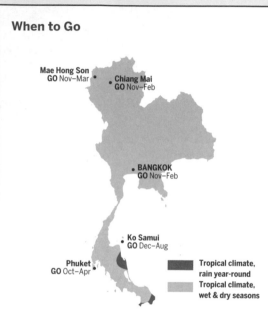

Mae Hong Son
GO Nov–Mar

Chiang Mai
GO Nov–Feb

BANGKOK
GO Nov–Feb

Ko Samui
GO Dec–Aug

Phuket
GO Oct–Apr

■ Tropical climate, rain year-round
■ Tropical climate, wet & dry seasons

High Season (Nov–Mar)

○ A cool and dry season follows the monsoons.

○ Christmas and New Year's holidays bring crowds and inflated rates.

Shoulder Season (Apr–Jun, Sep & Oct)

○ April–June is very hot and dry. Coastal areas get natural sea-breeze air-con.

○ September and October are ideal for the north and the gulf coast.

Low Season (Jul–Oct)

○ Monsoon season ranges from afternoon showers to major flooding.

○ Some islands shut down; boat service is limited during stormy weather.

○ Rain is usually in short, intense bursts.

Currency
Thai baht (B)

Language
Thai

Visas
International air arrivals receive a 30-day visa.

Money
ATMs are widespread and charge a 150B to 180B foreign-account fee; Visa and Master-Card accepted at most hotels and high-end restaurants but not at family-owned businesses.

Mobile Phones
Thailand is on a GSM network through inexpensive prepaid SIM cards; 4G is in urban areas.

Time
GMT plus seven hours.

Daily Costs

Budget: Less than 1000B

- Basic guesthouse room: 400–1000B
- Market/street stall meal: 40–100B
- One beer: 100B
- Public transport: 20–50B

Midrange: 1000–3000B

- Midrange hotel room: 1000–3000B
- Seafood dinner: 350B
- Organised tour or activity: 1000–1500B
- Motorbike hire: 150-250B

Top End: More than 3000B

- Boutique hotel room: 3000B
- Fine dining: 350–500B
- Private tour: 2000B
- Car hire: from 800B

Useful Websites

Bangkok Post (www.bangkokpost.com) English-language daily.
Lonely Planet (www.lonelyplanet.com/thailand) Country profile and what to do and see.
Thaivisa (www.thaivisa.com) Expat site for news and discussions.
Tourism Authority of Thailand (TAT; www.tourismthailand.org) National tourism department covering info and special events.

Opening Hours

All government offices and banks are closed on public holidays. Bars and clubs close during elections and certain religious holidays.
Banks 9.30am–3.30pm Monday to Friday; ATMs accessible 24 hours

Bars & clubs Open until midnight or 1am; 'entertainment zones' until 2am
Government offices 8.30am–4.30pm Monday to Friday
Restaurants 10am–8pm or 9pm
Stores 10am–7pm; shopping centres until 10pm

Arriving in Thailand

Suvarnabhumi International Airport (Bangkok) Taxis cost 220B to 380B plus tolls and 50B airport surcharge. An Airport Rail Link also provides service.
Chiang Mai International Airport Taxis are a flat 120B.
Phuket International Airport Buses and minivans run to Phuket Town (100–150B) and beaches (180B). Metered taxis cost 550B.

Getting Around

Air Domestic routes from Bangkok are plentiful.

Bus Intercity buses are convenient; purchase tickets at bus stations to avoid unscrupulous agents.

Hired transport Bangkok has metered taxis; elsewhere túk-túk and motorcycle taxis have negotiated fares. Motorcycles and cars are easily rented.

Public transport Bangkok has an extensive public transit system. Elsewhere sŏrng·tăa·ou (converted pick-up trucks) on fixed routes.

Train Slow but scenic.

For more on **getting around**, see p308 ➡

Plan Your Trip
Hotspots for...

Beaches

Bliss out on a tropical beach surrounded by jewel-coloured waters and brooding jungle-clad mountains.

Historic Sites

Follow the cultural trail through the historic capitals, evolving art and architecture and regional identities.

Thai Food

Zesty dishes of fresh spices and ingredients with a spicy sting from chillies make Thai food one of the globe's most beloved cuisines.

Shopping

An unofficial national pastime, shopping unfolds in exuberant street markets and high-end malls.

Ko Pha-Ngan
Master the art of hammock-hanging, rave till dawn during the lunar parties, or dive with the fishes and whale sharks.

Highlights
Full Moon parties and secluded east coast beaches.

Ko Samui
Quick and easy beach escape with gorgeous beaches, seaside yoga and loads of people-watching.

Highlights
Beach hopping and visiting island villages.

Phuket
International resort offering relaxation and adventure including watersports and day trips to mangrove forests.

Highlights
Andaman limestone scenery and Phuket Town (p226).

Sukhothai
Cycle among the ruins of an early Thai kingdom for a meditative journey into the past.

Top Site
Sukhothai Historical Park (p98)

Ayuthaya
Tumbledown temples of a former ancient capital now surrounded by a busy provincial town.

Top Site
Ayuthaya Historical Park (p84)

Chiang Mai
Teak treasures stand testament to the artistic legacy of the old Lanna kingdom.

Top Site
Old city temples and Wat Phra That Doi Suthep (p126).

Bangkok
A culinary superstar covering all the bases: humble noodles, haute cuisine and immigrant comfort food.

Best Dish
Máh hór, a citrus salad, served at nahm (p74).

Chiang Mai
This northern town excels in vegetarian cuisine and Thai cooking courses.

Best Dish
Any vegetarian dish at Pun Pun (p137).

Hua Hin
Thai-Chinese and southern seafood dishes eclipse the sea as an attraction for holidaying appetites.

Best Dish
Crab curry at Hua Hin's Night Market (p172).

Bangkok
From markets to malls, you can practically shop anywhere for just about anything.

Best Spot
Chatuchak, the mother of all markets (p50).

Chiang Mai
Homespun and chic handicrafts serve second fiddle to the fun-fair-like atmosphere of its outdoor markets.

Best Spots
Saturday (p120) and Sunday Walking Streets (p121).

Chiang Rai
The night markets and weekend bazaar peddle hill-tribe and northern crafts.

Best Spot
Saturday Walking Street (p153) for handicrafts.

Plan Your Trip
Local Life

PETER PTSCHELINZEW/GETTY IMAGES ©

Activities

Ko Pha-Ngan Swim with whale sharks and other big fish on a certificate or fun dive. Sail Rock and Chumphon Pinnacle are the Gulf of Thailand's premier dive spots.

Ko Phi-Phi Southern Andaman dive sites have colourful coral reefs, wrecks, pinnacles and loads of marine life.

Chiang Mai Hike to mountain villages, see elephant herds, raft down frothy rivers and zipline through the forest like a gibbon.

Railay Adrenalin junkies scale the limestone crags while kayakers take to the open water to inspect these rocky monuments.

Shopping

Bangkok Get a serious retail workout in the capital's mega-malls packed with designer gear and unique gifts and home decor. Then flex your shopping muscles in Chatuchak Weekend Market and other outdoor markets.

Chiang Mai The bustling Night Bazaar is filled with souvenirs and antiques. Boutique stores provide economic development opportunities for rural villagers and their handicrafts, such as silk textiles and basketry. And the weekend Walking Streets are retail amusement.

Nong Khai The beautiful Lao-influenced weaving traditions of *mát·mèe* can be found in this sleepy northeastern town.

Entertainment

Local festivals Traditional music and dance are performed in colourful street parades during local festivals in Chiang Mai, Chiang Rai and Nong Khai. These street parades are some of the best displays of the cultural arts.

Bangkok Sing and dance with the music-lovers of Bangkok at intimate clubs. See Thai boxing champions spar at the country's premier stadiums. Visit the cultural institutions for performances of traditional dance-dramas.

Chiang Mai Catch an open-mic night, jazz jam sessions and Thai folk music at cosy live music clubs.

Eating

Curries Each region whips up its own variation of this pungent, fiery and colourful dish.

Isan cuisine The northeast's triumvirate dishes – grilled chicken, spicy green papaya salad and sticky rice – have converts across the country.

Seafood Grilled prawns, crab curries – get thee to the coast and dine on the fruits of the sea.

Fruits Sweet-as-candy fruits are plucked from pyramid displays at markets or like precious jewels in glass-cased carts.

Cooking courses Learn the tricks of the trade in the cooking schools of Bangkok, Phuket or Chiang Mai.

Drinking & Nightlife

Bangkok International DJs spin the capital's clubs while cocktails flow from the city's sky bars. Thanon Khao San remains the backpacker favourite.

Phuket Clubs, live music bars and cabaret shows ensure there's plenty of post-beach action.

Ko Pha-Ngan Home of the Full Moon Party, whisky buckets and almighty hangovers nursed with lazy days on the beach.

Chiang Mai Hip uni students, boho NGOs and a prevailing artistic sensibility merges in big beer garden bars to toast the night way.

From left: Night market in Chiang Mai (p120); Sky Bar (p53), Bangkok

Plan Your Trip
Month by Month

January

The weather is cool and dry, ushering in the peak tourist season.

✷ Chinese New Year

Thais with Chinese ancestry celebrate the Chinese lunar new year *(drùt jeen)* with a week of house-cleaning and fireworks.

February

Still in the high season, snowbirds flock to Thailand for sun and fun.

✷ Makha Bucha

One of three holy days marking significant moments of Buddha's life, Makha Bucha *(mah·ká boo·chah)* commemorates the day when 1250 *arhants* (Buddhists who had achieved enlightenment) assembled to visit Buddha and received Buddhist principles. The festival falls on the full moon of the third lunar month. It's a public holiday.

✷ Flower Festival

Chiang Mai displays its floral beauty during a three-day period. The festival highlight is the flower-decorated floats that parade through town.

March

Hot and dry season approaches and the beaches start to empty out. This is also Thailand's semester break, and students head out on sightseeing trips.

✷ Kite-Flying Festivals

During the windy season, colourful kites battle it out over the skies of Sanam Luang in Bangkok and elsewhere in the country.

✷ Golden Mango Season

Luscious ripe mangoes come into season from March to June and are sliced before your eyes, packed in a container with sticky rice and accompanied with a sweet sauce.

TOPTEN22PHOTO/GETTY IMAGES ©

April

Hot, dry weather sweeps across the land. Although the tourist season is winding down, make reservations well in advance as the whole country is on the move for Songkran.

🌀 Songkran

Thailand's traditional new year (13–15 April) starts out as a respectful affair then devolves into a water war. Morning visits to the temple involve water-sprinkling ceremonies. After-wards, Thais load up their water guns and head out to the streets for battle. Chiang Mai and Bangkok are the theatres of war.

🌀 Poy Sang Long

This Buddhist ordination festival is held in late March/early April in Chiang Mai. Young Shan boys are paraded in festive costumes.

May

Leading up to the rainy season, festivals encourage plentiful rains and bountiful har-vests. Prices are low and tourists are few; it is still incredibly hot.

★ Best Festivals

Loi Krathong p24

Songkran p23

Vegetarian Festival p24

Rocket Festival p23

Flower Festival p22

🌀 Royal Ploughing Ceremony

This royal ceremony employs astrology and ancient Brahman rituals to kick off the rice-planting season. Sacred oxen are hitched to a wooden plough and part the ground of Sanam Luang in Bangkok.

🌀 Rocket Festival

In the northeast, where rain can be scarce, villagers craft bamboo rockets (*bâng fai*) that are fired into the sky to encourage precipitation. This festival is celebrated in Nong Khai.

From left: Chinese New Year celebration, Bangkok; Bamboo rockets on sale during the Rocket Festival

❸ Visakha Bucha

The holy day of Visakha Bucha (*wí·săh·kà boo·chah*) falls on the 15th day of the waxing moon in the sixth lunar month and commemorates the date of the Buddha's birth, enlightenment and *parinibbana* (passing away).

June

In some parts of the country, the rainy season is merely an afternoon shower, leaving the rest of the day for music and merriment. This month is a shoulder season.

❸ Hua Hin Jazz Festival

Jazz groups descend on this royal retreat for a musical homage to the king.

July

The start of the rainy season ushers in Buddhist Lent, a period of reflection and meditation. Summer holidays bring an upsurge in tourists.

❸ Asanha Bucha

The full moon of the eighth lunar month commemorates Buddha's first sermon, in which he described the religion's four noble truths. It is considered one of Buddhism's holiest days.

❸ Khao Phansaa

The day after Asanha Bucha marks the beginning of Buddhist Lent (the first day of the waning moon in the eighth lunar month), the traditional time for men to enter the monastery.

August

Overcast skies and daily showers mark the middle of the rainy season.

❸ HM the Queen's Birthday

The Thai Queen's Birthday (12 August) is a public holiday and national Mother's Day.

October

Religious preparations for the end of the rainy season and the end of Buddhist Lent begin. The monsoons are reaching the finish line (in most of the country).

❸ Vegetarian Festival

A holiday from meat is taken for nine days in adherence with Chinese beliefs of mind and body purification. In Phuket the festival gets extreme, with entranced marchers becoming human shish kebabs.

❸ Ork Phansaa

The end of the Buddhist lent (three lunar months after Khao Phansaa) is followed by the *gà·tĭn* ceremony, in which new robes are given to the monks by merit-makers. In Nong Khai and other river towns, long-boat races are held and Nong Khai's Mekong Fireball Festival.

❸ King Chulalongkorn Day

Rama V is honoured on the anniversary of his death (23 October) at Bangkok's Royal Plaza in Dusit.

November

The cool, dry season has arrived, and if you get here early enough, you'll beat the tourist crowds. The beaches are inviting and the landscape is lush.

❸ Loi Krathong

One of Thailand's most beloved festivals, Loi Krathong is celebrated on the first full moon of the 12th lunar month. Small origami-like boats (called *krathong* or *grà·tong*) festooned with flowers and candles are sent adrift in the waterways. Northern Thais call this festival Yi Peng, which is celebrated with illuminated floating lanterns.

December

The peak of the tourist season has returned with fair skies, busy beach resorts and a holiday mood.

❸ HM the King's Birthday

Honouring the King's birthday on 5 December, this public holiday hosts parades and merit-making events. It's also national Father's Day.

Plan Your Trip
Get Inspired

Above: Ko Phi-Phi (p245)

Read

Very Thai: Everyday Popular Culture (Philip Cornwel-Smith) Colourful compendium of the kingdom's whys and whats.

Fieldwork (Mischa Berlinski) A story about a fictional hill-tribe village in northern Thailand.

Sightseeing (Rattawut Lapcharoensap) Short fiction stories about Thai life.

The Beach (Alex Garland) The discovery of a secret backpacker utopia.

King Bhumibol Adulyadej: A Life's Work (Nicholas Grossman et al) Official biography of the king.

The Judgement (Chart Korbjitti) Award-winning novel about a village man wrongly accused of a crime.

Watch

Paradoxocracy (Pen-Ek Ratanaruang; 2013) Traces the country's political history from the 1932 revolution to today.

36 (Nawapol Thamrongrattanarit; 2012) Indie love affair remembered through 36 static camera set-ups.

Pee Mak Phra Khanong (Banjong Pisanthanakun; 2013) Perennial ghost story gets a comedy makeover.

Fah Talai Jone (Tears of the Black Tiger; 2000) Wisit Sasanatieng pays tribute to Thai action flicks.

Last Life in the Universe (Ruang Rak Noi Nid Mahasan; 2003) Directed by Pen-Ek Ratanaruang; unfurls a dark tale of two lost souls.

Listen

That Song (Modern Dog) Anthemic alt-rock.

Best (Pumpuang Duangjan) The best from the late country diva.

Boomerang (Bird Thongchai) Beloved album from the king of Thai pop.

Romantic Comedy (Apartment Khunpa) Leading post alt-rock.

The Sound of Siam: Leftfield Luk Thung, Jazz & Molam in Thailand 1964–1975 Compilation of vintage tunes.

Made in Thailand (Carabao) Thailand's classic classic-rock album.

Plan Your Trip
Five-Day Itineraries

Bangkok to Chiang Mai

Touch down in Bangkok, jet to Chiang Mai and escape the urban grind with an outing in the mountainous countryside.

2 Chiang Mai (p111) Visit the Old City, stroll the fashionable Th Nimmanhaemin, or visit an elephant sanctuary. 🚗 4 - 6 hrs to Mae Sa Valley

3 Mae Sa Valley (p134) Enjoy high altitude scenery while lunching on the edge of a mountain ridge. Frolic in Nam Tok Mae Sa waterfall.

1 Bangkok (p35) Explore the dynamic capital's dazzling temples and upscale restaurants, then shop till you drop, before kicking back at a rooftop bar.
✈ 1 hr to Chiang Mai

FROM LEFT: SEAN PAVONE/GETTY IMAGES ©, NIKADA/GETTY IMAGES ©

1 Bangkok (p35) Escape the urban mayhem, sightseeing historic temples along the river or visiting the Taling Chan Floating Market.
🚌 2½ hrs to Hua Hin

Bangkok to Hua Hin

Sample a little of everything – culture, nature, beaches and seafood – on this quick and convenient tour within a half-day's journey of Bangkok.

2 Phetchaburi (p174) Mix in a little cultural sightseeing at Phetchaburi's royal summer palaces.
🚗🚌 1½ hrs to Hua Hin

3 Hua Hin (p167) Enjoy the ocean, lively seafood markets and restaurants, and a vineyard in the tropics.

FROM LEFT: COMZEAL/GETTY IMAGES ©; ILARI LEHTINEN/GETTY IMAGES ©

Plan Your Trip
10-Day Itinerary

Ko Samui to Railay

Soak up the tropical scenery by surveying the beaches and islands of Thailand's famous coasts: the Gulf of Thailand and the Andaman Sea.

2 Ko Pha-Ngan (p197) At full moon this relaxed island transforms into a party werewolf. 🚢 3 hrs to Surat Thani, then 🚍 2½ hrs o Krabi, then 🚢 45 mins to Railay

1 Ko Samui (p181) Fly into paradise and hit the beaches, or head offshore to the limestone crags of Ang Thong Marine National Park.
🚢 20 - 60 mins to Ko Pha-Ngan

3 Railay (p237) It's worth the journey here to enjoy the stunning karst mountains jutting out of jewel-coloured seas; kayak amongst them or strap on a harness to climb the cliffs.

Plan Your Trip
Two-Week Itinerary

Ayuthaya to Chiang Rai

Follow the culture trail from the ancient capital of Ayuthaya to the Lanna headquarters of Chiang Mai and on to Chiang Rai.

5 Mae Salong (p149) An ethnic Chinese community perched on the spine of a mountain; an easy day trip (or overnighter).

4 Chiang Rai (p143) Visit Wat Rong Khun, peruse the Night Bazaar for hill-tribe crafts, and take an NGO-led trekking tour over three or four days.
🚌 transfer to sŏrng·tăa·ou 1½ hrs to Mae Salong

3 Chiang Mai (p111) Leave three or more days for wandering around old city temples, handicraft shops or fashionable Th Nimmanhaemin.
🚌 3 - 4 hrs to Chiang Rai

2 Sukhothai (p95) Spend two days in Sukothai visiting the Sukhothai Historical Park and the Si Satchanalai-Chaliang Historical Park.
🚌 6 hrs to Chiang Mai

1 Ayuthaya (p81) Balance out Bangkok's conspicuous consumption with a two-day cultural tour in the Unesco World Heritage–listed Ayuthaya Historical Park.
🚌 7hrs to Sukhothai

Plan Your Trip
Family Travel

Thais are so family focused that even grumpy taxi drivers want to pinch your baby's cheeks and play a game of peekaboo (called *já ǎir*). On crowded buses, adults will stand so that children can sit, and hotel and restaurant staff willingly set aside chores to become a child's playmate.

Sights & Activities

Children will especially enjoy the beaches, as most are in gentle bays good for beginner swimmers. For the more experienced, some of the Gulf and Andaman islands have near-shore reefs for snorkelling. Some beaches have strong currents and riptides, especially during the monsoon season.

Crocodile farms, monkey shows and tiger zoos abound in Thailand, but conditions are inhumane. Eco-tour projects in Chiang Mai provide a better alternative. The elephant sanctuaries are excellent places to see the revered pachyderm in a dignified setting. Older children will enjoy jungle tours and other outdoor activities. Many of the beach resorts, such as Phuket, also have waterfall spotting and water sports.

In urban areas, kids might feel cooped up, in which case a hotel swimming pool will provide necessary play space. Playgrounds are neither widespread nor well maintained, though every city has an exercise park where runners and families go in the early evening. Though Bangkok is lean on green, it is still fun for little ones in awe of construction sites and for older ones obsessed with shopping malls. If you're worried about long-distance journeys with a fussy passenger, opt for the train. Kids can walk around the carriage and visit the friendly locals; they are assigned the lower sleeping berths which have views of the stations and dust-kicking motorcycles.

Kid-Friendly Eats

In general, Thai children don't start eating spicy food until primary school; before then they seemingly survive on rice and junk food. Child-friendly meals include chicken in all of its nonspicy permutations – *gài yâhng* (grilled chicken), *gài tôrt* (fried chicken) and *gài pàt mét má·môo·ang* (chicken stir-fried with cashews).

Some kids will even branch out to *kôw pàt* (fried rice), though the strong odour of *nám plah* (fish sauce) might be a deal breaker. Helpful restaurant staff will recommend *kài jee·o* (Thai-style omelette), which can be made in a jiffy. If all else fails, tropical fruits and juices are ubiquitous and will keep the kids hydrated. Of course, most tourist centres also have Western restaurants catering to homesick eaters of any age.

Need to Know

Changing facilities Non-existent.

Cots By special request at midrange and top-end hotels.

Highchairs Sometimes available in resort areas.

Nappies (diapers) Minimarkets and 7-Elevens carry small sizes; try Tesco Lotus or Tops Market for size 3 or larger.

Strollers Bring a compact umbrella stroller.

Transport Car seats and seat belts are not widely available on public or hired transport.

Best Destinations for Kids

Ko Samui p181

Hua Hin p167

Ko Pha-Ngan p197

Health & Safety

For the most part, parents needn't worry too much about health concerns. It's a good idea to drink lots of water. Regular hand washing should be enforced. Children should be warned not to play with animals as rabies does occur and some pets (not to mention wild monkeys) may be aggressive.

Dengue is an increasing concern in Thailand and parents should take care to prevent mosquito bites (a difficult task) in children. See p299 for more information.

From left: Chiang Mai; fried rice with seafood

BANGKOK

Bangkok

Formerly the epitome of the steamy Asian metropolis, Bangkok has undergone decades worth of renovations and emerged an international starlet. The Bangkok of today is tidier and easier to navigate than ever before and will impress with awesome urban exploration, dining and nightlife. Supplement your fun with scholarly pursuits such as historic sightseeing and cooking courses. Come here for temples, palaces, malls, restaurants, nightclubs – all super-sized.

Two Days in Bangkok

Take the **Chao Phraya Express Boat** (p78) to explore the temples of **Ko Ratanakosin** (p38), followed by lunch in **Banglamphu**. Stick around for some shopping and imbibing on **Th Khao San**. On the next day visit **Jim Thompson House** (p48) and wrap up the daylight hours with a Thai massage. Visit a rooftop bar for cocktails, followed by an upscale Thai dinner at **nahm** (p74).

Four Days in Bangkok

Spend a day at **Chatuchak Weekend Market** (p50), enrol in a cooking class, or jump aboard a **long-tail boat** (p47) to explore Thonburi's canals. Hit Chinatown for a street-food dinner. Escape Bangkok's chaos with a visit to **Dusit Palace Park** (p68). Splash out at one of Sukhumvit's international restaurants and then hang out with Bangkok's hipsters at Sukhumvit's bars and clubs.

Ko Ratanakosin & Banglamphu
Buddhist temples and royal palaces; leafy lanes; antique shop-houses and buzzing wet markets

CHAO PHRAYA RIVER

Chinatown
Bird's-nest restaurants; gold and jade shops; flashing neon signs in Chinese characters

CHATUCHAK WEEKEND MARKET

Sukhumvit
Japanese enclaves, burger restaurants, Middle Eastern nightlife zones, 'sexpat' haunts

JIM THOMPSON HOUSE

Siam Square
Open-air shopping zone; ground zero for teenage culture in Bangkok; great place to pick up labels and designs not found elsewhere

Silom & Riverside
Palpable history in the riverside's crumbling architecture; Silom is frenetic and modern

WAT PHO

WAT PHRA KAEW & GRAND PALACE

Ko Ratanakosin, Banglamphu & Chinatown (p62)
Siam Square, Silom & Riverside (p64)
Sukhumvit (p66)

Street market, Th Khao San

Arriving in Bangkok

Suvarnabhumi International Airport
The Airport Rail Link (45B, 30 minutes) operates from 6am to midnight. Meter taxis cost 200B to 300B, plus 50B airport surcharge and expressway tolls.

Don Mueang International Airport
Meter taxis cost 200B to 500B plus 50B airport surcharge.

Where to Stay

Bangkok is home to a diverse spread of modern hostels, guesthouses and hotels. To make matters better, much of Bangkok's accommodation offers excellent value, and competition is so intense that fat discounts are almost always available.

For more information on the best neighbourhood to stay in, see p79.

PHOTO BY PRASIT CHANSAREEKORN/GETTY IMAGES ©

Wat Phra Kaew & Grand Palace

Wat Phra Kaew (Temple of the Emerald Buddha) is architecturally fantastic and the spiritual core of Thai Buddhism and the monarchy, symbolically united in what is the country's most holy image, the Emerald Buddha.

Great For...

☑ **Don't Miss**

The **Ramakian Murals** depict the *Ramakian* (the Thai version of the Indian *Ramayana* epic) in its entirety.

Wat Phra Kaew

Wat Phra Kaew gleams and glitters with so much colour and glory that its earthly foundations seem barely able to resist the celestial pull. Attached to the temple complex is the former royal residence, once a sealed city of intricate ritual and social stratification, although most of it is off-limits to visitors.

The ground was consecrated in 1782, the first year of Bangkok rule, and is today Bangkok's biggest tourist attraction and a pilgrimage destination for devout Buddhists and nationalists. The 94.5-hectare grounds encompass more than 100 buildings that represent 200 years of royal history and architectural experimentation. Wat Phra Kaew and the Grand Palace are best reached either by a short walk south from Banglamphu, via Sanam Luang, or by Chao Phraya Express Boat to Chang Pier

Yaksha (guardian giant)

RMNUNES/GETTY IMAGES ©

❶ Need to Know

Wat Phra Kaew & Grand Palace (วัดพระ
แก้ว, พระบรมมหาราชวัง; Map p62; Th Na Phra
Lan; admission 500B; ⊙8.30am-3.30pm;
⊠Chang Pier, Maharaj Pier, Phra Chan Tai
Pier)

✕ Take a Break

Pa Aew (p70) is a basic, open-air curry
stall but it's one of our favourite places
to eat in this part of town.

★ Top Tip

Guides can be hired at the ticket kiosk;
ignore anyone outside. An audio guide
can be rented for 200B for two hours.

or Maharaj Pier. From the Siam Sq area (in
front of the MBK Center, Th Phra Ram I),
take bus 47.

Ramakian Murals

Outside the main *bòht* (ordination hall) is a
stone statue of the Chinese goddess of mercy,
Kuan Im. In the 2km-long cloister that defines
the perimeter of the complex are 178 murals
depicting the *Ramakian* (the Thai version
of the Indian *Ramayana* epic) in its entirety,
beginning at the north gate and moving
clockwise around the compound. If the temple
grounds seem overrun by tourists, the mural
area is usually mercifully quiet and shady.

Emerald Buddha

Upon entering Wat Phra Kaew you'll meet
the *yaksha*, brawny guardian giants from
the *Ramakian*. Beyond them is a courtyard

where the central *bòht* houses the Emerald
Buddha. The spectacular ornamentation
inside and out does an excellent job of
distracting first-time visitors from paying
their respects to the image. Here's why: the
Emerald Buddha is only 66cm tall and sits
so high above worshippers in the main temple building that the gilded shrine is more
striking than the small figure it cradles. No
one knows exactly where it comes from
or who sculpted it, but it first appeared
on record in 15th-century Chiang Rai (in
northern Thailand). Photography inside the
bòht is not permitted.

Grand Palace

Adjoining Wat Phra Kaew is the Grand
Palace (Phra Borom Maharatchawang), a
former royal residence that is today only
used on ceremonial occasions. Visitors
can survey a portion of the Grand Palace
grounds, but are allowed to enter only one
of the remaining palace buildings.

Wat Phra Kaew & Grand Palace

EXPLORE BANGKOK'S PREMIER MONUMENTS TO RELIGION AND REGENCY

The first area tourists enter is the Buddhist temple compound generally referred to as Wat Phra Kaew. A covered walkway surrounds the area, the inner walls of which are decorated with the **murals of the _Ramakian_** **1** and **2**. Originally painted during the reign of Rama I (r 1782–1809), the murals, which depict the Hindu epic the _Ramayana_, span 178 panels that describe the struggles of Rama to rescue his kidnapped wife, Sita.

After taking in the story, pass through one of the gateways guarded by **_yaksha_** **3** to the inner compound. The most important structure here is the **_bòht,_ or ordination hall** **4**, which houses the **Emerald Buddha** **5**.

ALINA_ZIENEA / GETTY IMAGES ©

Kinaree
These graceful half-swan, half-women creatures from Hindu-Buddhist mythology stand outside Prasat Phra Thep Bidon.

Amarindra Hall

Borombhiman Hall

Prasat Phra Thep Bidon

Phra Si Ratana

The Murals of the _Ramakian_
These wall paintings, which begin at the eastern side of Wat Phra Kaew, often depict scenes more reminiscent of 19th-century Thailand than of ancient India.

ANTONIO D'ALBORE / GETTY IMAGES ©

Hanuman
Rows of these mischievous monkey deities from Hindu mythology appear to support the lower levels of two small _chedi_ near Prasat Phra Thep Bidon.

Head east to the so-called Upper Terrace, an elevated area home to the **spires of the three primary *chedi*** ⑥. The middle structure, Phra Mondop, is used to house Buddhist manuscripts. This area is also home to several of Wat Phra Kaew's noteworthy mythical beings, including beckoning *kinaree* ⑦ and several grimacing **Hanuman** ⑧.

Proceed through the western gate to the compound known as the Grand Palace. Few of the buildings here are open to the public. The most noteworthy structure is **Chakri Mahaprasat** ⑨. Built in 1882, the exterior of the hall is a unique blend of Western and traditional Thai architecture.

The Three Spires
The elaborate seven-tiered roof of Phra Mondop, the Khmer-style peak of Prasat Phra Thep Bidon, and the gilded Phra Si Ratana *chedi* are the tallest structures in the compound.

Emerald Buddha
Despite the name, this diminutive statue (it's only 66cm tall) is actually carved from nephrite, a type of jade.

The Death of Thotsakan
The panels progress clockwise, culminating at the western edge of the compound with the death of Thotsakan, Sita's kidnapper, and his elaborate funeral procession.

Chakri Mahaprasat
This structure is sometimes referred to as *fà·ràng sài chá·dah* (Westerner in a Thai crown) because each wing is topped by a *mon·dòp*: a spire representing a Thai adaptation of a Hindu shrine.

Dusit Hall

Bòht
(Ordination Hall)
This structure is an early example of the Ratanakosin school of architecture, which combines traditional stylistic holdovers from Ayuthaya along with more modern touches from China and the West.

Yaksha
Each entrance to the Wat Phra Kaew compound is watched over by a pair of vigilant and enormous *yaksha*, ogres or giants from Hindu mythology.

Reclining Buddha

NOA199/GETTY IMAGES ©

Wat Pho

Of all Bangkok's temples, Wat Pho is arguably the one most worth visiting, for both its remarkable Reclining Buddha image and its sprawling, stupa-studded grounds. The temple compound houses the oldest and largest wát in Bangkok and the largest collection of Buddha images in Thailand.

Great For...

☑ **Don't Miss**

The Reclining Buddha, the granite statues and the massage pavilions.

Reclining Buddha

In the northwest corner of the site you'll find Wat Pho's main attraction, the enormous Reclining Buddha. The figure was originally commissioned by Rama III (King Phranangklao; r 1824–51), and illustrates the passing of the Buddha into nirvana. It is made of plaster around a brick core and finished in gold leaf, which gives it a serene luminescence that keeps you looking, and looking again, from different angles.

Phra Ubosot

Phra Ubosot, the compound's main ordination hall or *bòht,* is constructed in Ayuthaya style and is strikingly more subdued than Wat Phra Kaew's. A temple has stood on this site since the 16th century, but in 1781 Rama I ordered the original Wat Photharam to be completely rebuilt as part of his new capital.

Monks at Wat Pho

SHAUN EGAN/GETTY IMAGES ©

ⓘ Need to Know

Wat Pho (วัดโพธิ์/วัดพระเชตุพน, Wat Phra Chetuphon; Map p62; Th Sanam Chai; admission 100B; ☺8.30am-6.30pm; 🚢Tien Pier)

✗ Take a Break

Sip a cocktail at Amorosa (p53), while enjoying views of the river and Wat Arun.

★ Top Tip

Enter via Th Chetuphon or Th Sanam Chai to avoid the touts and tour groups at the main entrance on Th Thai Wang.

Rama I's remains are interred in the base of the presiding Buddha figure in Phra Ubosot. The images on display in the four *wí·hǎhn* (sanctuaries) surrounding Phra Ubosot are worth investigation, as is a low marble wall with 152 bas-reliefs depicting scenes from the *Ramakian*. You'll recognise some of these figures when you exit the temple past the hawkers with mass-produced rubbings for sale: these are made from cement casts based on Wat Pho's reliefs.

Royal Chedi

On the western side of the grounds is a collection of four towering tiled *chedi* (stupa) commemorating the first four Chakri kings. The surrounding wall was built on the orders of Rama IV (King Mongkut; r 1851–68), who for reasons we can only speculate about decided he didn't want any future kings joining the memorial. Among the compound's additional 91 smaller *chedi* are clusters containing the ashes of lesser royal descendants.

Massage Pavilions

A small pavilion west of Phra Ubosot has Unesco-awarded inscriptions detailing the tenets of traditional Thai massage. These and other similar inscriptions led Wat Pho to be regarded as Thailand's first university. Today it maintains that tradition as the national headquarters for the teaching and preservation of traditional Thai medicine, including Thai massage. The famous school has two massage pavilions (p66) located within the temple area and additional rooms within the training facility (p66) outside the temple.

Gardens

Small Chinese-style rock gardens and hill islands interrupt the compound's numerous tiled courtyards providing shade, greenery and quirky decorations depicting daily life. Keep an eye out for the distinctive rockery festooned with figures of the hermit Khao Mor – who is credited with inventing yoga – in various healing positions.

Wat Pho

A WALK THROUGH THE BIG BUDDHAS OF WAT PHO

The logical starting place is the main *wí·hǎhn* (sanctuary), home to Wat Pho's centrepiece, the immense **Reclining Buddha ❶**. Apart from its huge size, note the **mother-of-pearl inlays ❷** on the soles of the statue's feet. The interior walls of the *wí·hǎhn* are covered with murals depicting previous lives of the Buddha, and along the south side of the structure are 108 bronze monk bowls; for 20B you can buy 108 coins, each of which is dropped in a bowl for good luck.

Exit the *wí·hǎhn* and head east via the two **stone giants ❸** who guard the gateway to the rest of the compound. Directly south of these are the four towering **royal *chedi* ❹**.

Continue east, passing through two consecutive **galleries of Buddha**

Southern *wí·hǎhn*

Buddha Galleries
The two series of covered hallways that surround the Phra Ubosot feature no fewer than 394 gilded Buddha images, many of which display classic Ayuthaya or Sukhothai features.

Phra Ubosot
Built during the reign of Rama I, the imposing *bòht* (ordination hall) as it stands today is the result of renovations dating back to the reign of Rama III (r 1824–51).

Eastern *wí·hǎhn*

Massage Pavilions
If you're hot and footsore, the two air-conditioned massage pavilions are a welcome way to cool down while experiencing high-quality and relatively inexpensive Thai massage.

❽

❻

❼

Phra Buddha Deva Patimakorn
On an impressive three-tiered pedestal that also holds the ashes of Rama I is this Ayuthaya-era Buddha statue originally brought to the temple by the monarch.

Northern *wí·hǎhn*

Western *wí·hǎhn*

states **5** linking four *wí·hǎhn*, two of which contain notable Sukhothai-era Buddha statues; these comprise the exterior of **Phra Ubosot 6**, the immense ordination hall that is Wat Pho's second-most noteworthy structure. The base of the building is surrounded by bas-relief inscriptions, and inside is the notable Buddha statue, **Phra Buddha Deva Patimakorn 7**.

Wat Pho is often referred to as Thailand's first university, a tradition that continues today in an associated traditional Thai medicine school and, at the compound's eastern extent, two **massage pavilions 8**.

Interspersed throughout the eastern half of the compound are several additional minor *chedi* and rock gardens.

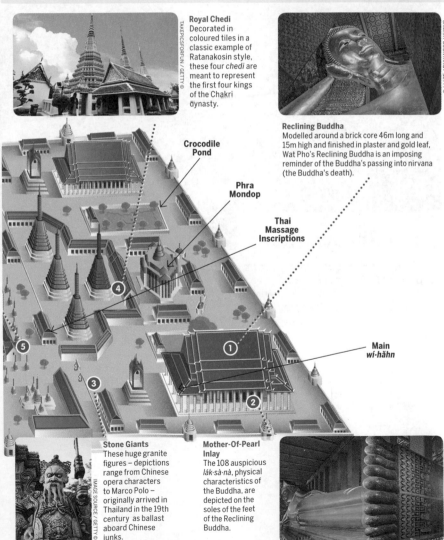

Royal Chedi
Decorated in coloured tiles in a classic example of Ratanakosin style, these four *chedi* are meant to represent the first four kings of the Chakri dynasty.

Reclining Buddha
Modelled around a brick core 46m long and 15m high and finished in plaster and gold leaf, Wat Pho's Reclining Buddha is an imposing reminder of the Buddha's passing into nirvana (the Buddha's death).

Crocodile Pond

Phra Mondop

Thai Massage Inscriptions

Main *wí·hǎhn*

Stone Giants
These huge granite figures – depictions range from Chinese opera characters to Marco Polo – originally arrived in Thailand in the 19th century as ballast aboard Chinese junks.

Mother-Of-Pearl Inlay
The 108 auspicious *lák·sà·nà*, physical characteristics of the Buddha, are depicted on the soles of the feet of the Reclining Buddha.

Chao Phraya River, with Wat Arun in the background

Chao Phraya River

The River of Kings is the symbolic lifeblood of the Thai nation. Revered riverside temples stand sentry as boats and barges industriously move cargo and passengers, and cool breezes provide evening refreshment.

Great For...

☑ Don't Miss

Catch the Chao Phraya Express Boat as the sun sets across this throbbing metropolis.

Wat Arun

Claiming a powerful riverside position, **Wat Arun** (วัดอรุณฯ; Map p62; www.watarun.net; off Th Arun Amarin; admission 50B; ⊘8am-6pm; ⛴cross-river ferry from Tien Pier) marks the rebirth of the Thai nation after the fall of Ayuthaya to the invading Burmese army in the 1700s. The temple's facade is decorated with delicate porcelain mosaics, a common temple adornment from the days when Chinese porcelain was used for ship ballasts.

Thonburi's Canals

Bangkok's past as the Venice of the East lives, bathes and plays along Thonburi's network of canals, including Khlong Bangkok Noi and Khlong Mon. Traditional homes are built on stilts with front doors leading to the water.

Taling Chan Floating Market

KAREN MASSIER/GETTY IMAGES ©

❶ Need to Know

Tour the river and riverside attractions aboard chartered long-tail boats (1½ to two hours, 1300-1500B) or the Chao Phraya Express commuter boats.

✕ Take a Break

Make a dinner date with the river at **Khinlom Chom Sa-Phan** (Map p62; ☑02 628 8382; www.khinlomchomsaphan. com; 11/6 Soi 3, Th Samsen; mains 95-2500B; ⊙11.30am-midnight; 🚢Thewet Pier).

★ Top Tip

Women shouldn't sit in the last seats on the commuter boats; these are reserved for monks.

Royal Barges National Museum

Travel by boat used to be a majestic affair. Historic vessels dating back to the Ayuthaya period are on display at the **Royal Barges National Museum** (พิพิธภัณฑสถาน แห่งชาติ เรือพระราชพิธี/เรือพระที่นั่ง; Map p62; Khlong Bangkok Noi or 80/1 Th Arun Amarin; admission 100B, camera 100B; ⊙9am-5pm; 🚢Phra Pin Klao Bridge Pier). *Suphannahong* (the king's personal barge) is bestowed with a huge swan head carved into the bow. Lesser barges feature bows that are carved into other Hindu-Buddhist mythological shapes such as the *naga* (mythical sea serpent) and *garuda* (Vishnu's bird mount).

Floating Market

The nearly extinct floating markets (*dà·làht nám*) have been rescued by nostalgic Thais and tourists. **Taling Chan Floating Market**

(ตลาดน้ำตลิ่งชัน; Khlong Bangkok Noi, Thonburi; ⊙7am-4pm Sat & Sun; ⑤Wongwian Yai exit 3 & taxi), located along Khlong Bangkok Noi, is a hybrid market with fruit vendors on the road and floating docks serving as informal dining rooms. Meals are prepared aboard tethered canoes.

Ko Kret

An easy rural getaway, Ko Kret is a car-free island and home to the Mon people, known for their hand-thrown terracotta pots. Locals flock to Ko Kret on weekends to snack and shop. Ko Kret is in Nonthaburi, about 15km north of central Bangkok. Take bus 166 from the Victory Monument or a taxi to Pak Kret, before boarding the cross-river ferry (2B, from 5am to 9pm) that leaves from Wat Sanam Neua.

Interior of Jim Thompson House

Jim Thompson House

The former home of an American silk entrepreneur is a beautiful repository for Thai art and architecture. On display are museum-quality examples of Thai craftsmanship, Buddhist sculpture and textiles.

Great For...

☑ **Don't Miss**

Wandering the lushly landscaped grounds.

A socialite and former spy, Jim Thompson's life is as intriguing as his belongings. He served briefly in the Office of Strategic Services (the forerunner to the CIA) in Thailand during WWII. Settling in Bangkok after the war, he established a successful Thai silk export business, introducing the textile to international fashion houses. He mysteriously disappeared in 1967 while out for a walk in Malaysia's Cameron Highlands. His disappearance was never explained and some suspect foul play.

Art

A collector with eclectic tastes, Thompson bought art and antiques from travelling merchants and neighbouring countries. He collected objects that were not well known at the time, including from the Dvaravati period.

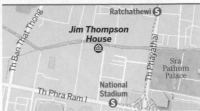

❶ Need to Know

(Map p64; www.jimthompsonhouse.com; 6 Soi Kasem San 2; adult/student 150/100B; ⏱9am-6pm, compulsory tours every 20 min; 🚤klorng boat to Sapan Hua Chang Pier, 🅂National Stadium exit 1)

✕ Take a Break

MBK Food Island (Map p64; 6th fl, MBK Center, cnr Th Phra Ram I & Th Phayathai; mains 35-150B; ⏱10am-10pm; ❄🖉; 🅂National Stadium exit 4) is a quintessential mall food court selling Thai and international dishes.

★ Top Tip

Read *The Ideal Man* by Joshua Kurlantzick for a profile of Jim Thompson.

Architecture

As an architect, Thompson was drawn to traditional Thai houses instead of the modern, Western-style homes popular at the time. He collected six teak houses from different regions in the country as a showcase for his art collection. Some of the houses were brought from Ayuthaya, while others were transported across the canal from Baan Khrua. The homes were given a landscaped jungle garden to further highlight Thailand's natural beauty. The home, however, is organised like a Western residence with an entrance hall and all rooms arranged on the same level overlooking the terrace and the canal.

Baan Khrua

Just across the canal is the silk-weaving community of **Baan Khrua** (บ้านครัว; Map p64; 🚤klorng boat to Sapan Hua Chang Pier,

🅂Ratchathewi exit 1, National Stadium exit 1). This neighborhood was settled by Cham Muslims from Cambodia and Vietnam, who relocated to Bangkok after fighting on the side of the Thai king during the wars of the end of the 18th century. Their silk-weaving skills attracted the attention of Jim Thompson in the 1950s and '60s when he hired the weavers for his burgeoning silk export business. Since then commercial silk production and many of the original families have moved elsewhere, but two family-run outfits, **Phamai Baan Krua** (Map p64; www.phamaibaankrua.com; Soi 9, Soi Phaya Nak; ⏱8.30am-5pm; 🚤klorng boat to Sapan Hua Chang Pier, 🅂Ratchathewi exit 1, National Stadium exit 1) and **Aood Bankrua Thai Silk** (Map p64; 📞02 215 9864; Soi 9, Soi Phaya Nak; ⏱9am-8pm; 🚤klorng boat to Sapan Hua Chang Pier, 🅂Ratchathewi exit 1, National Stadium exit 1), continue the tradition. Baan Khrua can be reached by the bridge over the canal at the end of Soi Kasem San 3.

Stalls selling arts and crafts

MADDOG99/SHUTTERSTOCK ©

Chatuchak Weekend Market

An outdoor market on steroids, Chatuchak Weekend Market sells everything under the sun. Vendors are packed into claustrophobic warrens. It is crowded and chaotic but one-of-a-kind.

Great For...

☑ **Don't Miss**

If you aren't in town on the weekend, visit **Or Tor Kor Market** (องค์กรตลาดเพื่อ เกษตรกร; Map p64; Th Kamphaengphet 1; ⊙8am-6pm; Ⓜ Kamphaeng Phet exit 3), a huge fruit and vegetable market.

A little pre-planning goes a long way. Nancy Chandler's *Map of Bangkok* has a handy schematic map and the clock tower provides an essential landmark.

Antiques, Handicrafts & Souvenirs

Section 1 is the place to go for Buddha statues, old LPs and other random antiques. More secular arts and crafts, such as musical instruments and hill-tribe items, can be found in Sections 25 and 26.

Clothing & Accesories

Clothing dominates most of Chatuchak, starting in Section 8 and continuing through the even-numbered sections to 24. Sections 5 and 6 deal in used clothing for every youth subculture, from punks to cowboys, while Soi 7, where it transects

Thai bracelets

MICHAEL LUHRENBERG/GETTY IMAGES ©

Th Kamphaengphet

Th Kamphaengphet 2

Chatuchak
Weekend
Market

Chatuchak
Park ⑤ Mo Chit

Ⓜ Chatuchak
Park

Kamphaeng
Phet

Th Phahonyothin

Th Kamphaengphet 1 Ⓜ

ⓘ Need to Know

Chatuchak Weekend Market (ตลาด
นัดจตุจักร, Talat Nat Jatujak; Map p64; www.
chatuchak.org; Th Phahonyothin; ⓧ9am-6pm
Sat & Sun; ⓜChatuchak Park exit 1, Kamphaeng Phet exits 1 & 2, ⓢMo Chit exit 1)

✕ Take a Break

Sections 6 and 8 have food and drink
vendors, a necessary antidote to
Chatuchak fatigue.

★ Top Tip

Come early to beat the crowds and
the heat. Or check out the low-key
Friday nights (8pm to midnight) for
clothing and live music.

Sections 12 and 14, is heavy on hip-hop and
skate fashions. More sophisticated independent labels can be found in Sections
2 and 3, while tourist-sized clothes and
textiles are in Sections 8 and 10.

Housewares & Decor

The western edge of the market, particularly Sections 8 to 26, specialises in
housewares, from cheap plastic buckets
to expensive brass woks. This area is a
particularly good place to stock up on
inexpensive Thai ceramics, ranging from
celadon to the traditional rooster-themed
bowls from Lampang. For less utilitarian
goods, Section 7 is a virtual open-air gallery
with stalls selling Bangkok-themed murals
and other unique art work. Burmese lacquerware can be found in Section 10, while
Section 26 has dusty collections of real and
reproduction antiques from Thailand and
Myanmar.

Eating & Drinking

Lots of Thai-style eating and snacking will
stave off Chatuchak rage, and numerous
food stalls set up shop between Sections
6 and 8. Long-standing favourites include
Foontalop, a popular Isan restaurant; Café
Ice, a Western-Thai fusion joint that does
good, if overpriced, *pàt tai* (fried noodles)
and tasty fruit shakes; Toh-Plue, which does
all the Thai standards; and Saman Islam, a
Thai-Muslim restaurant that serves a tasty
chicken biryani. Viva 8 features a DJ and,
when we stopped by, a chef making huge
platters of paella. And as evening draws
near, down a beer at Viva's, a cafe-bar that
features live music.

Sky Bar

VISIONS OF OUR LAND/GETTY IMAGES ©

Bangkok Nightlife

Bangkok wins all the awards in the nightlife category, embracing every party trend invented, from sweaty bars and sophisticated clubs to late-night dance parties.

Great For ...

☑ **Don't Miss**

Toasting the stars from a rooftop bar.

Bars

Bangkok's watering holes range from bare-bones beer gardens with plastic chairs to chic cocktail dens. Backpackers and young Thais congregate in Th Khao San. Romantic evenings can be found at riverside restaurants or rooftop bars. Th Sukhumvit has an eclectic collection of expats and hipster Thais. Only the rooftop bars enforce a dress code: no shorts or sandals.

○ **WTF** (Map p66; www.wtfbangkok.com; 7 Soi 51, Th Sukhumvit; ⊘6pm-1am Tue-Sun; 🕿; ⑤Thong Lo exit 3) A sophisticated yet friendly local boozer.

○ **Hippie de Bar** (Map p62; www.facebook.com/hippie.debar; 46 Th Khao San; ⊘3pm-2am; 🚤Phra Athit/Banglamphu Pier) This is a fun, retro-themed bar in the middle of Th Khao San.

Clubs

Bangkok's club scene is fickle, and venues that were pulling in thousands a night last year might be just a vague memory this year. Clubs also tend to heave on certain nights – Friday and Saturday, during a visit from a foreign DJ, or for a night dedicated to the music flavour of the month – then hibernate every other night.

The streets that extend from Th Sukhumvit are home to many of Bangkok's most popular clubs. Ravers of uni age tend to head to Soi 63/Ekamai, while the pampered elite play at Soi 55/Thong Lor, and expats, sexpats and tourists head to the clubs around Soi 11.

○ Route 66 (www.route66club.com; 29/33-48 RCA/Royal City Ave; admission 300B; ◷8pm-2am; Ⓜ Phra Ram 9 exit 3 & taxi) Long-standing megaclub.

○ Arena 10 (Map p66; Soi Thong Lor 10/Soi Ekamai 5; Ⓢ Ekkamai exit 2 & taxi) The current club queen.

Live Music

Bangkok is the music capital of a musically inclined country. The city has a thriving indie music scene and a cover band for every genre, especially reggae.

Banglamphu is home to Bangkok's greatest concentration of live music bars. The western stretch of Th Phra Athit in particular is home to half a dozen back-to-back, pint-sized music pubs that offer

○ Moon Bar (Map p64; www.banyantree.com/en/web/banyantree/ap-thailand-bangkok/vertigo-and-moon-bar; 61st fl, Banyan Tree Hotel, 21/100 Th Sathon Tai/South; ◷5pm-1am; Ⓜ Lumphini exit 2) Stunning views make this our fave of Bangkok rooftop bars.

○ Sky Bar (Map p64; www.lebua.com/sky-bar; 63rd fl, State Tower, 1055 Th Silom; ◷6pm-1am; ⛴ Sathon/Central Pier, Ⓢ Saphan Taksin exit 3) Go on, order a 'hangovertini' at this movie star rooftop bar.

○ Amorosa (Map p62; www.arunresidence.com; rooftop, Arun Residence, 36-38 Soi Pratu Nokyung; ◷5pm-midnight Mon-Thu, to 1am Fri-Sun; ⛴ Tien Pier) Sip the splendour of old Bangkok from this rooftop cocktail bar.

○ Smalls (Map p64; 186/3 Soi Suan Phlu; ◷8.30pm-late; Ⓜ Lumphini exit 2 & taxi) Cheeky new bar that feels like an old favourite.

lots of loud Thai pop, but not a whole lot of breathing room. Others are outside of central Bangkok.

○ **Brick Bar** (Map p62; www.brickbarkhao san.com; basement, Buddy Lodge, 265 Th Khao San; admission Sat & Sun 150B; ☺8pm-1.30am; 🛳Phra Athit/Banglamphu Pier) Live-music den, famous among locals for dancing on the tables.

○ **Ad Here the 13th** (Map p62; www.face book.com/adhere13thbluesbar; 13 Th Samsen; ☺6pm-midnight; 🛳Phra Athit/Banglamphu Pier) A Bangkok blues veteran.

○ **Brown Sugar** (Map p62; www.brownsugar bangkok.com; 469 Th Phra Sumen; ☺5pm-1am Tue-Thu, to 2am Sat & Sun; 🛳klorng boat to Phanfa Leelard Pier, Phra Athit/Banglamphu Pier) A jazz matron with a new home in Banglamphu.

○ **Living Room** (Map p66; ☎02 649 8888; www.thelivingroomatbangkok.com/en; Level 1, Sheraton Grande Sukhumvit, 250 Th Sukhumvit; ☺6pm-midnight; Ⓜ Sukhumvit exit 3, Ⓢ Asok exit 2) As the name implies, live jazz in a comfortable setting.

○ **Raintree** (Map p64; Soi Ruam Chit; ☺6pm-1am Mon-Sat; Ⓢ Victory Monument exit 2) Thai folk music in a rustic 'country' bar.

○ **Parking Toys' Watt** (Map p66; www.face book.com/Wattparkingtoys; 164 Soi Sun Wichai 14; ☺6pm-2am; Ⓢ Ekkamai exit 4 & taxi) Quirky live music spot.

After-Hours Spots

Speakeasies have sprung up all over the city, so follow the crowds. Here are a few reliable night owls.

Th Khao San

○ **Wong's Place** (Map p64; 27/3 Soi Si Bamphen; ⊘9pm-late Tue-Sun; Ⓜ️Lumphini exit 1) Open from midnight until the last punter crawls out.

○ **The Bank** (Map p62; 3rd fl, 44 Th Chakraphatdi Phong; ⊘6pm-late; 🚢Phra Athit/Banglamphu Pier) Puff on *shisha* or dance into the wee hours on Th Khao San.

○ **Narz** (Map p66; www.narzclubbangkok.net; 112 Soi 23; admission from 400B; ⊘9pm-2am;

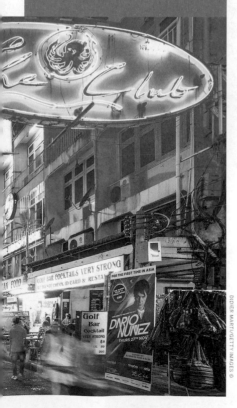

DIDIER MARTI/GETTY IMAGES ©

Ⓜ️Sukhumvit exit 2, Ⓢ️Asok exit 3) Clubbers rave 'til dawn.

○ **Levels** (Map p66; www.levelsclub.com; 6th fl, Aloft, 35 Soi 11, Th Sukhumvit; admission 500B; ⊘9pm-late; Ⓢ️Nana exit 3) Soi 11 late-night spot.

LGBT Scene

Bangkok has a notoriously pink vibe to it. Unlike elsewhere in Southeast Asia, homosexuality is not criminalised in Thailand and the general attitude remains extremely laissez-faire.

○ **Telephone Pub** (Map p64; www.telephone pub.com; 114/11-13 Soi 4, Th Silom; ⊘6pm-1am; 📞; Ⓜ️Si Lom exit 2, Ⓢ️Sala Daeng exit 1) An old favourite in Bangkok's pinkest zone.

○ **Balcony** (Map p64; www.balconypub.com; 86-88 Soi 4, Th Silom; ⊘5.30pm-2am; 📞; Ⓜ️Si Lom exit 2, Ⓢ️Sala Daeng exit 1) Streetside watering hole.

○ **Maggie Choo's** (Map p64; www.facebook. com/maggiechoos; basement, Novotel Bangkok Fenix Silom, 320 Th Silom; ⊘7.30pm-2am Sun-Thu, to 3am Fri & Sat; Ⓢ️Surasak exit 1) Sunday is gay day.

○ **DJ Station** (Map p64; www.dj-station.com; 8/6-8 Soi 2, Th Silom; admission from 150B; ⊘10pm-2am; Ⓜ️Si Lom exit 2, Ⓢ️Sala Daeng exit 1) Bangkok's most popular gay club.

○ **G Bangkok** (Guys on Display; Map p64; Soi 2/1, Th Silom; admission 300B; ⊘11pm-late; Ⓜ️Si Lom exit 2, Ⓢ️Sala Daeng exit 1) Where to go after-hours in Silom.

○ **Castro** (Map p66; www.facebook.com/Castro. rca.bangkok; RCA/Royal City Ave; admission 200B; ⊘9.30pm-2am; Ⓜ️Phra Ram 9 exit 3 & taxi) The only gay destination in RCA.

Egg noodle soup with wontons

QUYNH ANH NGUYEN/GETTY IMAGES ©

Culinary Bangkok

Nowhere else is the Thai reverence for food more evident than in Bangkok. Life appears to be a never-ending meal with a little bit of work and commuting thrown into the mix. For more Eating options, see p69.

Great For ...

☑ **Don't Miss**

You don't need a restaurant and linens to have a fine meal in this city. Bangkok foodies adore several famous street vendors.

Dining Scene

All of Thailand's culinary traditions converge in Bangkok. Simple market meals fuel the working class and transform the sidewalk into a communal dining room. High-end makeovers of Thai classics and royal recipes define the fine-dining scene. Mum-and-pop restaurants anchor a neighborhood, be it an immigrant community from Arabia or from southern Thailand.

Bangkok's Must-Have Meals

○ **Pàt tai** Thailand's famous noodle dish at **Thip Samai** (Map p62; 313 Th Mahachai; mains 50-250B; ☺5pm-2am; 🚤klorng boat to Phanfa Leelard Pier).

○ **Gǒo•ay đěe•o reua** Pork/beef 'boat noodle' soups at **Bharani** (Sansab Boat Noodle; Map p66; 96/14 Soi 23, Th Sukhumvit; mains

Street-food vendor

DESIGN PICS/RAY LASKOWITZ/GETTY IMAGES ©

ℹ️ Need to Know

Restaurants are generally open from 10am to 8pm. Street vendors are prohibited from operating on Monday.

✕ Take a Break

Mall food courts offer a great introduction to Thai street food.

MBK Center (p67) has an extensive food court
SYLVAIN SONNET/GETTY IMAGES ©

★ Top Tip

Thais use their spoon like a fork, held with the right hand, and hold the fork in the left hand. They only use chopsticks for noodle dishes.

19-115B; ⊙9am-10pm Tue-Sun; ❄️🖋; 🚢Phra Athit/Banglamphu Pier).

Cooking Courses

Better than a souvenir, Thai cooking courses teach students how to recreate standard dishes back home. Courses are half-day and include a recipe book and lunch.

○ **Helping Hands** (📞080 434 8686; www. cookingwithpoo.com; 1500B; ⊙lessons 8.30am-1pm)

○ **Silom Thai Cooking School** (Map p64; 📞084 726 5669; www.bangkokthaicooking.com; 68 Soi 13, Th Silom; courses 1000B; ⊙lessons 9am-1pm, 1.40-5.30pm & 6-9pm; 🚇Chong Nonsi exit 3)

○ **Bangkok Bold Cooking Studio** (Map p62; 📞098 829 4310; www.bangkokbold.com; 503 Th Phra Sumen; courses 2000B; ⊙lessons 9am-1pm & 2-5pm; 🚢klorng boat to Phanfa Leelard Pier)

60-250B; ⊙11am-10pm; ❄️; 🚇Sukhumvit exit 2, 🚉Asok exit 3).

○ **Mèe gròrp** A palace recipe for crispy noodles at **Chote Chitr** (Map p62; 146 Th Phraeng Phuthon; mains 60-200B; ⊙11am-10pm; 🚢klorng boat to Phanfa Leelard Pier).

○ **Kôw man gài** Chicken rice at **Boon Tong Kiat Singapore Hainanese Chicken Rice** (Map p66; 440/5 Soi 55/Thong Lor, Th Sukhumvit; mains 65-300B; ⊙10am-10pm; ❄️; 🚉Thong Lo exit 3 & taxi).

○ **Or sòo·an** Oyster crepe, a Bangkok Chinatown staple, at **Nai Mong Hoi Thod** (Map p62; 539 Th Phlap Phla Chai; mains 50-70B; ⊙5-10pm Tue-Sun; 🚢Ratchawong Pier, 🚇Hua Lamphong exit 1 & taxi).

○ **Má·dà·bà** Meat-filled flatbread, a Southeast Asian Muslim favourite, at **Roti-Mataba** (Map p62; 136 Th Phra Athit; dishes

Bangkok Walking Tour

Stroll around the former royal district of Ko Ratanakosin. Start early to beat the heat, dress modestly for the temples, and ignore shopping advice from well-dressed touts.
Start Wat Phra Kaew
Distance 5km
Duration 3 hours

5 Wander along Trok Mahathat, the alley leading to the **Amulet Market** (p60), to appreciate how extensive the market for small talismans is.

Take a Break...Savoey (p70) Provides an air-conditioned rest stop.

4 Return to the east bank to explore the classic architecture and riverside accoutrements in the narrow alleyway of Trok Tha Wang.

3 Catch the cross-river ferry from Tien Pier to the military-looking **Wat Arun** (p46) temple, boasting a Khmer-style *chedi* (stupa).

Thammasat University

Th Phra Chan

Th Maha Rat

Silpakorn University

Th Na Phra Lan

Th Maha Rat

Mae Nam Chao Phraya

(N) 0 / 0
800 m
0.4 miles

6 Exit at Th Phra Chan, and continue east until you reach the Sanam Luang (Royal Field), which hosts the annual Ploughing Ceremony.

Gold garuda decoration at Wat Phra Kaew

1 OUTCAST85/GETTY IMAGES ©, 2. PREECHA9423/GETTY IMAGES ©

1 Start with the city's most famous attraction, the architecturally flamboyant and domestically revered **Wat Phra Kaew & Grand Palace** (p38).

2 Head to the shady and peaceful **Wat Pho** (p42) temple where you can enjoy a traditional healing massage.

◉ SIGHTS

◎ Ko Ratanakosin & Banglamphu

Amulet Market   Market
(ตลาดพระเครื่องวัดมหาธาตุ; Map p62; Th Maha Rat; ⊘7am-5pm; 🚢Chang Pier, Maharaj Pier, Phra Chan Tai Pier) This arcane and fascinating market claims both the footpaths along Th Maha Rat and Th Phra Chan, as well as a dense network of covered market stalls that run south from Phra Chan Pier; the easiest entry point is clearly marked Trok Maha That. The trade is based around small talismans carefully prized by collectors, monks, taxi drivers and people in dangerous professions.

Potential buyers, often already sporting many amulets, can be seen bargaining and flipping through magazines dedicated to the amulets, some of which command astronomical prices. It's a great place to just wander and watch men (because it's rarely women) looking through magnifying glasses at the tiny amulets, seeking hidden meaning and, if they're lucky, hidden value.

National Museum   Museum
(พิพิธภัณฑสถานแห่งชาติ; Map p62; 4 Th Na Phra That; admission 200B; ⊘9am-4pm Wed-Sun; 🚢Chang Pier, Maharaj Pier, Phra Chan Tai Pier) Often touted as Southeast Asia's biggest museum, Thailand's National Museum is home to an impressive, albeit occasionally dusty, collection of items, best appreciated on one of the museum's twice-weekly **guided tours** (free with museum admission; ⊘9.30am Wed & Thu).

Most of the museum's structures were built in 1782 as the palace of Rama I's viceroy, Prince Wang Na. Rama V turned it into a museum in 1874, and today there are three permanent exhibitions spread out over several buildings. At the time of research some of the exhibition halls were being renovated.

Lak Meuang   Monument
(ศาลหลักเมือง; Map p62; cnr Th Sanam Chai & Th Lak Meuang; ⊘6.30am-6.30pm; 🚢Chang Pier, Maharaj Pier, Phra Chan Tai Pier) Serving as the spiritual keystone of Bangkok, Lak Meuang is a phallus-shaped wooden pillar erected by Rama I during the foundation of the

Amulet Market

DAVID C PHILLIPS/GETTY IMAGES ©

city in 1782. Part of an animistic tradition, the city pillar embodies the city's guardian spirit (Phra Sayam Thewathirat) and also lends a practical purpose as a marker of a town's crossroads and measuring point for distances between towns.

If you're lucky, *lá·kon gâa bon* (a commissioned dance) may be in progress. Brilliantly costumed dancers measure out subtle movements as gratitude to the guardian spirit for granting a worshipper's wish.

Museum of Ṣiam　　　Museum

(สถาบันพิพิธภัณฑ์การเรียนรู้แห่งชาติ; Map p62; www.museumsiam.org; Th Maha Rat; admission 300B; ⊙10am-6pm Tue-Sun; 🚇: 🚤Tien Pier) This fun museum employs a variety of media to explore the origins of the Thai people and their culture. Housed in a European-style 19th-century building that was once the Ministry of Commerce, the exhibits are presented in a contemporary, engaging and interactive fashion not typically found in Thailand's museums. They are also refreshingly balanced and entertaining, with galleries dealing with a range of questions about the origins of the nation and its people.

Golden Mount & Wat Saket　　　Buddhist Temple

FREE **Golden Mount** (ภูเขาทอง, Phu Khao Thong; Map p62; off Th Boriphat; admission to summit of Golden Mount 10B; ⊙7.30am-5.30pm; 🚤klorng boat to Phanfa Leelard Pier) was commissioned by Rama III, who ordered that the earth dug out to create Bangkok's expanding *klorng* network be piled up to build an enormous, 100m-high, 500m-wide *chedi*.

Next door, seemingly peaceful **Wat Saket** (วัดสระเกศ; Map p62; off Th Boriphat; 🚤klorng boat to Phanfa Leelard Pier) FREE contains murals that are among both the most beautiful and the goriest in the country; proceed to the pillar behind the Buddha statue for explicit depictions of Buddhist hell.

In November there's a festival in the grounds that includes an enchanting

candlelight procession up the Golden Mount.

◉ Chinatown

Wat Traimit (Golden Buddha)　Buddhist Temple

(วัดไตรมิตร, Temple of the Golden Buddha; Map p62; Th Mittaphap Thai-China; admission 40B; ⊙8am-5pm; 🚤Ratchawong Pier, Ⓜ Hua Lamphong exit 1) The attraction at Wat Traimit is undoubtedly the impressive 3m-tall, 5.5-tonne, **solid-gold Buddha image**, which gleams like, well, gold. Sculpted in the graceful Sukhothai style, the image was 'discovered' some 40 years ago beneath a stucco/plaster exterior, when it fell from a crane while being moved to a new building within the temple compound.

The 2nd floor of the building is home to the **Phra Buddha Maha Suwanna**

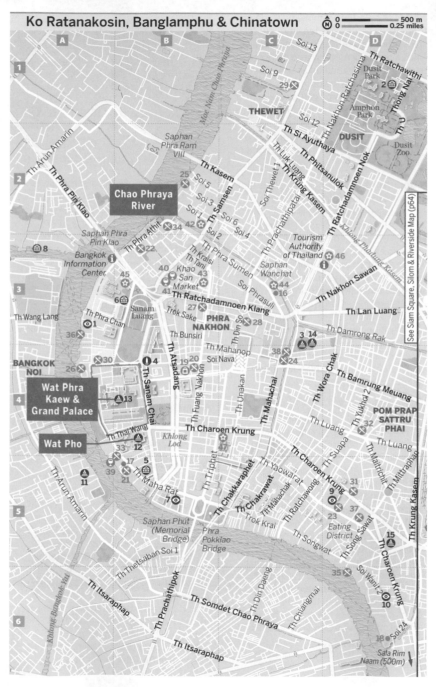

Ko Ratanakosin, Banglamphu & Chinatown

N 0 — 500 m
   0 — 0.25 miles

Ko Ratanakosin, Banglamphu & Chinatown

Patimakorn Exhibition (admission 100B; ⏱8am-4pm Tue-Sun), which has exhibits on how the statue was made, discovered and came to arrive at its current home, while the 3rd floor is home to the **Yaowarat Chinatown Heritage Center** (admission 100B; ⏱8am-4pm Tue-Sun), a small but engaging museum with multimedia exhibits on the history of Bangkok's Chinatown and its residents.

Talat Mai   Market
(ตลาดใหม่; Map p62; Soi Yaowarat 6/Charoen Krung 16; ⏱6am-6pm; 🚢Ratchawong Pier, Ⓜ Hua Lamphong exit 1 & taxi) With nearly two centuries of commerce under its belt, New Market is no longer an entirely accurate name for this strip of com-

merce. Regardless, this is Bangkok's, if not Thailand's, most Chinese market, and the dried goods, seasonings, spices and sauces will be familiar to anyone who's ever spent time in China. Even if you're not interested in food, the hectic atmosphere (be on guard for motorcycles squeezing between shoppers) and exotic sights and smells culminate in something of a surreal sensory experience.

While much of the market centres on cooking ingredients, the section north of Th Charoen Krung (equivalent to Soi 21, Th Charoen Krung) is known for selling incense, paper effigies and ceremonial sweets – the essential elements of a traditional Chinese funeral.

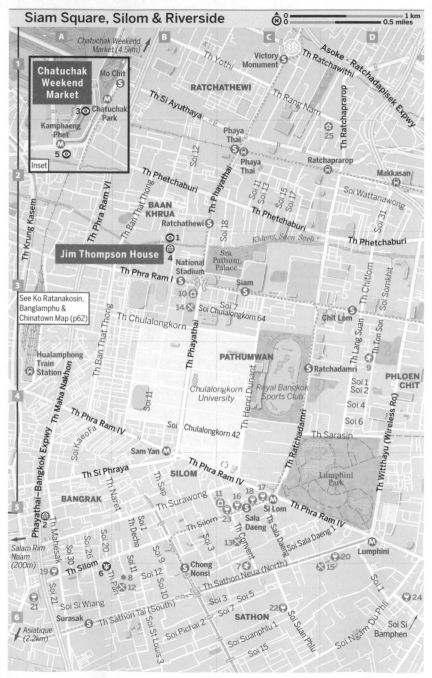

Siam Square, Silom & Riverside

0 — 1 km
0 — 0.5 miles

Chatuchak Weekend Market (4.5km)

Chatuchak Weekend Market

Mo Chit

Chatuchak Park

Kamphaeng Phet

3

5

Inset

Th Yothi

Victory Monument

Th Ratchawithi

Asoke - Ratchadapisek Expwy

RATCHATHEWI

Th Si Ayuthaya

Th Rang Nam

Th Ratchaprarop

25

Phaya Thai

Phaya Thai

Ratchaprarop

Makkasan

Th Phetchaburi

Soi Wattanawong

Th Phra Ram VI

Th Ban That Thong

Th Phetchaburi

BAAN KHRUA

Ratchathewi

Soi 11
Soi 13
Soi 15
Soi 17

Th Phetchaburi

Soi 31

Th Krung Kasem

Th Phayathai

Soi 18

Soi 12

Khlong Saen Saeb

Th Phetchaburi

1

Jim Thompson House

4

National Stadium

Sra Pathum Palace

Th Chitlom

Soi Somkhit

Th Phra Ram I

See Ko Ratanakosin, Banglamphu & Chinatown Map (p62)

10

14

Soi Chulalongkorn 64

Soi 7

Siam

Chit Lom

Th Lang Suan

Th Ton Son

Th Chulalongkorn

Th Ban That Thong

Th Phayathai

PATHUMWAN

Th Henri Dunant

Ratchadamri

9

PHLOEN CHIT

Hualamphong Train Station

Soi 11

Chulalongkorn University

Royal Bangkok Sports Club

Soi 1
Soi 2

Soi 4

Th Witthayu (Wireless Rd)

Th Maha Nakhon

Th Phra Ram IV

Soi Kaeo Fa

Soi Chulalongkorn 42

Soi 6

Sam Yan

Th Ratchadamri

Th Sarasin

Phayathai–Bangkok Expwy

Th Si Phraya

SILOM

Th Phra Ram IV

Lumphini Park

BANGRAK

Th Naret

Th Sap

Th Surawong

11
16
18
17

Si Lom

2

Salam Rim Naam (200m)

Soi 1
Th Decho

Th Silom

23

Sala Daeng

Th Sala Daeng

M

Th Phra Ram IV

Soi 20

Soi 26

Soi 30

Soi 9

Soi 3

Th Convert

13

Soi Sala Daeng 1

Lumphini

19

Th Silom

6
Th Pan

8
12

Soi 11

Soi 12

Soi 10

Chong Nonsi

7

Th Sathon Neua (North)

20

15

21

Soi 21

Soi Si Wiang

Surasak

Th Sathon Tai (South)

Soi St Louis 3

Soi 3

Soi 5

22

SATHON

Soi Suan Phlu

24

Asiatique (2.2km)

Soi Pichai 2

Soi 7

Soi Suanphlu 1

Soi 15

Soi Ngam Du Phli

Soi Si Bamphen

Soi 1

Siam Square, Silom & Riverside

Pak Khlong Talat Market

(ปากคลองตลาด, Flower Market; Map p62; Th Chakkaraphet; ⊙24hr; ⊛Pak Klong Talad Pier, Saphan Phut/Memorial Bridge Pier) This sprawling wholesale flower market has become a tourist attraction in its own right. The endless piles of delicate orchids, rows of roses and stacks of button carnations are a sight to be seen, and the shirtless porters wheeling blazing piles of colour set the place in motion. The best time to come is late at night, when the goods arrive from upcountry.

During the daytime, Pak Khlong Talat is one of the city's largest wholesale vegetable markets.

⊙ Silom & Riverside

Sri Mariamman Temple Hindu Temple

(วัดพระศรีมหาอุมาเทวี/วัดแขก, Wat Phra Si Maha Umathewi; Map p64; cnr Th Silom & Th Pan; ⊙6am-8pm; ⑤Surasak exit 3) **FREE** Arrestingly flamboyant, the Sri Mariamman Hindu temple is a wild collision of colours, shapes and deities. It was built in the 1860s by Tamil immigrants and features a 6m facade of intertwined, full-colour Hindu deities. While most of the people working in the temple hail from the Indian subcontinent, you will likely see plenty of Thai and Chinese devotees praying here as well. This is because the Hindu gods figure just as prominently in their individualistic approach to religion.

Bangkokian Museum Museum

(พิพิธภัณฑ์ชาวบางกอก; Map p64; 273 Soi 43, Th Charoen Krung; admission by donation; ⊙10am-4pm Wed-Sun; ⊛Si Phraya/River City Pier) A collection of three antique structures built during the early 20th century, the Bangkokian Museum illustrates an often-overlooked period of Bangkok's history.

The main building was built in 1937 as a home for the Surawadee family and, as the signs inform us, was finished by Chinese carpenters on time and for less than the budgeted 2400B (which would barely buy a door handle today). This building and the large wooden one to the right, which was added as a boarding house to help cover costs, are filled with the detritus of postwar family life and offer a fascinating window into the period.

The third building, at the back of the block, was built in 1929 as a surgery for a British doctor, though he died soon after arriving in Thailand.

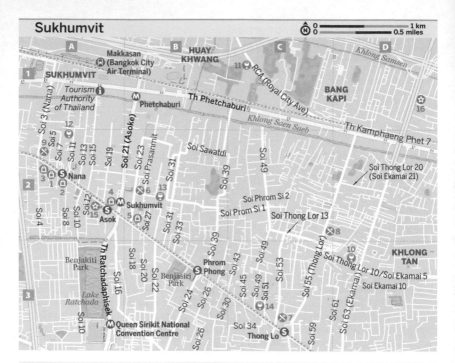

Sukhumvit

⊙ **Shopping**
1 Nickermann's.....................................A2
2 Raja's Fashions.................................A2
3 Rajawongse.......................................A2
   Ricky's Fashion House...................(see 9)
4 Terminal 21.......................................A2
5 ThaiCraft Fair...................................B2

⊗ **Eating**
6 Bharani...B2
7 Bo.lan...C3
8 Boon Tong Kiat Singapore
   Chicken Rice..................................C2
9 Nasir Al-Masri.................................A2

◯ **Drinking & Nightlife**
10 Arena 10..D3
11 Castro..C1
12 Levels...A2
13 Narz..B2
14 WTF..C3

✪ **Entertainment**
15 Living Room......................................A2
16 Parking Toys' Watt..........................D1

✚ ACTIVITIES

Ruen-Nuad Massage Studio
Massage

(Map p64; ☑ 02 632 2662; 42 Th Convent; massage per hr 350B; ⊙10am-9pm; Ⓜ Si Lom exit 2, Ⓢ Sala Daeng exit 2) Set in a refurbished wooden house, this charming place successfully avoids both the tackiness and New Agedness that characterise most Bangkok Thai-massage joints. Prices are reasonable, too.

Massage Pavilions
Massage

(Map p62; Wat Pho, Th Sanam Chai; Thai massage per hr 420B; ⊙9am-6pm; ⊉Tien Pier) These two air-conditioned *săh·lah* (pavilions) located near the eastern entrance to the Wat Pho grounds are run by the **massage school** (Map p62; ☑ 02 622 3551;

www.watpomassage.com; 392/32-33 Soi Phen Phat; lessons from 2500B, Thai massage per hour 420B; ☺lessons 9am-4pm, massage 9am-6pm; ♨Tien Pier) affiliated with Wat Pho, which is the country's primary training centre for Thai traditional massage. The menu is short but the quality is guaranteed, and after a day of temple sightseeing it's hard to think of a better way to cool down and chill out.

Spa 1930   Spa

(Map p64; ☎02 254 8606; www.spa1930.com; 42 Th Ton Son; Thai massage from 1000B, spa packages from 3500B; ☺9.30am-9.30pm; ⒮Chit Lom exit 4) Discreet and sophisticated, Spa 1930 rescues relaxers from the contrived spa ambience of New Age music and ingredients you'd rather see at a dinner party. The menu is simple (face, body care and body massage) and the scrubs and massage oils are logical players.

☻ TOURS

Although the pollution and heat are significant obstacles, Bangkok is a fascinating city to explore on foot. If you'd rather do it with an expert guide, **Bangkok Private Tours** (www.bangkokprivatetours.com; tours from US$150) and **Co van Kessel Bangkok Tours** (Map p62; ☎02 639 7351; www.covankessel.com; ground fl, River City, 23 Th Yotha; tours from 950B; ☺6am-7pm; ♨River City Pier) conduct themed walking tours of the city. Foodies will appreciate the offerings at **Bangkok Food Tours** (☎095 943 9222; www.bangkokfoodtours.com; tours from 1150B) or **Chili Paste Tours** (☎085 143 6779, 094 552 2361; www.foodtoursbangkok.com; tours from 1800B), both of which offer half-day culinary tours of Bangkok's older neighbourhoods.

ⓐ SHOPPING

MBK Center   Shopping Centre

(Map p64; www.mbk-center.com; cnr Th Phra Ram I & Th Phayathai; ☺10am-10pm; ⒮National Stadium exit 4) This colossal shopping mall underwent an extensive renovation in 2015 and is set to retain its role as one of Bangkok's top attractions. On any given weekend half of Bangkok's residents (and most of its tourists) can be found here combing through a seemingly inexhaustible range of small stalls and shops that span a whopping eight floors.

MBK is Bangkok's cheapest place to buy mobile phones and accessories (4th floor). It's also one of the better places to stock up on camera gear (ground floor and 5th floor), and the expansive food court (6th floor) is one of the best in town.

Terminal 21   Shopping Centre

(Map p66; www.terminal21.co.th; cnr Th Sukhumvit & Soi 21/Asoke; ☺10am 10pm, Ⓜ Sukhumvit exit 3, ⒮Asok exit 3) Seemingly catering to a Thai need for wacky objects to be photographed in front of, this new mall is worth a visit for the spectacle as much as the shopping. Start at the basement-level 'airport' and proceed upwards through 'Paris', 'Tokyo' and other city-themed floors. Who knows, you might even buy something.

Asiatique   Market

(www.thaiasiatique.com; Soi 72-76, Th Charoen Krung; ☺4-11pm; ♨shuttle boat from Sathon/Central Pier) One of Bangkok's more popular night markets, Asiatique takes the form of warehouses of commerce next to Mae Nam Chao Phraya. Expect clothing, handicrafts, souvenirs and quite a few dining and drinking venues.

To get here, take one of the frequent, free shuttle boats from Sathon/Central Pier that run from 4pm to 11.30pm.

Patpong Night Market   Souvenirs

(Map p64; Th Phat Phong & Soi Phat Phong 2; ☺6pm-midnight; Ⓜ Si Lom exit 2, ⒮Sala Daeng exit 1) You'll be faced with the competing distractions of strip-clubbing and shopping in this infamous area. And true to the area's illicit leanings, pirated goods (in particular watches) make a prominent appearance even amid a wholesome crowd of families and straight-laced couples. Bargain with determination, as first-quoted prices tend to be astronomically high.

 Dusit Palace Park

Following his first European tour in 1897, Rama V (King Chulalongkorn; r 1868–1910) returned with visions of European castles and set about transforming these styles into a uniquely Thai expression, today's **Dusit Palace Park** (วังสวนดุสิต; Map p62; bounded by Th Ratchawithi, Th U Thong Nai & Th Nakhon Ratchasima; admission adult/child 100/20B, or free with Grand Palace ticket; ⊙9.30am-4pm Tue-Sun; ⛴Thewet Pier, ⑤Phaya Thai exit 2 & taxi).

The premier attraction is the Vimanmek Teak Mansion, which was originally constructed on Ko Si Chang in 1868 and moved to the present site in 1910. It contains 81 rooms, halls and anterooms, and is said to be the world's largest golden-teak building, allegedly built without the use of a single nail. The mansion was the first permanent building on the Dusit Palace grounds, and served as Rama V's residence in the early 1900s. The interior of the mansion contains various personal effects of the king and a treasure trove of early Ratanakosin-era art objects and antiques.

Compulsory tours (in English) leave every 30 minutes between 9.45am and 3.15pm, and last about an hour. Because this is royal property, visitors should wear shirts with sleeves and long pants (no cropped pants) or long skirts.

Vimanmek Teak Mansion

Heritage Craft   Handicrafts
(Map p62; 35 Th Bamrung Meuang; ⊙11am-6pm Mon-Fri; ⛴klorng boat to Phanfa Leelard Pier) Handicrafts with a conscience: this new boutique is an atmospheric showcase for the quality domestic wares of **ThaiCraft** (Map p66; www.thaicraft.org; L fl, Jasmine City Bldg, cnr Soi 23 & Th Sukhumvit; ⊙10am-3pm; Ⓜ Sukhumvit exit 2, ⑤Asok exit 3), some of which are produced via fair trade practices. Items include silks from Thailand's northeast, baskets from the south and jewellery from the north, and there's also an inviting on-site cafe.

❂ ENTERTAINMENT

Ratchadamnoen Stadium   Spectator Sport
(Map p62; off Th Ratchadamnoen Nok; tickets 3rd-class/2nd-class/ringside 1000/1500/2000B; ⛴Thewet Pier, ⑤Phaya Thai exit 3 & taxi) Ratchadamnoen Stadium, Bangkok's oldest and most venerable venue for *moo·ay tai* (Thai boxing; also spelt *muay thai*), hosts matches on Monday, Wednesday and Thursday from 6.30pm to around 11pm, and Sunday at 3pm and 6.30pm. Be sure to buy tickets from the official ticket counter, not from the touts and scalpers who hang around outside the entrance.

Lumpinee Boxing Stadium   Spectator Sport
(✆02 282 3141; www.muaythailumpinee.net/en; 6 Th Ramintra; tickets 3rd-class/2nd-class/ringside 1000/1500/2000B; Ⓜ Chatuchak Park exit 2 & taxi, ⑤Mo Chit exit 3 & taxi) The other of Bangkok's two premier Thai boxing rings has moved to fancy new digs north of town. Matches occur on Tuesdays and Fridays from 6.30pm to 11pm, and on Saturdays at 4pm to 8.30pm and from 9pm to 12.30am. At time of research there were plans underway for a Thai boxing museum and a school for foreign fighters.

It's located well north of central Bangkok; the best way to get here is via taxi from BTS Mo Chit or MRT Chatuchak Park.

PETER STUCKINGS/GETTY IMAGES ©

Dancers performing at Sala Rim Naam

National Theatre
Theatre

(Map p62; ✆02 224 1342; 2 Th Ratchini; tickets 60-100B; ⛴Chang Pier, Maharaj Pier, Phra Chan Tai Pier) The National Theatre holds performances of *kŏhn* (masked dance-drama based on stories from the *Ramakian*) at 2pm on the first and second Sundays of the month from January to September, and *lá·kon* (Thai dance-dramas) at 2pm on the first and second Sundays of the month from October to December. Tickets go on sale an hour before performances begin.

Sala Rim Naam
Theatre

(✆02 437 3080; www.mandarinoriental.com/bangkok/fine-dining/sala-rim-naam; Mandarin Oriental Hotel, Soi 40/Oriental, Th Charoen Krung; tickets adult/child 1999/1700B; ◷dinner & show 8.15-9.30pm; ⛴Oriental Pier or hotel shuttle boat from Sathon/Central Pier) The historic Mandarin Oriental hosts dinner theatre in a sumptuous Thai pavilion located across the river in Thonburi. The price is well above the average, reflecting the means of the hotel's client base, but the performance gets positive reviews.

Sala Chalermkrung
Theatre

(Map p62; ✆02 222 0434; www.salachalermkrung.com; 66 Th Charoen Krung; tickets 800-1200B; ◷shows 7.30pm Thu & Fri; ⛴Saphan Phut/Memorial Bridge Pier, Ⓜ Hua Lamphong exit 1 & taxi) This Art Deco Bangkok landmark, a former cinema dating to 1933, is one of the few remaining places *kŏhn* can be witnessed. The traditional Thai dance-drama is enhanced here by laser graphics, high-tech audio and English subtitles. Concerts and other events are also held; check the website for details.

✖ EATING
⊗ Ko Ratanakosin & Banglamphu

Ming Lee
Chinese-Thai $

(Map p62; 28-30 Th Na Phra Lan, no roman-script sign; mains 70-100B; ◷11.30am-6pm; ⛴Chang Pier, Maharaj Pier, Phra Chan Tai Pier) Hidden in plain sight across from Wat Phra Kaew is this decades-old shophouse restaurant. The menu spans Western/Chinese dishes (stewed tongue, for example) and Thai standards (such as the impossibly tart and garlicky 'beef spicy salad'). Often closed before 6pm, Ming Lee is best approached as a post-sightseeing lunch option.

There's no English-language sign here; look for the last shophouse before Silpakorn University.

Pa Aew   Central Thai $

(Map p62; Th Maha Rat, no roman-script sign; mains 20-60B; ⏰10am-5pm Tue-Sat; 🚤Tien Pier) Pull up a plastic stool for some rich, seafood-heavy, Bangkok-style fare. It's a bare-bones, open-air curry stall, but for taste, Pa Aew is one of our favourite places to eat in this part of town.

There's no English-language sign; look for the exposed trays of food directly in front of the Krung Thai Bank near the corner with Soi Pratu Nokyung.

Kimleng   Thai $

(Map p62; 158-160 Th Tanao; mains 60-150B; ⏰10am-10pm Mon-Sat; ❄; 🚤klorng boat to Phanfa Leelard Pier) This tiny family-run restaurant specialises in the dishes and flavours of central Thailand. It's a good place

to dip your toes in the local cuisine via an authentic *yam* (Thai-style salad), such as *yam þlah dùk foo*, a mixture of catfish deep-fried until crispy and strands of tart, green mango.

Savoey   Thai $$

(Map p62; www.savoey.co.th; 1st fl, Maharaj Pier, Th Maha Rat; mains 125-1800B; ⏰10am-10pm; ❄; 🚤Maharaj Pier, Chang Pier) A chain with other branches across town, you're not going to find heaps of character here, but you will get consistency, river views, air-con, and a seafood-heavy menu that should appeal to just about everybody. Come cool evenings, take advantage of the open-air, riverside deck.

Hemlock   Thai $$

(Map p62; 56 Th Phra Athit; mains 75-280B; ⏰4pm-midnight Mon-Sat; ❄🖋; 🚤Phra Athit/ Banglamphu Pier) Taking full advantage of its cosy shophouse location, this perennial favourite has enough style to feel like a special night out, but doesn't skimp on flavour or preparation. And unlike at other similar places, the eclectic menu here

Thai street food

reads like an ancient literary work, reviving old dishes from aristocratic kitchens across the country, not to mention several meat-free items.

Err
Thai $$

(Map p62; www.errbkk.com; off Th Maha Rat; dishes 65-360B; ⏱11am-late Tue-Sun; 🅿; 🚤Tien Pier) Think of all those different smoky, spicy, crispy, meaty bites you've encountered on the street. Now imagine them assembled in one funky, retro-themed locale, and coupled with tasty Thai-themed cocktails and domestic microbrews. If Err (a Thai colloquialism for agreement) seems too good to be true, we empathise, but insist that it's true.

Krua Apsorn
Thai $$

(Map p62; www.kruaapsorn.com; Th Din So; mains 80-400B; ⏱10.30am-8pm Mon-Sat; 🅿; 🚤klorng boat to Phanfa Leelard Pier) This homely dining room is a favourite of members of the Thai royal family and restaurant critics alike. Just about all of the central and southern Thai dishes are tasty, but regulars never miss the chance to order the decadent stir-fried crab with yellow chilli or the *tortilla Española*–like omelette with crab.

There's another branch on Th Samsen in **Dusit** (Map p62; www.kruaapsorn. com; 503-505 Th Samsen; mains 80-400B; ⏱10.30am-7.30pm Mon-Fri, to 6pm Sat; 🅿; 🚤Thewet Pier).

Khunkung
Central Thai $$

(Navy Club; Map p62; 77 Th Maha Rat; mains 70-450B; ⏱11am-2pm & 6-10pm Mon-Fri, 11am-10pm Sat & Sun; 🅿; 🚤Chang Pier, Maharaj Pier, Phra Chan Tai Pier) The restaurant of the Royal Navy Association has one of the few coveted riverfront locations along this stretch of Mae Nam Chao Phraya. Locals come for the combination of views and cheap and tasty seafood-based eats – ostensibly not for the cafeteria-like atmosphere.

Khunkung is just off the main road; look for the sign on Th Maha Rat that says 'Navy Club'.

🍽 Vegetarian Festival in Chinatown

During the annual Vegetarian Festival in September/October, Bangkok's Chinatown becomes a virtual orgy of nonmeat cuisine. The festivities centre on Chinatown's main street, Th Yaowarat, and the **Talat Noi** (ตลาดน้อย; Map p62; off Th Charoen Krung; ⏱7am-7pm; 🚤Marine Department Pier) area, but food shops and stalls all over the city post yellow flags to announce their meat-free status.

Celebrating alongside the ethnic Chinese are Thais who look forward to the special dishes that appear during the festival period. Most restaurants put their normal menus on hold and instead prepare soy-based substitutes for standard Thai dishes like *dôm yam* (Thai-style spicy/sour soup) and *gaang kěe·o wǎhn* (green curry). Even Thai regional cuisines are sold (without the meat, of course). Yellow Hokkien-style noodles often make an appearance in the special festival dishes, usually in stir-frys along with meaty mushrooms and big hunks of vegetables.

Along with abstinence from meat, the 10-day festival is celebrated with special visits to the temple, often requiring worshippers to dress in white.

Vegetarian curry puff
JIRABU/GETTY IMAGES ©

Jay Fai
Central Thai $$$

(Map p62; 327 Th Mahachai; mains 180-1000B; ⏱3pm-2am Mon-Sat; 🚤klorng boat to Phanfa Leelard Pier) You wouldn't think so by looking at her bare-bones dining room, but Jay Fai

⚠ The Sex Industry

Prostitution has been widespread in Thailand since long before the country became famous for it. Throughout Thai history the practice was tolerated though not respected.

Due to pressure from the UN, prostitution was declared illegal in 1960, though entertainment places (go-go bars, beer bars, massage parlours, karaoke bars and bathhouses) are governed by a separate law passed in 1966. These establishments are licensed and can legally provide nonsexual services (such as dancing, massage, a drinking buddy); sexual services occur through these venues but they are not technically the businesses' purpose.

With the arrival of the US military in Southeast Asia in the 1960s and '70s, enterprising forces adapted prostitution to suit foreigners, in turn creating an industry that persists today. Indeed, this foreigner-oriented sex industry is still a prominent part of Thailand's tourist economy.

In 1998 the International Labour Organization, a UN agency, advised Southeast Asian countries, including Thailand, to recognise prostitution as an economic sector and income generator. It is estimated that one third of the entertainment establishments are registered with the government and the majority pay an informal tax in the form of police bribes.

is known far and wide for serving Bangkok's most expensive *pàt kêe mow* ('drunkard's noodles'; wide rice noodles fried with seafood and Thai herbs).

Jay Fai is located in a virtually unmarked shophouse on Th Mahachai, directly across from a 7-Eleven.

The *pàt kêe mow* price is justified by the copious fresh seafood, as well as Jay Fai's distinct frying style that results in an almost oil-free finished product.

⊗ Chinatown

Khun Yah Cuisine · Central Thai $
(Map p62; off Th Mittaphap Thai-China, no roman-script sign; mains from 40B; ⊘6am-1.30pm Mon-Fri; ⛴Ratchawong Pier, ⓜHua Lamphong exit 1) Strategically located for a lunch break after visiting Wat Traimit (Golden Buddha), Khun Yah specialises in the full-flavoured curries, relishes, stir-fries and noodle dishes of central Thailand. But be sure to get here early; come noon many dishes are already sold out.

Khun Yah Cuisine has no English-language sign but is located just east of the Golden Buddha, in the same compound.

Nay Hong · Chinese-Thai $
(Map p62; off Th Yukol 2, no roman-script sign; mains 35-50B; ⊘4-10pm; ⛴Ratchawong Pier, ⓜHua Lamphong exit 1 & taxi) The reward for locating this hole-in-the-wall is one of the best fried noodle dishes in Bangkok. The dish in question is *gǒo·ay dĕe·o kôo·a gài*, flat rice noodles fried with garlic oil, chicken and egg.

To find it, proceed north from the corner of Th Suapa and Th Luang, then turn right into the first side-street; it's at the end of the narrow alleyway.

Thanon Phadungdao Seafood Stalls · Thai $$
(Map p62; cnr Th Phadungdao & Th Yaowarat; mains 100-600B; ⊘4pm-midnight Tue-Sun; ⛴Ratchawong Pier, ⓜHua Lamphong exit 1 & taxi) After sunset, these two opposing open-air restaurants – each of which claims to be the original – become a culinary train

wreck of outdoor barbecues, screaming staff, iced seafood trays and messy sidewalk seating. True, the vast majority of diners are foreign tourists, but this has little impact on the cheerful setting, the fun experience and the cheap bill.

Hoon Kuang Chinese-Thai $$
(Map p62; 381 Th Yaowarat; mains 90-240B; ☺11am-7.45pm Mon-Sat; ✷; ⛴Ratchawong Pier, ⓜHua Lamphong exit 1 & taxi) Serving the food of Chinatown's streets in air-con comfort is this low-key, long-standing staple. The must-eat dishes are pictured on the door, but it'd be a pity to miss the 'prawn curry flat rice noodle', a unique mash-up of two Chinese-Thai dishes – crab in curry powder and flash-fried noodles – that will make you wonder why they were ever served apart.

Samsara Japanese, Thai $$
(Map p62; Soi Khang Wat Pathum Khongkha; mains 110-320B; ☺4pm-midnight Tue-Thu, to 1am Fri-Sun; ✐; ⛴Ratchawong Pier, ⓜHua Lamphong exit 1 & taxi) Combining Japanese and Thai dishes, Belgian beers and an artfully ramshackle atmosphere, Samsara is easily Chinatown's most eclectic place to eat. It's also very tasty, and the generous riverside breezes and views simply add to the package.

The restaurant is at the end of tiny Soi Khang Wat Pathum Khongkha, just west of the temple of the same name.

❌ Silom & Riverside

Chennai Kitchen Indian $
(Map p64; 107/4 Th Pan; mains 70-150B; ☺10am-3pm & 6-9.30pm; ✷✐; ⓢSurasak exit 3) This thimble-sized mom-and-pop restaurant puts out some of the best southern Indian vegetarian food in town. Yard-long *dosai* (a crispy southern Indian bread) is always a good choice, but if you're feeling indecisive (or exceptionally famished) go for the banana-leaf *thali* (set meal) that seems to incorporate just about everything in the kitchen.

Eat Me International $$$
(Map p64; ✐02 238 0931; www.eatmerestaurant.com; Soi Phiphat 2; mains 275-1400B;

Chillies for sale in a Chinatown market

⊘3pm-1am; ※⧠; Ⓜ Si Lom exit 2, Ⓢ Sala Daeng exit 2) The dishes here, with descriptions like 'charred whitlof and mozzarella salad with preserved lemon and dry aged Cecina beef' may sound all over the map or perhaps somewhat pretentious, but they're actually just plain tasty. A casual-yet-sophisticated atmosphere, excellent cocktails, a handsome wine list, and some of the city's best desserts also make this one of our favourite places in Bangkok to dine.

nahm Thai $$$

(Map p64; ✆02 625 3388; www.comohotels. com/metropolitanbangkok/dining/nahm; ground fl, Metropolitan Hotel, 27 Th Sathon Tai/South; set lunch 550-1500B, set dinner 2300B, dishes 280-750B; ⊘noon-2pm Mon-Fri, 7-10.30pm daily; ※; Ⓜ Lumphini exit 2) Australian chef-author David Thompson is the man behind one of Bangkok's – and if you believe the critics, the world's – best Thai restaurants. Using ancient cookbooks as his inspiration, Thompson has given new life to previously extinct dishes with exotic descriptions such as 'smoked fish curry with prawns, chicken livers, cockles, chillies and black pepper'.

Dinner is best approached via the multi-course set meal, while lunch means *kà·nŏm jeen*, thin rice noodles served with curries.

If you're expecting bland, gentrified Thai food meant for foreigners, prepare to be disappointed. Reservations recommended.

⊗ Sukhumvit

Nasir Al-Masri Middle Eastern $$

(Map p66; 4/6 Soi 3/1, Th Sukhumvit; mains 160-370B; ⊘24hr; ※⧠; Ⓢ Nana exit 1) One of several Middle Eastern restaurants on Soi 3/1, Nasir Al-Masri is easily recognisable by its floor-to-ceiling stainless steel 'theme'. Middle Eastern food often means meat, meat and more meat, but the menu here also includes several delicious vegie-based *mezze* (small dishes).

Bo.lan Thai $$$

(Map p66; ✆02 260 2962; www.bolan.co.th; 24 Soi 53, Th Sukhumvit; set meals 980-2680B; ⊘noon-2.30pm & 7-10.30pm Thu-Sun, 11.30am-10.30pm Tue & Wed; ※⧠; Ⓢ Thong Lo

Bangkok cityscape

exit 1) Upscale Thai is often more garnish than flavour, but Bo.lan has proven to be the exception. Bo and Dylan (Bo.lan is a play on words that also means 'ancient') take a scholarly approach to Thai cuisine, and generous set meals featuring full-flavoured Thai dishes are the results of this tuition (à la carte is not available; meat-free meals are). Reservations recommended.

🍸 DRINKING & NIGHTLIFE

See Bangkok Nightlife Top Experience for bar and club information.

ℹ️ INFORMATION

Bangkok has two organisations that handle tourism matters: the Tourism Authority of Thailand (TAT) for countrywide information, and Bangkok Information Center for city-specific information. Also be aware that travel agents in the train station and near tourist centres co-opt 'T.A.T.' and 'Information' as part of their name to lure in commissions. These places are not officially sanctioned information services, but just agencies registered with the TAT.

Bangkok Information Center (Map p62; ☑02 225 7612-4; www.bangkoktourist.com; 17/1 Th Phra Athit; ⊙9am-7pm Mon-Fri, to 5pm Sat & Sun; 🚤Phra Athit/Banglamphu Pier) City-specific tourism office providing maps, brochures and directions. Kiosks and booths are found around town; look for the green-on-white symbol of a mahout on an elephant.

Tourism Authority of Thailand Head office (TAT; Map p66; ☑02 250 5500, call centre 1672; www.tourismthailand.org; 1600 Th Phetchaburi Tat Mai; ⊙8.30am-4.30pm; 🚇Phetchaburi exit 2); **Banglamphu** (TAT; Map p62; ☑02 283 1500, call centre 1672; cnr Th Ratchadamnoen Nok & Th Chakraphatdi Phong; ⊙8.30am-4.30pm; 🚤klorng boat Phanfa Leelard Pier); **Suvarnabhumi International Airport** (TAT; ☑02 134 0040, call centre 1672; www.tourismthailand.org; 2nd fl, btwn Gates 2 & 5, Suvarnabhumi International Airport; ⊙24hr).

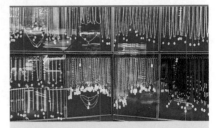

⚠️ Bangkok Street Smarts

Keep the following in mind to survive the traffic and avoid joining the list of tourists sucked in by Bangkok's numerous scam artists.

● Ignore 'helpful,' often well-dressed, English-speaking locals who tell you that tourist attractions and public transport are closed for a holiday or cleaning; it's the beginning of a con, most likely a gem scam.

● Skip the 50B túk-túk ride unless you have the time and willpower to resist a heavy sales pitch in a tailor or gem store.

● Good jewellery, gems and tailor shops aren't found through a túk-túk driver.

● Don't expect any pedestrian rights; put a Bangkokian between you and any oncoming traffic, and yield to anything with more metal than you.

● Walk away from the tourist strip to hail a taxi that will actually use the meter. Tell the driver 'meter.' If the driver refuses to put the meter on, get out.

Gold jewellery for sale
ZHYKOVA/GETTY IMAGES ©

ℹ️ GETTING THERE & AWAY

AIR

Suvarnabhumi International Airport (p307) The Airport Rail Link runs from Phaya Thai station to Suvarnabhumi (45B, 30 minutes, from 6am to midnight). Meter taxis run 24 hours and cost approximately 200B to 300B plus 50B airport surcharge and optional expressway tolls.

Don Mueang International Airport (p308) There are two bus lines from Bangkok's de facto budget airport: bus A1 makes stops at BTS Mo Chit (30B, frequent from 7.30am to 11.30pm), while bus A2 makes stops at BTS Mo Chit and BTS Victory Monument (30B, half-hourly from 7.30am to 11.30pm). Meter taxis from Don Mueang also charge an airport surcharge (50B); trips to town start at approximately 200B.

BUS

Eastern Bus Terminal (☎02 391 2504; Soi 40, Th Sukhumvit; ⑤Ekkamai exit 2) The departure point for buses to points east, except for the border crossing at Aranya Prathet. Most people call it *sà·tăh·nee èk·gà·mai* (Ekamai station). Accessible via Ekkamai BTS station.

Southern Bus Terminal (Sai Tai Mai; ☎02 422 4444, call centre 1490; Th Boromaratchachonanee) The departure point to all points south of Bangkok as well as western Thailand. It is commonly called *săi đâi mài*. A taxi to central Bangkok costs 120B.

Northern & Northeastern Bus Terminal (Mo Chit; ☎northeastern routes 02 936 2852, ext 602/605, northern routes 02 936 2841, ext 325/614; Th Kamphaeng Phet; Ⓜ Kamphaeng Phet exit 1 & taxi, ⑤Mo Chit exit 3 & taxi) North of Chatuchak Park, this hectic bus station is commonly called *kŏn sòng mŏr chít* (Mo Chit station) – not to be confused with Mo Chit BTS station. Buses depart for all northern and northeastern destinations, as well as some international destinations. It is a short taxi or motorcycle ride from Mo Chit BTS station or Chatuchak Park MRT station.

TRAIN

Hualamphong (☎02 220 4334, call centre 1690; www.railway.co.th; off Th Phra Ram IV; Ⓜ Hua Lamphong exit 2) is the city's main train terminus. It's advisable to ignore all touts here and avoid the travel agencies. Call or check the website to get destination timetable and price information. The station is connected to the MRT.

Túk-túk transport

ⓘ GETTING AROUND

Bangkok may seem impenetrable at first, but its transport system is gradually improving. Taxis are the most expedient choice – although it's important to note that Bangkok traffic is nothing if not unpredictable. During rush hour, opt for public transport.

BTS & MRT

The elevated **BTS** (📞02 617 6000, tourist information 02 617 7341; www.bts.co.th), also known as the Skytrain (*rót fai fáa*), whisks you through 'new' Bangkok (Silom, Sukhumvit and Siam Sq). The interchange between the two lines is at Siam station. Most ticket machines only accept coins, but change is available at the information booths.

Bangkok's **MRT** (📞02 354 2000; www.bangkokmetro.co.th), or Metro, is most helpful for people staying in the Sukhumvit or Silom area to reach the train station at Hualamphong.

BUS

Bangkok's public buses are run by the **Bangkok Mass Transit Authority** (📞02 246 0973, call centre 1348; www.bmta.co.th).

As the routes are not always clear, and with Bangkok taxis being such a good deal, you'd really have to be pinching pennies to rely on buses as a way to get around Bangkok. However, if you're determined, air-con bus fares range from 10B to 23B, and fares for fan buses start at 6.50B.

Most of the bus lines run between 5am and 10pm or 11pm, except for the 'all-night' buses, which run from 3am or 4am to mid-morning.

You'll most likely require the help of thinknet's *Bangkok Bus Guide*.

TAXI

All taxis are required to use their meters, which start at 35B, and fares to most places within central Bangkok cost 60B to 90B. Freeway tolls – 25B to 70B – must be paid by the passenger.

Never agree to take a taxi that won't use the meter. If a driver refuses to take you somewhere, it's probably because he needs to return his hired cab before a certain time. Very few Bangkok taxi drivers speak much English, so an address written in Thai is helpful.

🔲 Public Transport at a Glance

BTS The elevated Skytrain runs from 6am to 11.45pm. Tickets 15B to 52B or 140B for a one-day pass.

MRT The metro runs from 6am to midnight. Tickets 16B to 42B or 120B for a one-day pass.

Taxi Outside of rush hours, Bangkok taxis are a great bargain. Flag fall 35B.

Chao Phraya Express Boat Run from 6am to 8pm, charging from 10B to 40B.

Klorng boat Bangkok's canal boats run from 5.30am to 7.15pm most days. Tickets from 9B to 19B.

Bus Cheap but slow and confusing. Tickets 6.50B to 30B.

Chao Phraya Express cruises past Wat Arun
MANFRED GOTTSCHALK/GETTY IMAGES

Older cabs may be less comfortable but typically have more experienced drivers because they are driver-owned, as opposed to the new cabs, which are usually rented.

Taxi Radio (📞1681; www.taxiradio.co.th) and other 24-hour 'phone-a-cab' services are available for 20B above the metered fare.

If you leave something in a taxi your best chance of getting it back (still pretty slim) is to call 📞1644.

TÚK-TÚK

Bangkok's iconic túk-túk (pronounced *đúk đúk;* a type of motorised rickshaw) are used by Thais for short hops not worth paying the taxi flag fall. For foreigners, however, they are part of the Bangkok experience, despite their inflated prices. The vast majority of túk-túk drivers ask too much from tourists. A short hop should cost 60B.

Reputable Tailors

Bangkok has fabulous tailors but commission-hungry túk-túk drivers, shoddy workmanship and inferior fabrics make bespoke tailoring in Bangkok a potentially disappointing investment. Most reliable tailors will ask for two to five sittings.

Raja's Fashions (Map p66; ✆02 253 8379; www.rajasfashions.com; 160/1 Th Sukhumvit; ☺10.30am-8pm Mon-Sat; ⓈNana exit 4) Bobby will make you feel as important as the long list of ambassadors, foreign politicians and officers he's fitted over his family's decades in the business.

Rajawongse (Map p66; ✆02 255 3714; www.dress-for-success.com; 130 Th Sukhumvit; ☺10.30am-8pm Mon-Sat; ⓈNana exit 2) Another legendary and long-standing Bangkok tailor; Jesse and Victor's creations are particularly renowned among American visitors and residents.

Ricky's Fashion House (Map p66; ✆02 254 6887; www.rickysfashionhouse.com; 73/5 Th Sukhumvit; ☺11am-10pm Mon-Sat & 1-5.30pm Sun; ⓈNana exit 1) Ricky gets positive reviews from locals and resident foreigners alike for his more casual styles of custom-made trousers and shirts.

Nickermann's (Map p66; ✆02 252 6682; www.nickermanns.net; basement, Landmark Hotel, 138 Th Sukhumvit; ☺10am-8.30pm Mon-Sat, noon-6pm Sun; ⓈNana exit 2) Corporate ladies rave about Nickermann's tailor-made power suits. Formal ball gowns are another area of expertise.

Tailor at work
VIVIANE PONTI/GETTY IMAGES ©

Túk-túk drivers are notorious for taking little 'detours' to commission-paying gem and silk shops and massage parlours. Ignore anyone offering too-good-to-be-true 20B trips.

BOAT

KLORNG

Canal boats run along Khlong Saen Saep (Banglamphu to Ramkhamhaeng) and are an easy way to get between Banglamphu and Jim Thompson House and the Siam Sq shopping centres. Disembark at Saphan Hua Chang Pier after changing boats at Pratunam Pier.

These boats are mostly used by daily commuters and pull into the piers for just a few seconds – jump straight on or you'll be left behind.

RIVER

The **Chao Phraya Express Boat** (✆02 623 6001; www.chaophrayaexpressboat.com) operates the main ferry service along Mae Nam Chao Phraya. The central pier is known as Tha Sathon, Saphan Taksin or sometimes Central Pier, and connects to the BTS at Saphan Taksin station.

❍ The most common boats are the orange-flagged express boats. These run between Wat Rajsingkorn, south of Bangkok, to Nonthaburi, north, stopping at most major piers (15B, frequent from 6am to 7pm).

❍ A blue-flagged tourist boat (40B, half-hourly from 9.30am to 5pm) runs from Sathon/Central Pier to Phra Athit/Banglamphu Pier, with stops at eight major sightseeing piers and barely comprehensible English-language commentary. Vendors at Sathon/Central Pier tout a 150B all-day pass, but unless you plan on doing a lot of boat travel, it's not great value.

❍ There are also dozens of cross-river ferries, which charge 3B and run every few minutes until late at night.

❍ Private long-tail boats can be hired for sightseeing trips at Phra Athit/Banglamphu Pier, Chang Pier, Tien Pier and Oriental Pier.

Where to Stay

Because Bangkok is a sprawling metropolis, it is best to pick your neighbourhood and then shop within your budget range. Otherwise pick a spot on the BTS for easy neighbourhood hopping.

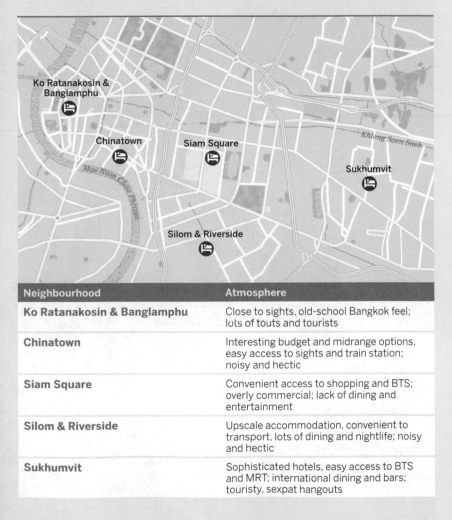

Neighbourhood	Atmosphere
Ko Ratanakosin & Banglamphu	Close to sights, old-school Bangkok feel; lots of touts and tourists
Chinatown	Interesting budget and midrange options, easy access to sights and train station; noisy and hectic
Siam Square	Convenient access to shopping and BTS; overly commercial; lack of dining and entertainment
Silom & Riverside	Upscale accommodation, convenient to transport, lots of dining and nightlife; noisy and hectic
Sukhumvit	Sophisticated hotels, easy access to BTS and MRT; international dining and bars; touristy, sexpat hangouts

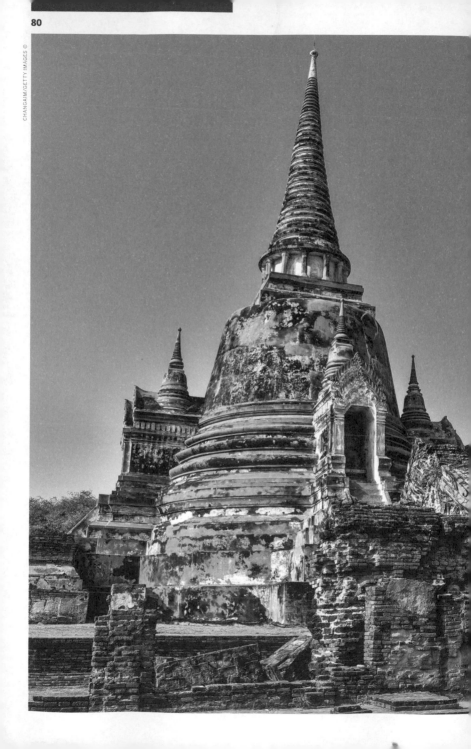

AYUTHAYA

Ayuthaya

Ayuthaya reigned as the Siamese capital for more than 400 years. The island city was an important stop along the seafaring trade route and was regaled at the time for its golden temples and architectural splendour. The kingdom fended off political intrigue and expansionist European powers, but after frequent wars with the Burmese, the city eventually fell in 1767. War, looting and gravity took their toll on Ayuthaya's once great temples and today the remaining ruins are designated as a Unesco World Heritage Site. A quiet provincial town sprung up around the ruins, providing a glimpse into ordinary Thai life with an historic backdrop.

Two Days in Ayuthaya

Visit the interactive exhibition at the **Ayutthaya Tourist Center** (p86) and discover why the city was once so great. Cycle around **Ayuthaya Historical Park** (p84), then stop at **Lung Lek** (p85) for the best noodles in town. The following day wander among the ruins then finish your visit by sampling locally made produce at the **Ayuthaya Floating Market** (p90).

Four Days in Ayuthaya

On your third day head out of the city to visit **Bang Pa In Palace** (p88) and the nearby **Bang Sai Arts & Crafts Centre** (p90). On the way back, drop by at **Wat Phanan Choeng** (p86) to ensure good luck by releasing fish back into the river and return to the island in time to visit the brilliantly nostalgic **Million Toy Museum** (p90).

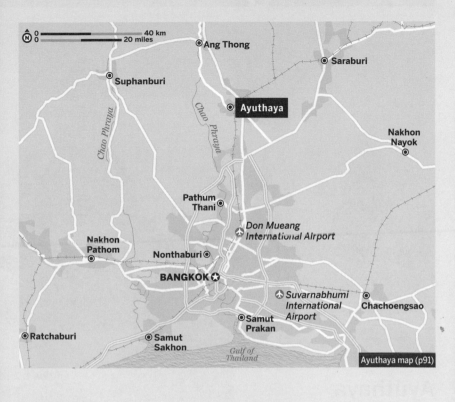

N 0 — 40 km
0 — 20 miles

⊚ Ang Thong

⊚ Saraburi

⊚ Suphanburi

Chao Phraya

Chao Phraya

⊚ **Ayuthaya**

Nakhon Nayok ⊚

Pathum Thani ⊚

✈ *Don Mueang International Airport*

Nakhon Pathom ⊚

Nonthaburi ⊚

BANGKOK ✪

✈ *Suvarnabhumi International Airport*

⊚ Chachoengsao

⊚ **Samut Prakan**

⊚ Ratchaburi

⊚ **Samut Sakhon**

Gulf of Thailand

Ayuthaya map (p91)

Arriving in Ayuthaya

Bus stop Most visitors arrive via bus or minivan from Bangkok. The bus stop is in the centre of town.

Train station Services from Bangkok's Hualamphong station make the journey here. Ayuthaya's train station is across the river from the centre of town.

Where to Stay

Being so close to Bangkok, many travellers visit Ayuthaya as a day trip, and as a result the town's sleeping options are somewhat limited. The primary guesthouse zone is on the island around Soi 2, Th Naresuan – a convenient location with easy access to the historical park, restaurants, markets and transport – and there are also budget options close to the train station. Midrange and top-end hotels typically congregate around the river.

★

Wat Chai Wattanaram

PHOTO BY VICHAN SRISEANGNIL/GETTY IMAGES ©

Ayuthaya Historical Park

At its zenith, Ayuthaya was home to over 400 temples. Today dozens of them have been partially restored, leaving the naked stupas, roofless chapels and headless Buddha images to evocatively tell the kingdom's tale of war with enemies and time.

Great For...

☑ **Don't Miss**

At night the temple ruins are dramatically lit up, providing great photo-ops.

The park is divided into two parts: sites on the island and sites off the island. You can visit the island on a bicycle but will need a motorcycle or chartered transport to go beyond.

Wat Phra Si Sanphet

One of the holiest sites, **Wat Phra Si Sanphet** (วัดพระศรีสรรเพชญ; admission 50B; ⊙8am-6pm) has three magnificent stupas and served as the model for Bangkok's Wat Phra Kaew. The temple was built in the late 15th century inside the palace grounds. It was Ayuthaya's largest temple and once contained a 16m-high standing Buddha (Phra Si Sanphet) covered with approximately 143kg gold. The Burmese conquerors melted down the gold.

Wihan Phra Mongkhon Bophit

Next to Wat Phra Si Sanphet, this **sanctuary hall** (วิหารพระมงคลบพิตร; ⊙8am-5pm)

ⓘ Need to Know

A one-day pass for most sites costs 220B and can be bought at the museums or ruins.

✕ Take a Break

Lung Lek (Th Chee Kun; mains 30-50B; ⊘8.30am-4pm) serves old-fashioned style 'boat noodles,' a recipe from the days of floating markets.

★ Top Tip

The temple ruins are revered symbols of royalty and religion; dress modestly and behave respectfully.

houses one of Thailand's largest bronze Buddha images. The 12.5m-high figure (17m with the base) was badly damaged by a lightning-induced fire around 1700, and again when the Burmese sacked the city. The Buddha and the building were repaired in the 20th century. In 1956 the Burmese Prime Minister donated 200,000B to restore the building, an act of atonement for his country's invasion 200 years before.

Wat Mahathat

Founded in 1374, during the reign of King Borom Rachathirat I, **Wat Mahathat** (วัด มหาธาตุ; Th Chee Kun; admission 50B; ⊘8am-6pm) was the seat of the supreme patriarch and the kingdom's most important temple. Today the ruins are best known for a curious interplay between nature and art: a sandstone Buddha head is held above the

ground by entangled bodhi tree roots. Be prepared to stand in line for the opportunity to photograph the phenomenon. And remember to act respectfully because it is a Buddha head that should be given reverence.

Wat Ratchaburana

The prang in this **temple** (วัดราชบูรณะ; admission 50B; ⊘8am-6pm) is one of the best extant versions in the city, with detailed carvings of lotus and mythical creatures. You can climb inside the prang to visit the brightly painted crypt, if you aren't afraid of heights, small spaces or bats. The temple was founded in 1424 by King Borom Rachathirat II on the cremation site for his two brothers who died fighting each other for the throne.

Wat Chai Wattanaram

This is the most impressive **off-island site** (วัดไชยวัฒนาราม; admission 50B; ⊘8am-6pm), thanks to its 35m-high Khmer-style central prang and overall good condition. It was built by King Prasat Thong beginning in 1630 (and taking around 20 years) to honour his mother, and the resemblance to Cambodia's Angkor Wat is intentional.

Wat Phanan Choeng

A bevy of popular merit-making ceremonies makes this **temple** (วัดพนัญเชิง; admission 20B; ☉dawn-dusk) a bustling place on weekends. The temple marks the historic location of a Chinese community which settled in Ayuthaya in the 14th century and is often associated with Zheng He (known as Sam Po Khong in Thailand), the Chinese emissary who explored Southeast Asia in the 15th century.

The signature attraction is the 19m-high Phra Phanan Choeng Buddha, which was created in 1324 and sits inside a sanctuary surrounded by 84,000 small buddha images. The Chinese shrine facing the river is especially colourful.

Wat Na Phra Men

This **temple** (วัดหน้าพระเมรุ; admission 20B; ☉dawn-dusk; P) was one of the few to escape the wrath of Burma's invading army in 1767 since it served as their main base. The *bòht* is massive, larger than most modern ones, and the very holy main Buddha image wears royal attire, which was very common in the late Ayuthaya era. Despite what the English sign inside says, it's made of bronze, not gold.

Ayutthaya Tourist Center

This multi-purpose building houses the **tourist information centre** (ศูนย์ท่องเที่ยว อยุธยา; ☎035 246076; ☉8.30am-4.30pm) FREE on the ground floor. But the reason for

Wat Phanan Choeng

a visit is the excellent upstairs museum, which puts Ayuthaya history into context with displays about the temples and daily life. Also upstairs is the tiny but interesting Ayutthaya National Art Museum.

Ayuthaya Historical Study Centre

This modern **museum** (ศูนย์ศึกษาประวัติศาสตร์ อยุธยา; Th Rotchana; adult/child 100/50B; ☺9am-4pm; [P]) funded by Japan features exhibitions on the lives of traditional villagers and the foreign communities during the Ayuthaya kingdom, plus a few dioramas of the city's former glories.

✕ Take a Break

Drop in to Bang Ian Night Market (p90) if you're visiting the park in the late afternoon to evening.

MARTINHOSMART/GETTY IMAGES ©

Chao Sam Phraya National Museum

The largest **museum** (พิพิธภัณฑสถานแห่ง ชาติเจ้าสามพระยา; cnr Th Rotchana & Th Si Sanphet; adult/child 150B/free; ☺9am-4pm; [P]) in the city displays many of the treasures unearthed during excavations of the ruins, including the golden treasures found in the crypts of Wat Mahathat and Wat Ratchaburana. Despite these treasures, the building lacks English signs and is a bit outdated.

Wat Yai Chai Mongkhon

King U Thong founded this **temple** (วัดใหญ่ ชัยมงคล; admission 20B; ☺6am-6pm) in 1357 to house monks returning from ordination in Sri Lanka. In 1592 King Naresuan built its fantastic bell-shaped *chedi* after a victory over the Burmese. The landscaped gardens make this one of Ayuthaya's most photogenic ruins. There's a 7m-long reclining Buddha near the entrance and the local belief is that if you can get a coin to stick to the Buddha's feet, good luck will come your way.

Phu Khao Thong

Phu Khao Thong (เจดีย์ภูเขาทอง; ☺dawn-dusk; [P]) is a huge white stupa built by the Burmese to commemorate their occupation of Ayuthaya in 1569. The larger-than-life statue is a memorial to the all-conquering Thai King Naresuan, who ousted the Burmese. Surrounding him are reliefs of his heroic exploits, including wrestling a crocodile, and dozens of statues of fighting cockerels.

King Naresuan is a celebrated Thai king who defeated the Burmese prince in an epic elephant battle. A lush movie trilogy first released in 2007 celebrated his exploits.

★ Did You Know?

Bicycles are a great way of getting around more rural, less-trafficked corners of Thailand like Ayuthaya Historical Park.

Aisawan Thiphya-At

MMEEE/GETTY IMAGES ©

Bang Pa In Palace

A former summer palace for the Thai kings, Bang Pa In is an eclectic assortment of architectural styles ranging from Chinese throne rooms to Gothic churches.

Great For...

☑ **Don't Miss**

Feeding the fish that live in the palace lake – it is an act of merit-making for Thai Buddhists and is believed to bring luck.

Bang Pa In was built beside the Chao Phraya River in the 17th century during the reign of King Prasat Thong. The palace was abandoned by the Ayuthaya kings and later revived by the Bangkok kings. The European formal gardens, statuary and residences were introduced by King Rama V (Chulalongkorn), an enthusiast of Western art and architecture. At the time of use, the property was divided into two sectors by an artificial lake – the outer was for ceremonial use and inner for the royal family only.

Saphakhan Ratchaprayun

A striking European-style residence originally built for the King's brothers now houses a small history museum about the palace.

❶ Need to Know

Bang Pa In Palace (พระราชวังบางปะอิน; admission 100B; ⊘8am-4pm, last entrance 3.15pm)

✕ Take a Break

Drinks and snacks are served at the small cafe by the Therawat Khanlai Gate, which overlooks the lake.

★ Top Tip

This is royal property so dress modestly.

Ho Withun Thatsana

'Sages' Lookout' is a brightly painted lookout tower. Climb the spiral staircase to reach King Rama V's favourite lookout spot.

Wat Niwet Thamaprawat

King Rama V loved mixing Thai and Western styles. This Buddhist temple located on an island across the river is a Gothic-church replica complete with stained-glass windows, a steeple and statues of knights in shining armour standing among buddha images. Take the cable car across the river.

Phra Thinang Warophat Phiman

Built in 1876, this neoclassical building served as King Rama V's residence and throne hall. Historical paintings decorate the chambers. During the current royal family's infrequent visits, they stay here.

Aisawan Thiphya-At

A classical Thai-style pavilion is scenically situated in the palace lake. Inside is a statue of King Rama V.

Phra Thinang Wehut Chamrun

A grand Chinese-style palace, known as the 'Residence of Heavenly Light,' was a gift to King Rama V from the Chinese Chamber of Commerce in 1889. On the ground floor is an ornate throne room.

Memorial to Queen Sunanda

A marble obelisk remembers King Rama V's consort Queen Sunanda, who drowned on the boat journey to the palace. Thai law forbade courtiers from touching the queen, so nobody dared jump in to save her. The law was later changed.

◉ SIGHTS

Bang Sai Arts & Crafts Centre — Cultural Centre

(ศูนย์ศิลปาชีพบางไทร; adult/child 100/50B; bird park additional 20B; ⊘9am-5pm) This centre preserves traditional Thai art by offering 30 training courses, ranging from ceramics to silks to *kǒhn* masks, and visitors can walk around and see them all. Other attractions on the 180-hectare site include **Sala Phra Ming Kwan** pavilion, which has galleries and sells a wide range of goods; a park with traditional houses from around the kingdom; a bird park and an aquarium. Avoid coming on non-holiday Mondays, when most things are closed.

There's no public transport from Ayuthaya.

Ayothaya Floating Market — Market

(ตลาดน้ำอโยธยา; ⊘9am-5pm Mon-Fri, to 6pm Sat & Sun; 𝐏) **FREE** Not an actual floating market, rather a highly kitsch tourist trap full of souvenir shops and selfie-snapping spots set on wooden platforms above the water. It is, however, a good place for snacking and there are afternoon cultural shows. Avoid the neighbouring Ayodia Inter Market with its dubious animal attractions.

Million Toy Museum — Museum

(พิพิธภัณฑ์ล้านของเล่นเกริกยุ้นพันธ์; ☏081 890 5782; www.milliontoymuseum.com; Th U Thong; adult/child 50/20B; ⊘9am-4pm Tue-Sun; 𝐏) Chances are your favourite childhood toy is enjoying retirement here among the tin soldiers, dolls and Godzillas, all lovingly displayed in this two-storey museum. It isn't just toys; the collection of pottery and old coconut scrapers is also of interest.

◉ TOURS

Ayutthaya Boat & Travel — Tour

(☏081 733 5687; www.ayutthaya-boat.com; Th Chee Kun; ⊘9am-5pm Mon-Sat) A variety of cycling and paddling tours are available through Ayutthaya Boat and Travel, off Th Rotchana. Two-day trips around the countryside involve staying overnight with a local family and a canal cruise.

◉ EATING

Bang Ian Night Market — Market $

(Th Bang Ian; ⊘4pm-8.30pm) This big, busy night market at the end of its namesake street is a great noshing destination. It's also ideally situated for a visit either before or after seeing the ruins illuminated at night.

Talat Nam Wat Tha Ka Rong — Market $

(⊘8am-5pm Sat & Sun) Buying your food at this floating market, where vendors serve from boats tied up to large rafts, is a great experience, though finding space at a table is less fun. It's on the Chao Phraya river behind its namesake temple (วัดท่าการ้อง).

Ayuthaya

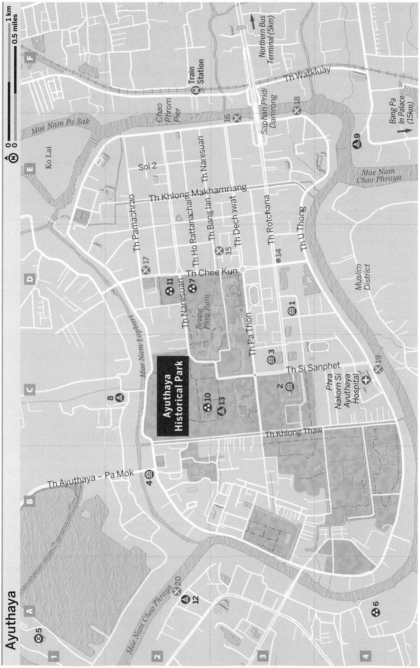

Ayuthaya

Ayuthaya Historical Park

Th Ayuthaya – Pa Mok

Mae Nam Chao Phraya

Th Khlong Thaw

Th Si Sanphet

Phra Nakorn Si Ayuthaya Hospital

Muslim District

Th U Thong

Th Rotchana

Th Pa Thon

Bueng Phra Ram

Th Chee Kun

Th Naresuan

Th Dechawat

Th Bang Ian

Th Ho Rattanachai

Th Khlong Makhamriang

Th Pamaphrao

Soi 2

Th Naresuan

Ko Lai

Mae Nam Lopburi

Mae Nam Pa Sak

Chao Phrom Pier

Train Station

Th Watkluay

Northern Bus Terminal (5km)

Saphan Pridi Damrong

Mae Nam Chao Phraya

Bang Pa In Palace (15km)

Roti Sai Mai Stalls   Sweets $

(Th U Thong; ⏱8am-8pm) The dessert *roh-dee săi măi* (silk thread roti) was invented in Ayuthaya and is sold all over town, though the shops fronting the hospital are the most famous. Buy a bag then make your own by rolling together thin strands of melted palm sugar and wrapping them inside the roti.

Bann Kun Pra   Thai $$

(📞035 241978; www.bannkunpra.com; Th U Thong; dishes 70-420B; ⏱11am-9.30pm) Far more intimate than most of Ayuthaya's riverside restaurants, this century-old teak house is a great place to sit and watch river life pass by. The inventive menu is loaded with seafood and has several versions of the local river prawn, including grilled with herbs and fried with tamarind sauce. There are some lovely but pricey guestrooms here, too.

Pae Krung Gao   Thai $$

(Th U Thong; dishes 60-1000B; ⏱10am-9.30pm; 🛜) A wonderfully cluttered riverside restaurant serving top-notch Thai food – seemingly half the crowd is here for the grilled river prawns. The English-language menu is limited, so if you know what you like, just ask.

📔🖊 **Foreign Quarter**

Ayuthaya's rulers were adroit diplomats and welcomed international merchants and immigrants. At its peak, over 40 ethnic groups resided here. The Mon, Lao and Khmer, as well as the Chinese, lived among the locals. The Indians, Persians, Javanese and Malay were given land, mostly to the south of the island. The Portuguese, who arrived in 1511, were the first Europeans to reach Siam. The **Portuguese Village** (หมู่บ้าน โปรตุเกส; ⏱9am-4pm) **FREE**, south of the island, contains a Catholic church and excavation site. Later, the Dutch, English, Spanish and French arrived, bringing arms and other luxuries and returning mostly with tin, deerskins, sappan wood and rice.

ℹ INFORMATION

Phra Nakorn Si Ayuthaya Hospital (📞035 211888; Th U Thong) Has an emergency centre and English-speaking doctors.

Tourism Authority of Thailand (TAT; 📞035 246076; tatyutya@tat.or.th; Th Si Sanphet; ⏱8.30am-4.30pm) Has an information counter with maps and good advice at the Ayutthaya Tourist Center (p86).

ℹ GETTING THERE & AWAY

BUS

Minivans to Bangkok's Victory Monument (60B, 1½ hours, frequent) leave from two central stops south of the backpacker strip around Soi 2, Th Naresuan.

TRAIN

For Bangkok, most trains stop at Bang Sue station (convenient for Banglamphu) before arriving at Hualamphong. Destinations include:

Bang Pa In (12B, 1¼ hour, 18 daily)

Bangkok (15B to 66B, 1½ to 2½ hours, frequent)

Chiang Mai (211B to 1398B, 11 to 14 hours, five daily)

Nong Khai (202B to 1262B, nine to 11 hours, four daily)

ℹ GETTING AROUND

Cycling is the ideal way to see the city. Most guesthouses hire bicycles (40B to 50B per day) and motorcycles (250B to 300B).

For most túk-túk trips on the island, the rate should be around 50B. The going rate per hour is 200B.

The river ferries cost 5B plus 5B for a bike. The ferry nearest the train station operates 5am to 7.30pm, and the western-most can carry motorcycles.

Short elephant rides past the temples are available, but it's worth considering the animal welfare issues involved with elephant rides.

Clockwise from top: Phra Thinang Wehut Chamrun (p89); statue on the grounds of Bang Pa In Palace (p88); Ho Withun Thatsana (p89)

SUKHOTHAI

In this Chapter

Sukhothai

Sukhothai is widely regarded as the first capital of Siam. After breaking away from the imperial Khmer kingdom in 1238, the newly founded state established itself as a regional power and a cultural leader. Beautiful temples mixing Khmer and unique Sukhothai styles were built to honour the newly adopted Theravada Buddhism and the new dynasty. Today the old city is sheltered in a quiet parklike setting that creates a meditative calm, perfect for enjoying the gravity of the majestic monuments. Despite its popularity, Sukhothai never feels crowded but there are off-the-beaten-path corners like Si Satchanalai-Chaliang, where you can be a solo adventurer.

Two Days in Sukothai

Spend two days exploring the **Sukhothai Historical Park** (p98). The central and northern zones are easily visited by bicycle. Come early in the morning to beat the heat and return for an evening photo shoot. The next day hire a motorcycle to explore the less-visited western and southern zones.

Four Days in Sukothai

Spend day three catching a local bus or hiring a motorcycle to **Si Satchanalai-Chaliang Historical Park** (p102). The park is in the country so enjoy life in the slow lane. On your last day sign up for a **cycling tour** (p106) of Sukhothai for a guided adventure to unexplored corners.

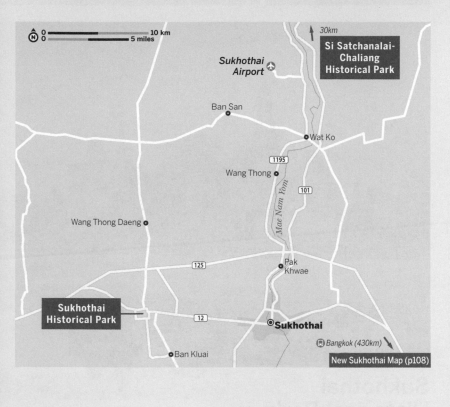

Sukhothai Airport

Si Satchanalai-Chaliang Historical Park

30km

Ban San

Wat Ko

1195

Wang Thong

101

Mae Nam Yom

Wang Thong Daeng

125

Pak Khwae

Sukhothai Historical Park

12

Sukhothai

Bangkok (430km)

New Sukhothai Map (p108)

Ban Kluai

Arriving in Sukothai

Sukhothai Airport Most visitors arrive by bus from Bangkok though there is an airport in Sukhothai and in nearby Phitsanulok. Minivan services link both airports to accommodations in Sukhothai.

Bus station Located 1km northwest of New Sukhothai. Accessible to town by chartered and public transport.

Where to Stay

Most accommodation is in New Sukhothai, which is home to some of the best-value budget accommodation in northern Thailand. Clean, cheerful hotels and guesthouses abound, with many places offering attractive bungalows, free pick-up from the bus station, and free use of bicycles. There are an increasing number of options near the park, many of them in the upscale bracket. Prices tend to go up during the Loi Krathong festival.

Wat Mahathat

TAMVISUT/GETTY IMAGES ©

Sukhothai Historical Park

Crumbling temple ruins and serene Buddha statues provide a meditative journey through this ancient Thai capital, designated a Unesco World Heritage site. The central leafy compound is one of the country's most impressive and peaceful historical parks.

Great For...

☑ **Don't Miss**

Renting a bicycle and cycling around the ruins is the best way to explore the central zone.

The Sukhothai Kingdom ('Sukhothai' means 'rising happiness') flourished from the mid-13th century to the late-14th century, as the imperial Angkor Kingdom in Cambodia was loosing its grip on its western frontier. This period is often viewed as the golden age of Thai civilisation. Sukhothai's dynasty lasted 200 years and spanned nine kings. By 1438 Sukhothai was absorbed by Ayuthaya.

Lesser ruins in the east and south appear in the Sights section; see p106.

Central Zone

The pockmarked ruins of the kingdom, believed to be the administrative centre, are concentrated here in an area known as *meuang gòw* (old city), a 45-sq-km compound.

❶ Need to Know

The historical park is divided into five zones (open 7.30am to 5.30pm). The central, northern and eastern zones have a separate 100B admission fee, plus a 10B to 50B surcharge for vehicles.

✕ Take a Break

Coffee Cup (Rte 12; dishes 30-150B; ☺8am-10pm; 🛜) serves fresh breads, drinks and other cafe fare.

★ Top Tip

The soft light and cooler temperatures of evening make it a perfect time to visit the central zone.

Ramkhamhaeng National Museum

A good starting point for exploring the historical park is this **museum** (พิพิธภัณฑสถาน แห่งชาติรามคำแหง; admission 150B; ☺9am-4pm), named for the third Sukhothai king. King Ramkhmahaeng is considered to be the founding father of the nation. He is credited with creating the Thai script and establishing Theravada Buddhism as the kingdom's primary religion. A replica of the famous Ramkhamhaeng inscription, said to be the earliest example of Thai writing, is kept here among an impressive collection of Sukhothai artefacts.

Religious art and architecture of the era are considered to be the most classic of Thai styles, influenced by the preceding Khmer period but adapted with graceful elements found in the features and gestures of the Buddha sculptures

of the time. Other hallmarks are the shape of the *chedi* and stucco relief work. The temple ruins of the historic park are viewed by historians as a transition between Khmer and Thai art.

Admission to the museum is not included in the ticket to the central zone.

Wat Mahathat

The largest temple in the historic park, **Wat Mahathat** (วัดมหาธาตุ) was completed in the 13th century and is considered to be the former spiritual and administrative centre of the old capital. It is a hybrid of Khmer and Sukhothai artistic styles. The temple is surrounded by brick walls (206m long and 200m wide) and a moat that is believed to represent the outer wall of the universe and the cosmic ocean, a common theme in Khmer architecture. Multiple *chedi* feature the famous lotus-bud motif, considered a distinctive Sukhothai artistic feature adapted from the Sri Lankan bell-shaped *chedi*. Some of the original stately Buddha figures still sit among the ruined columns of the old *wí·hǎhn* (sanctuary). There are 198 *chedi* within the monastery walls and many photogenic specimens.

Wat Si Sawai

Just south of Wat Mahathat, this Buddhist **shrine** (วัดศรีสวาย) dating from the 12th and 13th centuries features three Khmer-style towers and a picturesque moat. It was originally built by the Khmers as a Hindu temple. Sukhothai craftspeople added stucco reliefs depicting mythical creatures, such as *apsara* and *naga*.

Wat Sa Si

Wat Sa Si (วัดสระศรี, Sacred Pond Monastery) sits on an island west of the bronze

monument of King Ramkhamhaeng (the third Sukhothai king). It's a simple, classic Sukhothai-style wát containing a large Buddha, one bell-shaped *chedi* and the columns of the ruined *wí·hǎhn*. Bell-shaped *chedi,* an artistic inheritance from Sri Lanka, migrated to Sukhothai thanks to the adoption of Buddhism.

Wat Trapang Thong

Next to the Ramkhamhaeng National Museum, this small, still-inhabited **wát** (วัดตระพังทอง) with fine stucco reliefs is reached by a footbridge across the large lotus-filled pond that surrounds it. This reservoir, the original site of Thailand's Loi Krathong festival, supplies the Sukhothai community with most of its water.

Seated Buddha at Wat Si Chum

Northern Zone

This zone is 500m north of the old city walls and is easily reached by bicycle. It rivals the central zone with important architectural ruins.

Wat Si Chum

Beloved by shutterbugs, this **temple** (วัดศรี ชุม; Northern Zone) is northwest of the old city and contains an impressive *mon·dòp* (pavilion) with a 15m, brick-and-stucco seated Buddha. The Buddha's elegant, tapered fingers are much photographed and larger than life. Archaeologists theorise that this

> ★ **Did You Know?**
> The park includes the remains of 21 historical sites and four large ponds within the old walls, with an additional 70 sites within a 5km radius.

MARTIN M3D3/GETTY IMAGES ©

image is the 'Phra Atchana' mentioned in the famous Ramkhamhaeng inscription. A passage in the *mon·dòp* wall that leads to the top has been blocked so that it's no longer possible to view the *Jataka* inscriptions that line the tunnel ceiling.

Wat Phra Phai Luang

Often viewed as an architectural companion to Wat Si Sawai in the central zone, this somewhat isolated **temple** (วัดพระพายหลวง; Northern Zone) featured three 12th-century Khmer-style towers. All but one tower has collapsed and the remaining structure is decorated with time-worn stucco relief indicative of Sukhothai style. This may have been the centre of Sukhothai when it was ruled by the Khmers of Angkor prior to the 13th century.

Western Zone

This zone is about 2km from the old city and is rarely crowded. The road here leads past scenic countryside.

Wat Saphan Hin

Located on the crest of a hill that rises about 200m above the plain, the name of the **wát** (วัดสะพานหิน; Western Zone), which means 'stone bridge,' is a reference to the slate path and staircase that leads up to the temple, which are still in place. All that remains of the original temple are a few *chedi* and the ruined *wí·hǎhn*, consisting of two rows of laterite columns flanking a 12.5m-high standing Buddha image on a brick terrace. The site is 3km west of the former city wall and gives a good view of the Sukhothai ruins to the southeast and the mountains to the north and south.

> ★ **Did You Know?**
> The establishment of Sukhothai in 1238 is often described as marking the first thai kingdom, however the kingdom of Chiang Saen had already been established 500 years earlier so this is technically incorrect.

Wat Chang Lom

PRASIT PHOTO/GETTY IMAGES ©

Si Satchanalai-Chaliang Historical Park

Picturesque countryside and forests frame the ruins of this satellite city of the Sukhothai kingdom, dating to the 13th to 15th centuries. You're likely to encounter fewer visitors here.

Great For...

☑ **Don't Miss**

Climbing the stairs to the hilltop temple of Wat Khao Phanom Phloeng is a sightseeing workout.

As Sukhothai's influence grew, it expanded to this strategic position on the banks of the Mae Nam Yom (Yom River) between two lookout hills. Si Satchanalai hosted many of the Sukhothai kingdom's monasteries and temples as well as ceramics factories that exported to neighbouring countries. The town was linked by what historians refer to as Thailand's first highway. After the fall of Sukhothai, this area continued to be used by the rival forces of Lanna and Ayuthaya. Si Satchanalai, along with Sukhothai, was recognized as a Unesco World Heritage site. The park covers roughly 720 hectares and is surrounded by a 12m-wide moat. The complex is more sprawling and rural than Sukhothai and provides a glimpse into village life.

evocative of temples in Angkor. The figure
depicts the Hindu god Brahma.

The temple is believed to have been
founded in 1237 during the Khmer empire
and later renovated by Sukhothai and Ayuthaya rulers. An active monastery occupies
the grounds and contains a golden Buddha
image in the seated position surrounded by
smaller Buddhist figurines.

Wat Chang Lom

This fine **temple** (วัดช้างล้อม), marking the
centre of the old city of Si Satchanalai, is
encircled by elephant statues and a towering bell-shaped *chedi* that is somewhat
better preserved than its counterpart in
Sukhothai. The elephants' entire bodies
are intact giving the visual appearance of
the structure being carried on the backs
of the elephants. In Buddhist iconography,
elephants are often regarded as guardians,
and they were a common motif in Sukhothai temples. An inscription states that
the temple was built by King Ramkhamhaeng between 1285 and 1291.

Wat Khao Phanom Phloeng

On the hill overlooking Wat Chang Lom
are the remains of **Wat Khao Phanom
Phloeng** (วัดเขาพนมเพลิง), meaning Holy
Fire Mountain Temple. The forest closes

Wat Phra Si Ratana Mahathat

Si Satchanalai's main attraction, **Wat Phra
Si Ratana Mahathat** (วัดพระศรีรัตนมหาธาตุ;
admission 20B; ⊙8am-4.30pm) sits outside
the entrance to the historical park on the
banks of the Mae Nam Yom. The impressive
central tower poses peacefully amongst the
surrounding greenery and is framed by a
large seated Sukhothai Buddha and pillars.
Nearby is a smaller standing image and a
bas-relief of the famous walking Buddha,
exemplary of the flowing, boneless Sukhothai style. The tower is a corn-cob shape,
suggestive of Khmer style, but it is actually
an Ayuthaya style because it has a smooth
curvature rather than the Khmer 'steps'.
Near the main entrance, look for a pillar
topped by a Khmer-style four-faced figure,

in among a *chedi,* a large seated Buddha and stone columns that once supported the roof of the *wí·hǎhn.* From here you can make out the general design of the once-great city. It is a sweaty walk up the 44 steps made of laterite blocks to the top, but the surrounding forest adds a mystique of adventure. A small shrine to a local goddess receives supplications of dresses from devotees. The hilltop is also a nesting site for waterbirds, including egrets and cranes; locals often carry umbrellas to protect themselves from bird droppings.

The slightly higher hill west of Phanom Phloeng is capped by a large Sukhothai-style *chedi* – all that remains of Wat Khao Suwan Khiri.

Wat Chedi Jet Thaew

A strong contender for Si Satchanalai's best, **Wat Chedi Jet Thaew** (วัดเจดีย์เจ็ดแถว), next to Wat Chang Lom, is so named because of its seven rows of *chedi,* the largest of which is a copy of one at Wat Mahathat in Sukhothai. An interesting brick-and-plaster *wí·hǎhn* features barred windows designed to look like lathed wood (an ancient Indian technique used all over Southeast Asia).

The temple dates back to the 14th century and contains a mix of styles: Khmer, Lanna and Sukhothai. Inspect the niches to find a *naga*-canopied Buddha, which refers to the story of Buddha being protected from a rain storm by the mythical *naga.*

Wat Chao Chan

Wat Nang Phaya

One of the youngest temples in the collection, **Wat Nang Phaya** (วัดนางพญา), south of Wat Chedi Jet Thaew, has a bell-shaped Sinhalese *chedi* and was built in the 15th or 16th century. Stucco reliefs on the large laterite *wí·hăhn* in front of the *chedi* – now sheltered by a tin roof – date from the Ayuthaya period when Si Satchanalai was known as Sawankhalok. Goldsmiths in the district still craft a design known as *nahng pá·yah,* modelled after these reliefs. Local legend says that the temple was named for a princess.

★ **Don't Miss**

When visiting the park, make sure to check out the excavated kilns along Mae Nam Yom.

LUISMIX/GETTY IMAGES ©

Wat Chao Chan

Sheltered by woods, **Wat Chao Chan** (วัดเจ้าจันทร์; admission 100B; ⊗8am-5pm) is a large Khmer-style tower similar to later towers built in Lopburi and probably constructed during the reign of Khmer King Jayavarman VII (1181–1217). The tower has been restored and is in fairly good shape. The roofless *wí·hăhn* on the right contains the laterite outlines of a large standing Buddha that has all but melted away from exposure and weathering. Admission isn't always collected here.

Si Satchanalai Centre for Study & Preservation of Sangkalok Kilns

At one time, more than 200 huge pottery kilns lined the banks of the Mae Nam Yom in the area around Si Satchanalai. The kilns produced glazed ceramics that were exported to other Asian countries. In China – the biggest importer of Thai pottery during the Sukhothai and Ayuthaya periods – the pieces produced here came to be called Sangkalok, a mispronunciation of Sawankhalok, the original name of the region.

Excavated kilns can be visited at the **Si Satchanalai Centre for Study & Preservation of Sangkalok Kilns** (ศูนย์ศึกษาและอนุรักษ์เตาสังคโลก; admission 100B; ⊗8am-4.30pm), located 5km northwest of the Si Satchanalai ruins. There are also many intact pottery samples and interesting displays despite the lack of English labels. Ceramics are still made in the area, and a local ceramic artist even continues to fire his pieces in an underground wood-burning oven.

★ **Did You Know?**

Wat Phra Si Ratana Mahathat is one of the largest, oldest and most historically important in the park and received the status of royal property after a visit by the current king.

◎ SIGHTS

Sangkhalok Museum Museum
(พิพิธภัณฑ์สังคโลก; Rte 1293; adult/child
100/50B; ☺8am-5pm) This small but
comprehensive museum is an excellent
introduction to ancient Sukhothai's most
famous product and export, its ceramics.

The ground floor displays an impressive
collection of original Thai pottery found
in the area, plus some pieces traded from
Vietnam, Burma and China. The 2nd floor
features examples of non-utilitarian pottery
made as art, including some beautiful and
rare ceramic Buddha statues.

The museum is about 2.5km east of the
centre of New Sukhothai; a túk-túk here will
cost about 100B.

Wat Chang Lom Historic Site
(วัดช้างล้อม; off Rte 12) FREE Off Rte 12 in the
eastern zone, Wat Chang Lom (Elephant
Circled Monastery) is about 1km east of
the main park entrance. A large bell-shaped
chedi is supported by 36 elephants sculpted into its base.

Wat Chetupon Historic Site
(วัดเชตุพน) FREE Located 1.4km south of
the old city walls, this temple once held a
four-sided *mon·dòp* featuring the four classic poses of the Buddha (sitting, reclining,
standing and walking). The graceful lines of
the walking Buddha can still be made out
today.

Wat Chedi Si Hong Historic Site
(วัดเจดีย์สี่ห้อง) FREE Directly across from
Wat Chetupon, the main *chedi* here has
retained much of its original stucco relief
work, which shows still vivid depictions of
elephants, lions and humans.

⊕ TOURS

Cycling Sukhothai Bicycle Tour
(☏055 612519, 08 5083 1864; www.cycling-sukho
thai.com; off Th Jarodvithithong; half-day 750B,
full day 950-990B, sunset tour 400B) A resident
of Sukhothai for nearly 20 years, Belgian
cycling enthusiast Ronny Hanquart's rides
follow themed itineraries such as the His-

torical Park Tour, which also includes stops
at lesser-seen wát and villages. Its office is
based about 1.2km west of Mae Nam Yom,
in New Sukhothai; free transport can be
arranged.

Sukhothai Bicycle Tour Bicycle Tour
(☏08 6931 6242; www.sukhothaibicycletour.com;
34/1 Th Jarodvithithong; half-day 750B, full day
1050-1150B) A bicycle-based tour outfit that
gets overwhelmingly positive feedback.

⊗ EATING

Night Market Market $
(Th Ramkhamhaeng; mains 30-60B; ☺6-11pm) A
wise choice for cheap eats is New Sukhothai's tiny night market. Most vendors here
are accustomed to accommodating foreigners and even provide bilingual menus.

Jayhae Thai $
(Th Jarodvithithong; dishes 30-50B; ☺8am-
4pm) You haven't been to Sukhothai if you
haven't tried the noodles at Jayhae, an extremely popular restaurant that also serves
pàt tai and tasty coffee drinks.

Poo Restaurant International, Thai $
(24/3 Th Jarodvithithong; mains 30-150B;
☺11am-midnight; ☎) Unfortunately named
and deceptively simple, Poo has a small
selection of Belgian beers.

Fueang Fah Thai $
(107/2 Th Khuhasuwan, no roman-script sign;
dishes 50-350B; ☺10am-10pm) Pretend you're
a local in-the-know and take a meal at this
long-standing riverside restaurant. The
speciality is freshwater fish dishes, such
as the tasty fried fish, the first item on the
barely comprehensible English-language
menu. It's just after the bridge on Th
Khuhasuwan.

Dream Café Thai $$
(86/1 Th Singhawat; mains 80-350B; ☺5-11pm;
❄☎) A meal at Dream Café is like dining
in an antique shop. Eclectic but tasteful
furnishings and knick-knackery abound,
staff are equal parts competent and

Clockwise from top: Wat Si Sawai (p100); performance during Loi Krathong (p24), Sukhothai Historical Park; close-up of a Buddha statue, Sukhothai Historical Park (p98)

New Sukhothai

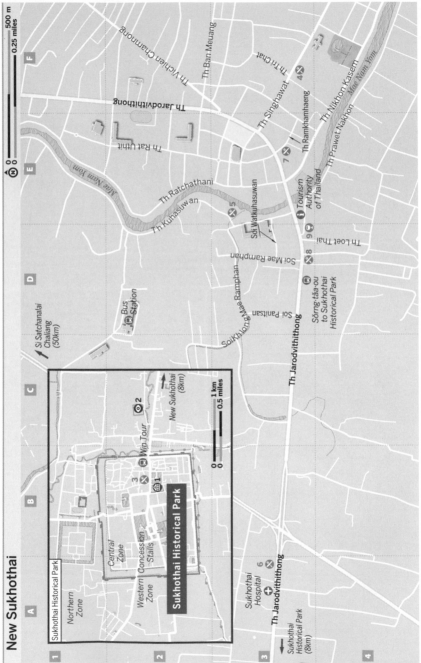

Sukhothai Historical Park

Northern Zone

Central Zone

Western Concession Stalls Zone

Sukhothai Historical Park

Win Tour

New Sukhothai (8km)

1 km
0.5 miles

Sukhothai Hospital

6

Th Jarodvithithong

Sukhothai Historical Park (8km)

Bus Station

Si Satchanalai Chaliang (50km)

Mae Nam Yom

Th Kuhasuwan

Th Ratchathani

Th Rat Uthit

Th Jarodvithithong

Th Vichien Chamnong

Th Ban Meuang

Th Singthawat

Th Tri Chat

4

7

Th Ramkhamhaeng

Th Nikhon Kasem

Mae Nam Yom

Th Prawet Nakhon

Tourism Authority of Thailand

5

Soi Watkuhasuwan

9

Th Loet Thai

8

Soi Mae Ramphan

Sŏrng·tăa·ou to Sukhothai Historical Park

Soi Panitsan

Soi Khlong Mae Ramphan

Th Jarodvithithong

500 m
0.25 miles

New Sukhothai

friendly, and, most importantly of all, the food is good. Try one of the well-executed *yam* (Thai-style 'salads'), or one of the dishes that feature freshwater fish, a local speciality.

🍸 DRINKING & NIGHTLIFE

Chopper Bar   Bar
(Th Prawet Nakhon; ◷10am-12.30am; 🛜) Both travellers and locals congregate at this restaurant-bar from morning till hangover for food (mains 30B to 150B), drinks and live music. Take advantage of Sukhothai's cool evenings on the rooftop terrace.

ℹ️ INFORMATION

Sukhothai Hospital (✆055 610280; Th Jarodvithithong) Located just west of New Sukhothai.

Tourism Authority of Thailand (TAT; ✆055 616228, nationwide 1672; Th Jarodvithithong; ◷8.30am-4.30pm) Near the bridge in New Sukhothai, this new office has a pretty good selection of maps and brochures.

ℹ️ GETTING THERE & AWAY

AIR
Sukhothai's airport is a whopping 27km north of town off Rte 1195. **Bangkok Airways** (✆Sukho-

thai Airport 0 5564 7224, nationwide 1771; www.bangkokair.com; Sukhothai Airport; ◷7.30-11.30am & 12.30-5.30pm) operates flights to Bangkok's Suvarnabhumi International Airport (1695B, one hour 15 minutes, two daily).

BUS
Sukhothai's **minivan and bus station** (✆055 614529; Rte 101) is 1km northwest of New Sukhothai; a motorcycle taxi should cost around 50B. Buses to Si Satchanalai (49B, 1½ hour, hourly) leave from here.

Win Tour (Rte 12; ◷6am-9.40pm) has an office near the historical park where you can board buses to Bangkok (342B, six hours, 8.20am, 12.30pm and 9.50pm) and Chiang Mai (228B, five hours, six departures from 6.50am to 2pm).

ℹ️ GETTING AROUND

Frequent *sŏrng·tăa·ou* run between New Sukhothai and Sukhothai Historical Park (30B, 30 minutes, from 6am to 6pm), leaving from a stop on Th Jarodvithithong. Motorcycle taxis do the trip for 120B. The best way to get around the historical park is by bicycle, which can be rented at shops outside the park entrance for 30B per day. Motorbike rental starts at about 250B per day.

CHIANG MAI

Chiang Mai

The cultural capital of the north, Chiang Mai is beloved by temple-spotters, culture vultures and adventure-loving families. The narrow streets steeped in history provide an atmosphere more like a country town than a modern city. Beyond the old city, modern Chiang Mai offers fantastic dining thanks to imports from Burma and Japan, as well as local specialities. Great escapes from the city lie just an hour away and tours shuttle visitors to jungle treks, elephant sanctuaries and minority villages.

Two Days in Chiang Mai

Visit the temples and museums of the **old city**. Have dinner at **Huen Phen** (p137) and finish the evening at **Riverside Bar & Restaurant** (p140). Spend your second day doing a Thai cooking course, then visit the **Saturday Walking Street** (p120) or **Sunday Walking Street** (p121), if you're here for a weekend.

Four Days in Chiang Mai

On your third day join a full-day outdoor activity, such as trekking, ziplining or mountain biking. The next day, tour the shops and restaurants of **Th Nimmanhaemin** – try **I-Berry** (p125) for icecream and **Tong Tem Toh** (p124) for Northern Thai cuisine – and stay for the nightlife.

Central Chiang Mai map (p132)

Arriving in Chiang Mai

Chiang Mai International Airport Airport taxis charge a flat 160B fare. Some hotels also provide hotel transfer.

Arcade Bus Terminal A chartered *rót daang* ('red truck') to the centre costs about 60B; a túk-túk, 80B to 100B.

Chiang Mai Railway Station A chartered *rót daang* costs about 60B; a túk-túk, 80B to 100B.

Where to Stay

Chiang Mai's most charming area to stay is the centrally located old city, even though it is touristy and crowded. The Riverside area and east of the old city may lack personality but boast waterside accommodation and proximity to the Night Bazaar. Lodging is overpriced west of the old city, but you'll be close to dining options and nightlife.

Wat Chedi Luang

Old City's Temples

Chiang Mai's temples showcase traditional Lanna art and architecture, using teak harvested in the once-dense frontiers and demonstrating traditions inherited from Burma and China.

Great For...

☑ Don't Miss

Learn about Buddhism and being a monk at Wat Chedi Luang's Monk Chat.

The highlight of any visit to the old city is exploring the temples that burst out on almost every street corner, attracting hordes of pilgrims, tourists and local worshippers. For a calmer experience, visit late in the afternoon, when the tourist crowds are replaced by monks attending evening prayers.

Exploring these temples is easily done on bicycle, giving you a chance to cruise the old city's side roads and residential areas. The temples featured here are all located in the old city, but other beautiful temples lie outside of the city walls.

Wat Phra Singh

Chiang Mai's most revered temple, **Wat Phra Singh** (วัดพระสิงห์; Th Singharat; admission to main wí·hǎhn 20B; ⏰5am-8.30pm) sits regally at the end of Th Ratchadamnoen. Behind its whitewashed walls are lavish

Decoration at Wat Phra Singh

JOHN W BANAGAN/GETTY IMAGES ©

National Museum and one in Nakhon Si Thammarat. Regardless of its provenance, the statue has become a focal point for religious celebrations during the Songkran festival, when it is ceremoniously paraded for worshippers to bathe.

As you wander the monastery grounds, note the raised temple library, housed in a dainty teak and stucco pavilion known as Ho Trai, decorated with bas-relief angels. The temple's main *chedi,* rising over a classic Lanna-style octagonal base, was constructed by King Pa Yo in 1345; it's often wrapped in bolts of orange cloth by devotees.

Wat Chedi Luang

Wat Chedi Luang (วัดเจดีย์หลวง; Th Phra Pok-klao; donations appreciated; ⊗6am-6pm) **FREE** is not quite as grand as Wat Phra Singh, but its towering, ruined Lanna-style *chedi* (built in 1441) is much taller and the sprawling compound is powerfully atmospheric. The famed Phra Kaew (Emerald Buddha), now held in Bangkok's Wat Phra Kaew, resided in the eastern niche of the *chedi* until 1475; today, you can view a jade replica, given as a gift from the Thai king in 1995 to celebrate the 600th anniversary of the *chedi.*

In the main *wí·hǎhn* is a revered standing Buddha statue, known as Phra Chao Attarot, flanked by two disciples. There are more chapels and statues in teak pavilions at the rear of the compound, including a

monastic buildings and immaculately trimmed grounds, dotted with coffee stands and massage pavilions. Pilgrims flock here to venerate the famous Buddha image known as Phra Singh (Lion Buddha), housed in Wihan Lai Kham, a small chapel immediately south of the *chedi* (stupa) to the rear of the temple grounds.

This elegant image is said to have come to Thailand from Sri Lanka and was enshrined in 1367. The chapel is similarly striking, with gilded *naga* gables and sumptuous *lai·krahm* (gold-pattern stencilling) inside.

Despite Phra Singh's exalted status, very little is actually known about the image, which has more in common with images from northern Thailand than with Buddha statues from Sri Lanka. Adding to the mystery, there are two nearly identical images elsewhere in Thailand, one in the Bangkok

huge reclining Buddha and a handsome Chinese-influenced seated Buddha barely contained by his robes. The daily Monk Chat under a tree in the grounds always draws a crowd of interested travellers.

Next to the main entrance on Th Phra Pokklao, you'll pass Wat Chedi Luang's other claim to fame: the Lak Meuang (city pillar), allegedly raised by King Mengrai himself when Chiang Mai was founded in 1296. Buddhist rules dictate that only men can enter the pavilion to view the pillar. The gateway to the shrine on Th Phra Pokklao is flanked by *yaksha* (guardian demons), and Lanna warriors are depicted in bas-relief on the gates.

Wat Phan Tao

Without doubt the most atmospheric wát in the old city is **Wat Phan Tao** (วัดพันเถา; Th Phra Pokklao; donations appreciated; ⊘6am-6pm) FREE. This teak marvel sits in the shadow of Wat Chedi Luang. Set in a compound full of fluttering orange flags, the monastery is a monument to the teak trade, with an enormous prayer hall supported by 28 gargantuan teak pillars and lined with dark teak panels, enshrining a particularly graceful gold Buddha image. The juxtaposition of the orange monks' robes against this dark backdrop during evening prayers is particularly sublime.

Above the facade is a striking image of a peacock over a dog, representing the astrological year of the former royal resident's birth. The monastery is one of the focal points for celebrations during the Visakha Bucha festival in May or June, when monks light hundreds of butter lamps around the pond in the grounds.

Prayers during Makha Bucha (p22) at Wat Phan Tao

Wat Chiang Man

Chiang Mai's oldest temple, **Wat Chiang Man** (วัดเชียงมั่น; Th Ratchaphakhinai; donations appreciated; ⊘6am-6pm) **FREE**, was established by the city's founder, Phaya Mengrai, sometime around 1296. In front of the *ubosot* (ordination hall), a stone slab, engraved in 1581, bears the earliest known reference to the city's founding. The main *wí·hǎhn* also contains the oldest known Buddha image created by the Lanna kingdom, cast in 1465.

★ Did You Know?

Phra Singh is said to have come from Sri Lanka but it has more in common with images from northern Thailand than with Buddha statues from Sri Lanka.

ABILITYRIDDLE/GETTY IMAGES ©

A smaller second *wí·hǎhn* enshrines the city's guardian images: the bas-relief marble Phra Sila Buddha, believed to have been carved in Sri Lanka more than 1000 years ago, and the tiny crystal Phra Sae Tang Khamani Buddha, reportedly crafted for the king of Lopburi in around AD 200.

The sacred images are housed inside a handsome, *mon·dòp*-like altar known as a *khong phra chao,* a distinctive feature of ancient Lanna temples. The monastery has a glorious *chedi,* with an elephant-flanked stucco base and a gilded upper level.

Wat Inthakhin Saduemuang

Tucked to the side of the Chiang Mai City Arts & Cultural Centre, **Wat Inthakhin Saduemuang** (วัดอินทขิลสะดือเมือง; donations appreciated; ⊘6am-6pm) **FREE** was the original location of the Lak Meuang (city pillar); part of its name refers to the 'city navel,' or geographic centre, which was chosen some 700 years ago. The city pillar was moved to Wat Chedi Luang in 1800 after this temple fell into disrepair. It has since been given an intense makeover, making it one of the old city's most glittering temples. Marooned in the middle of Th Inthawarorot, its gilded teak *wí·hǎhn* is one of the most perfectly proportioned monuments in the city.

Temple Etiquette

Visitors are welcome but should follow the standard rules of Buddhist etiquette.

○ Stay quiet during prayers.

○ Keep your feet pointed away from Buddha images and monks.

○ Dress modestly (covering shoulders and knees).

○ Remove your shoes when you enter a temple building. Sit with your feet tucked behind you to avoid pointing the bottom of your feet at Buddha images.

○ Women should never touch a monk or a monk's belongings; step out of the way on footpaths and don't sit next to them on public transport.

Chiang Mai City Arts & Cultural Centre

Old City's Museums

Chiang Mai's museums are modern and provide an excellent introduction to the former Lanna kingdom's culture and history. These historical showcases are conveniently clustered near each other in colonial-style government buildings.

Great For...

☑ Don't Miss

A string of shops on Th Inthawarorot, near the museums, sells Thai sweets and other local dishes. It's packed with workers at lunchtime.

Just when you think you've got this country figured out, you land in a place like Chiang Mai and discover a whole new regional identity. Thankfully these museums explain the unique aspects of the Lanna kingdom, a closer cousin to southern China and Burma than Bangkok.

Chiang Mai City Arts & Cultural Centre

The **Chiang Mai City Arts & Cultural Centre** (หอศิลปวัฒนธรรมเชียงใหม่; www.cmocity. com; Th Phra Pokklao; adult/child 90/40B; ⊙8.30am-5pm Tue-Sun) provides an excellent primer on Chiang Mai history. Dioramas, photos, artefacts and audiovisual displays walk visitors through the key battles and victories in the Chiang Mai story, from the first settlements to wars with Burma and to the arrival of the railroad. Upstairs is a

ⓘ Need to Know

The museums are closed on Monday. They have a central location within walking distance to most old city accommodation.

✕ Take a Break

Get a massage and help inmates earn work skills at the Vocational Training Center of the Chiang Mai Women's Correctional Institution (p130).

★ Top Tip

Combination tickets (180B) gain entry to all three museums.

charming recreation of a wooden Lanna village.

The museum gift shop is exceptionally well stocked with lacquerware, jewellery and even decorative fingernails for the Thai traditional dance. The building previously housed the provincial hall and is a handsomely restored Thai-colonial-style building dating from 1927. Restoration of the building was recognised by the Royal Society of Siamese Architects in 1999.

Lanna Folklife Museum

A real gem, the **Lanna Folklife Museum** (พิพิธภัณฑ์พื้นถิ่นล้านนา; Th Phra Pokklao; adult/ child 90/40B; ⊗8.30am-5pm Tue-Sun) is set inside the former 1935 provincial court and recreates Lanna village life in a series of life-sized dioramas that explain everything

from *lai·krahm* stencilling and *forn lép* (traditional Lanna dance) to the intricate symbolism of different elements of Lanna-style temples. Each room is designed like an art installation with engaging lessons on cultural tidbits. You'll leave knowing a little more Lanna than before.

Chiang Mai Historical Centre

Housed in an airy building, this **museum** (หอประวัติศาสตร์เมืองเชียงใหม่; Th Ratwithi; adult/ child 90/40B; ⊗8.30am-5pm Tue-Sun) covers the history of Chiang Mai province, with displays on the founding of the capital, the Burmese occupation and the modern era of trade and unification with Bangkok. Downstairs is an archaeological dig of an ancient temple wall. There is a bit of overlap between the Chiang Mai City Arts & Culture Centre but sometimes an air conditioned building is all one really needs.

SOO HON KEONG/GETTY IMAGES ©

Shoppers browsing the Saturday Walking Street

Evening Shopping

The evening market is a popular fixture across Thailand but Chiang Mai invented the 'walking street,' which transforms streets into a pedestrian zone for itinerant vendors, a tradition that dates back to the Silk Road days.

Great For...

☑ **Don't Miss**

Local vendors selling refreshing ice cream, advertised as 'ancient' ice cream, at the walking streets.

Saturday Walking Street

The **Saturday Walking Street** (ถนนเดินวันเสาร์; Th Wualai; ◷4pm-midnight Sat) takes over Th Wualai, running southwest from Pratu Chiang Mai at the southern entrance to the old city. There is barely space to move as locals and tourists haggle for carved soaps, novelty dog collars, wood-carvings, Buddha paintings, hill-tribe trinkets and more.

The market unfolds along the city's historic silversmithing neighbourhood. Come early enough and you can see the craftspeople tapping out a rhythm as they impress decorative patterns into bowls, jewellery boxes and decorative plaques made from silver or, more often, aluminium.

Chiang Mai Night Bazaar

You don't have to wait for a weekend to scratch your shopping itch. The **Chiang Mai Night Bazaar** (Th Chang Khlan; ☉7pm-midnight) is one of the city's main night-time attractions and is the modern legacy of the original Yunnanese trading caravans that stopped here along the ancient trade route between China and Myanmar's Gulf of Martaban coast.

The night bazaar sells the usual tourist souvenirs. In true market fashion, vendors form a gauntlet along the footpath of Th Chang Khlan from Th Tha Phae to Th Loi Kroh. In between are dedicated shopping buildings: the Chiang Mai Night Bazaar Building is filled mainly with antique and handicraft stores. Across the street is the Kalare Night Bazaar selling upmarket clothes and home decor.

Sunday Walking Street

Thanon Ratchadamnoen is taken over by the boisterous **Sunday Walking Street** (ถนนเดินวันอาทิตย์; Th Ratchadamnoen; ☉4pm-midnight Sun), which feels even more animated than the Saturday Walking Street because of the energetic food markets that open up temple courtyards along the route. There's not a lot of breathing room as crowds slowly pass stalls selling wood-carvings, Buddha paintings, hill-tribe trinkets, Thai musical instruments, T-shirts, paper lanterns and umbrellas, silver jewellery and herbal remedies.

The market is a major source of income for local families and many traders spend the whole week hand-making merchandise to sell on Saturday and Sunday.

Elephant Nature Park

ISWEETRIVER/GETTY IMAGES ©

Outdoor Activities

Outdoor escapes are easy in Chiang Mai thanks to nearby looming mountains, rushing rivers, hill-tribe villages, and elephant sanctuaries and camps. Dozens of operators offer adventure tours on foot, bike, raft and zipline.

Great For ...

☑ **Don't Miss**

Chiang Mai's climate quickly transitions from the tropical plains to fern-filled mountain forests.

Trekking & Outdoor Adventuring

Thousands of visitors trek into the hills of northern Thailand hoping for adventure. Recommended companies include **Pooh Eco-Trekking** (☑053 208538; www.pooh-ecotrekking.com; 59 Th Ratchaphakhinai; 2-day tours per person from 3500B), which has a strong environmental ethos, and **Peak Adventure Tour** (☑053 800567; www.thepeakadventure.com; 302/4 Th Chiang Mai-Lamphun; tours 900-2500B), for soft-adventure. Everyone loves **Flight of the Gibbon** (☑053 010660; www.treetopasia.com; 29/4-5 Th Kotchasan; day tour 3599B), a nearly-2km zipline course through the forest.

Need To Know

Most tours travel about an hour outside of the city for full- and half-day tours. Trips usually include hotel transfer and lunch.

✕ Take a Break

After a sweaty adventure, reward yourself with a massage at **Lila Thai Massage** (☑053 327243; www.chiangmaimassage.com; Th Ratchadamnoen; standard/herbal massage from 200/300B; ☾10am-10pm).

★ Top Tip

Book your tickets directly with the tour operator to cut out agent commission charges.

Elephant Parks

Elephants have been used as beasts of burden in Thailand for thousands of years, hauling logs from the teak forests and transporting the carriages of Thai royalty. With the nationwide ban on logging in 1989, thousands of working elephants suddenly found themselves out of a job, and herders and mahouts (elephant drivers) looked for new ways to generate revenue from their animals.

Elephant camps can look a lot like a prison but Chiang Mai has many humane alternatives.

Elephant Nature Park (☑053 818754; www.elephantnaturepark.org; 1 Th Ratchamankha; 1-/2-day tour 2500/5800B) ✿ provides a semi-wild state where visitors observe

the natural interactions of elephants, while **Patara Elephant Farm** (☑081 992 2551; www.pataraelephantfarm.com; Baan Pong; day tour 3800-5800B) offers some of the traditional elephant experiences (bathing and learning mahout commands) in a forested setting with high animal welfare standards.

Bicycling

The city's closest green space, Doi Suthep, has mountain biking trails traversed by **Chiang Mai Mountain Biking & Kayaking** (☑053 814207; www.mountainbikingchiangmai. com; 1 Th Samlan; tours 1250-2300B). **Click and Travel** (☑053 281553; www.chiangmai cycling.com; tours 950-5350B; ⊕) cycles through cultural sights outside the city centre.

Water Sports

White-water rafting takes on the wild and frothy part of Mae Taeng (best from July to March). **Siam River Adventures** (☑089 515 1917; www.siamrivers.com; 17 Th Ratwithi; rafting per day from 1800B) has well-regarded safety standards for the 10km stretch. Chiang Mai Mountain Biking & Kayaking kayaks down a remote part of the Mae Ping.

Nám prík ong (chilli paste with vegetables for dipping)

SOMRAK JENDEE/GETTY IMAGES ©

Th Nimmanhaemin

The epicentre of 'new' Chiang Mai, Th Nimmanhaemin is the place to wine, dine and stay up all night (or at least until closing time). The main road and its tributary soi are frequented by hip uni students and NGO expats.

Great For...

☑ Don't Miss

The food stalls near Soi 10 sell fried chicken, cut fruit and noodle dishes. Simple is amazing in Thailand.

Dining

There is a bewildering array of food to be found on Nimman.

Tong Tem Toh (Soi 13, Th Nimmanhaemin; mains 50-170B; ⊙11am-9pm) is set in an old teak house and serves Northern Thai cuisine, such as *nám prík ong* (chilli paste with vegetables for dipping) and *gaang hang lay* (Burmese-style pork curry with peanut and tamarind).

Salad Concept (Th Nimmanhaemin; mains 50-170B; ⊙11am-10pm; 🖘🍴) has a colourful salad buffet with a big choice of chemical-free greens. Sounds a bit ho-hum, but in Thailand, this is exotic.

Nimman goes ga-ga for Japanese. **Ai Sushi** (Th Huay Kaew; mains 90-210B; ⊙5-11.30pm) pulls in droves of hungry students for fresh and delicious sushi, sashimi and

ⓘ Need to Know

Th Nimmanhaemin is accessible by *rót daang* travelling along Th Huay Kaew.

✕ Take a Break

Ristr8to (153/3 Th Nimmanhaemin; coffee 65-120B; ⊙8am-7pm Wed-Mon) treats coffee like wine, complete with tasting notes.

★ Top Tip

The soi branching off Th Nimmanhaemin don't have sidewalks so be careful as a pedestrian.

sides. But **Tengoku** (⌕053 215801; Soi 5, Th Nimmanhaemin; mains 130-1650B; ⊙11am-2pm & 5.30-10pm; ☏) leaves every other place in the shade of Mt Fuji. This sleek restaurant serves superior sushi, yakitori, spectacular sukiyaki and wonderful wagyu steaks, plus cheaper bento boxes.

Ice cream with star power, **I-Berry** (off Soi 17, Th Nimmanhaemin; ice creams & smoothies from 60B; ⊙10am-10pm; ☏) is owned by Thai comedian Udom Taepanich (nicknamed 'Nose' for his signature feature). This kitschy shop in a leafy garden is mobbed day and night.

Drinking & Nightlife

Nimman draws in an eclectic crowd of night owls, from rowdy uni students to Thai yuppies and in-the-know foreigners.

Check out the urban tribe at **Sangdee Gallery** (www.sangdeegallery.org; 5 Soi 5, Th Sirimungklajarn; ⊙11am-midnight Tue-Sat), part gallery, music club, bar and cafe.

The trendy spots change but the formula stays the same: beer garden venues with brews, food and friends. The more people can pack in, the merrier. **Beer Republic** (Soi 11, Th Nimmanhaemin; ⊙4pm-midnight Tue-Sun) offers 15 draught beers. **Year Garage** (www.facebook.com/oneyearatnimman; Soi 17, Th Nimmanhaemin; ⊙6pm-midnight) does good cheap eats and, of course, beer.

Blar Blar Bar (Soi 5, Th Nimmanhaemin; ⊙6pm-midnight) is a big and boozy bar popular with youthful punters. **Warmup Cafe** (www.facebook.com/warmupcafe1999; 40 Th Nimmanhaemin; ⊙6pm-2am) is a Nimman club survivor, rocking out since 1999. Each room does a different music genre: hip-hop, electronica and rock.

KANTAPAT PHUTTHAMKUL/GETTY IMAGES ©

Doi Suthep

Ascending Doi Suthep is something of a spiritual experience: switchback roads leave behind the lowland plains and ascend into the cool cloud belt filled with mosses and ferns. The mountain shelters a national park, holy temple, royal palace and hill-tribe villages.

Great For ...

☑ Don't Miss

The spectacular views of Chiang Mai from Wat Phra That Doi Suthep.

Wat Phra That Doi Suthep

Overlooking the city from its mountain throne, **Wat Phra That Doi Suthep** (วัด พระธาตุดอยสุเทพ; Th Huay Kaew, Doi Suthep; admission 30B; ⊙6am-6pm) is one of northern Thailand's most sacred temples, and its founding legend is learned by every school kid in Chiang Mai. The wát itself is a beautiful example of northern Thai architecture, reached via a strenuous, 306-step staircase flanked by mosaic-encrusted *naga* (serpents); the climb is intended to help devotees accrue Buddhist merit, but less energetic pilgrims can take a funicular lift (20B).

The monastery was established in 1383 by King Keu Naone to enshrine a piece of bone, said to be from the shoulder of the

historical Buddha. The bone shard was brought to Lanna by a wandering monk from Sukhothai and it broke into two pieces at the base of the mountain, with one piece being enshrined at Wat Suan Dok. The second fragment was mounted onto a sacred white elephant who wandered the jungle until it died, in the process selecting the spot where the monastery was later founded.

The terrace at the top of the steps is dotted with small shrines, rock gardens and a statue of the white elephant that carried the Buddha relic. Before entering the inner courtyard, children pay their respects to a lizard-like guardian statue known as 'Mom.'

Steps lead up to the inner terrace, where a walkway circumnavigates the gleaming golden *chedi* enshrining the relic. The crowning five-tiered umbrella marks the city's independence from Burma and its union with Thailand. Pilgrims queue to leave lotus blossoms and other offerings at the shrines surrounding the *chedi*.

Bhubing Palace

Above Wat Phra That Doi Suthep, the grounds of the royal family's **winter palace** (พระตำหนักภูพิงค์, Phra Tamnak Bhu Bing; www.bhubingpalace.org; Th Huay Kaew, Doi Suthep; admission 50B; ◷8.30-11.30am & 1-3.30pm) are open to the public. Thanks to the mountain's cool climate, the royal gardeners are able to raise 'exotic' species such as roses. More interesting is the reservoir, brought to life by fountains that dance to the king's own musical compositions.

Ban Kun Chang Kian

Ban Kun Chang Kian is a Hmong coffee-producing village about 500m down a dirt track just past the Doi Pui campground. You'll need private transport to reach the village.

Chiang Mai Walking Tour

Chiang Mai's famous temples reside in the historic old city. Start in the morning hours, dress modestly (covering shoulders and knees) and remove your shoes before entering and sit in the 'mermaid' position inside the sanctuary halls.

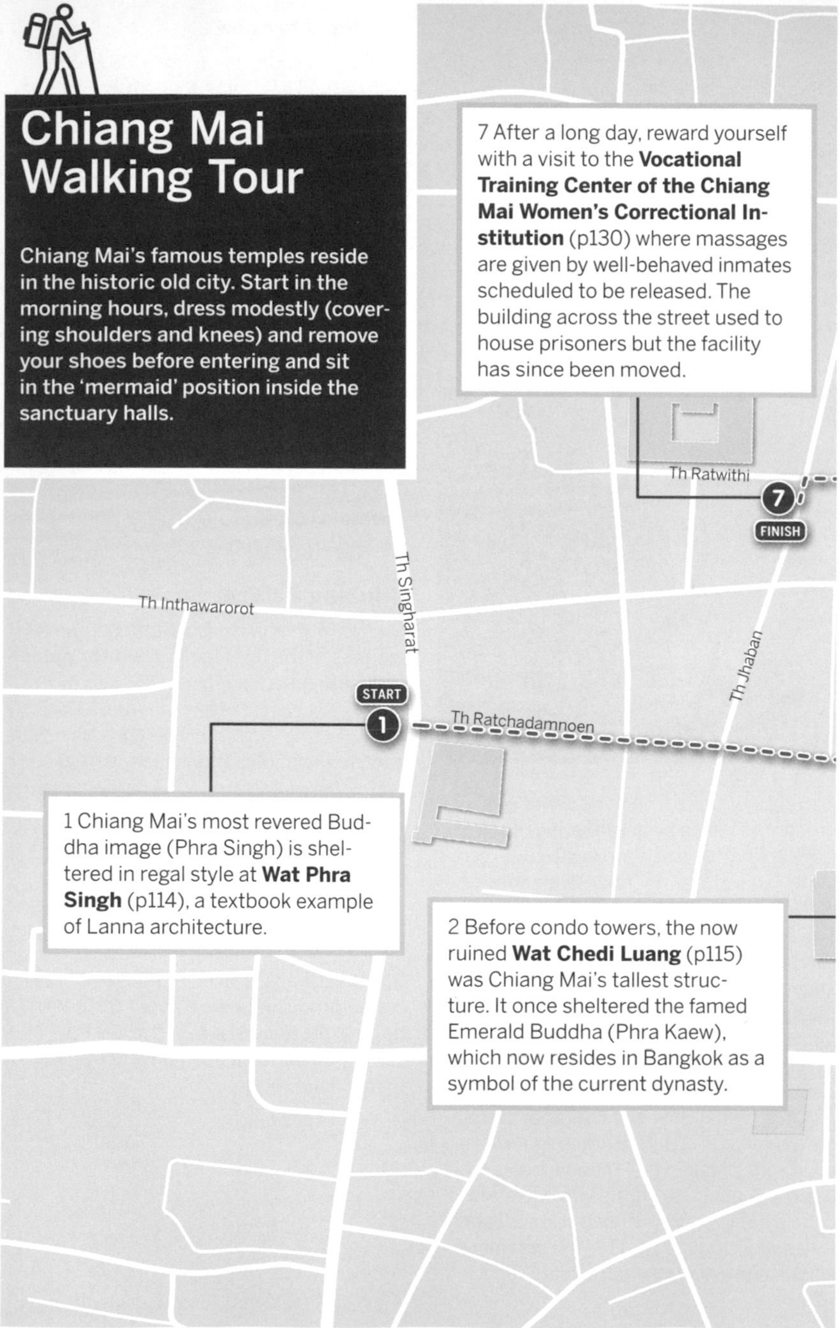

7 After a long day, reward yourself with a visit to the **Vocational Training Center of the Chiang Mai Women's Correctional Institution** (p130) where massages are given by well-behaved inmates scheduled to be released. The building across the street used to house prisoners but the facility has since been moved.

Th Ratwithi

7

FINISH

Th Singharat

Th Inthawarorot

Th Jhaban

START

1

Th Ratchadamnoen

1 Chiang Mai's most revered Buddha image (Phra Singh) is sheltered in regal style at **Wat Phra Singh** (p114), a textbook example of Lanna architecture.

2 Before condo towers, the now ruined **Wat Chedi Luang** (p115) was Chiang Mai's tallest structure. It once sheltered the famed Emerald Buddha (Phra Kaew), which now resides in Bangkok as a symbol of the current dynasty.

200 m
0.1 miles

Th Ratchaphakhinai

5 Synthesise the morning's art, architecture and history into a cohesive narrative at the informative and blissfully air-conditioned **Chiang Mai City Arts & Cultural Centre** (p118). The museum's building is recognised as an architectural stand-out.

6 Just across the street, the **Lanna Folklife Museum** (p119) is professionally run and provides a beautiful stroll through a well-restored historic building filled with informative and artistic displays

Th Inthawarorot

5

6

4

Soi 12

Th Phra Pokklao

Take a Break...Café de Museum has a full range of hot, cold and iced brews.

Th Ratchadamnoen

3

2

Soi 8

3 Next door is **Wat Phan Tao** (p116), a tiny teak temple that is more photogenic than venerated. Once you've seen this temple and its delicate ornamentation, you'll instinctively understand what is meant by 'classic Lanna style.'

APIGUIDE/SHUTTERSTOCK ©

4 The pretty, pint-sized **Wat In-thakhin Saduemuang** (p117) has been refurbished and is a popular subject among the camera-phone tourists. It used to house the city pillar thanks to its central 'navel' position.

◉ SIGHTS

Museum of World Insects & Natural Wonders   Museum

(www.thailandinsect.com; Th Ratchadamnoen; adult/child 100/70B; ⊙9.30am-4.30pm) Thailand's giant butterflies and creepy crawlies are showcased at this little museum operated by a malaria researcher and his entomologist wife. As well as pinned and mounted specimens, there are info panels on insect-borne diseases and surreal paintings of nudes with mosquitoes. There's a small **branch** (www.thailandinsect.com; Soi 13, Th Nimmanhaemin; adult/child 200/100B; ⊙9am-5pm Mon-Sat, 9am-4pm Sun) in the Th Nimmanhaemin zone.

Talat Warorot   Market

(ตลาดวโรรส; cnr Th Chang Moi & Th Praisani; ⊙6am-5pm) Chiang Mai's oldest public market, Warorot (also spelt 'Waroros') is a great place to connect with the city's Thai soul. Alongside souvenir vendors you'll find parades of stalls selling must-have items for ordinary Thai households: woks, toys, fishermen's nets, pickled tea leaves, wigs, sticky-rice steamers, Thai-style sausages, *kâap mŏo* (pork rinds), live catfish and tiny statues for spirit houses. It's easy to spend half a day wandering the covered walkways, watching locals browsing, and haggling for goods that actually have a practical use back home.

Wat Srisuphan   Buddhist Temple

(วัดศรีสุพรรณ; Soi 2, Th Wualai; donations appreciated; ⊙6am-6pm) **FREE** It should come as no surprise that the silversmiths along Th Wualai have decorated their patron monastery with the same fine craftsmanship shown in their shops. The 'silver' *ubosot* (ordination hall) at Wat Srisuphan is covered inside and out with silver, nickel and aluminium panels, embossed with elaborate repoussé-work designs. The effect is like a giant jewellery box, particularly after dark when the monastery is illuminated by coloured lights.

Wat Suan Dok   Buddhist Temple

(วัดสวนดอก; Th Suthep; donation appreciated; ⊙6am-10pm) **FREE** Built on a former flower garden in 1373, this important monastery enshrines the other half of the sacred Buddha relic that was transported by white elephant to Wat Phra That Doi Suthep. The main *chedi* is a gilded, bell-shaped structure that rises dramatically above a sea of immaculate white memorial *chedi* honouring members of the Thai royal family, with the misty ridge of Doi Suthep soaring behind.

Chiang Mai Night Safari   Zoo

(เชียงใหม่ไนท์ซาฟารี; ☑053 999000; www.chiangmainightsafari.com; Rte 121; tours adult/child 800/400B; ⊙11am-10pm; 👪) This expansive animal park is open day and night, but the real action happens after dark, when you can view all sorts of critters from the back of an open-sided tram. With animal shows and musical fountains, it's all a little bit Las Vegas. Despite having come under fire from animal welfare experts for alleged poor animal management, it remains popular with families, with lots of big predators and African herbivores on display. Predator Prowl and Savannah Safari tours leave at fixed times, day and night.

⊕ ACTIVITIES

Vocational Training Center of the Chiang Mai Women's Correctional Institution   Massage

(☑053 122340; 100 Th Ratwithi; foot/traditional massage from 150/180B; ⊙8am-4.30pm Mon-Fri, 9am-4.30pm Sat & Sun) Offers fantastic massages performed by female inmates participating in the prison's job-training rehabilitation program. The cafe next door is a nice spot for a post-massage brew.

Thai Massage Conservation Club   Massage

(☑053 904452; 99 Th Ratchamankha; massage 180-300B; ⊙8am-9pm) A collective of traditional Thai massage practitioners, the Thai Massage Conservation Club employs all blind masseuses, who are considered

Clockwise from top: Wat Srisuphan; food stall at Talat Warorot; Wat Phra That Doi Suthep (p126)

Central Chiang Mai

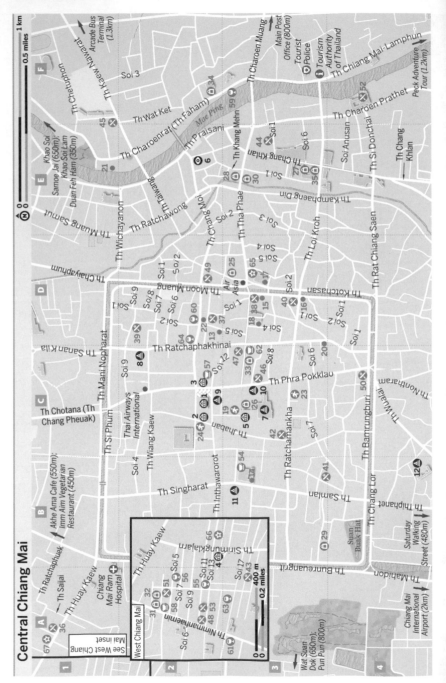

Central Chiang Mai

to be expert practitioners because of their heightened sense of touch.

Ban Hom Samunphrai   Massage
(☏053 817362; www.homprang.com; 93/2a Mu 12, Tawangtan, Saraphi; steam bath 200B, massage 600-1300B) Teacher Maw Hom ('Herbal Doctor') comes from a long line of herbalists and massage therapists; as well as traditional Thai massage here, you can try a traditional herbal steam bath. It's 9km

from Chiang Mai near the McKean Institute; check the website for directions.

⊙ TOURS

Chiang Mai Street Food Tours   Food
(☏085 033 8161; www.chiangmaistreetfoodtours. com; tours 750B) These foodie trips through the city's morning and night markets are a great introduction to Northern Thai cuisine.

👀 Mae Sa Valley

Just north of the city is the Mae Sa Valley and a 100km loop that winds through fantastic high-altitude scenery. It is a beautiful ride, often done on rented motorcycles.

The first stop is **Nam Tok Mae Sa** (adult/child 100/50B, car 30B; ⊙8am-4.30pm), a chain of cascades set in the fringes of Doi Suthep-Pui National Park on Rte 1096.

Further on **Queen Sirikit Botanic Gardens** (www.qsbg.org; Rte 1096; adult/child 100/50B, car 100B, motorcycle 30B; ⊙8.30am-4.30pm) has gardens and greenhouses full of exotic and local flora. The road eventually climbs into a high-altitude basin, once a centre for opium poppy production. With sponsorship from the Thai royal family, local hill-tribe farmers re-seeded their terraced fields with vegetables, fruits and flowers, processed under the Doi Kham label. The **Mon Cham Restaurant** (Nong Hoi Mai; mains 60-150B; ⊙7am-7pm), teetering on a ridgetop, cooks up tasty dishes with Doi Kham produce. You'll need a reasonably powerful motorcycle to get up the steep hill. From the main road, turn off at Ban Pong Yaeng to the Hmong village of Nong Hoi. Above the village, at around 1200m above sea level, you'll find the restaurant.

The rest of the route swings around the mountain ridge, passing spectacular viewpoints, and then begins its descent into Chiang Mai via Rte 1269 to Rte 121.

Mae Sa Valley
JGPHOTO76/GETTY IMAGES ©

Scorpion Tailed River Cruise
Boat Tour

(✆081 960 9398; www.scorpiontailedrivercruise.com; Th Charoenrat; cruise 500B) This river cruise focuses on the history of the Mae Ping river using traditional-style craft, known as scorpion-tailed boats. Informative cruises (five daily) last one to 1½ hours. They depart from Wat Srikhong pier near Rim Ping Condo and stop for a snack at the affiliated Scorpion Tailed Boat Village.

🏬 SHOPPING

🔒 Old City

Mengrai Kilns   Ceramics
(www.mengraikilns.com; 79/2 Th Arak; ⊙8am-5pm) In the southwestern corner of the old city, Mengrai Kilns keeps the tradition of Thai celadon pottery alive, with cookware, dining sets, ornaments and Western-style nativity scenes.

Chiang Mai Cotton   Clothing
(www.chiangmaicotton.com; Th Ratchadamnoen; ⊙10am-7pm Mon-Sat, 10am-11pm Sun) Close to Wat Chedi Luang and selling high-quality natural cotton cut for modern living. It's a good place to find clothes for people who wouldn't normally be seen dead in 'ethnic' clothing.

🔒 East of the Old City

Backstreet Books   Books
(2/8 Th Chang Moi Kao; ⊙8am-8pm) Backstreet, a rambling shop along 'book alley' (Th Chang Moi Kao), has a good selection of guidebooks and stacks of crime and thriller novels.

Kesorn Arts   Handicrafts
(154-156 Th Tha Phae; ⊙9am-6pm) The collector's best friend, this cluttered shop has been trading old bric-a-brac from the hills for years. It specialises mainly in textiles, lacquerware and jewellery.

Siam Celadon   Ceramics
(www.siamceladon.com; 158 Th Tha Phae; ⊙8am-6pm) This long-established com-

pany sells fine cracked-glazed celadon ceramics in a lovely fretwork-covered teak building from the time of the British teak concessionaires. After browsing, stop for a cuppa at the attached Raming Tea House (p138).

Praewphun Thai Silk   Clothing
(83-85 Th Tha Phae; ⊗10am-6pm) This 50-year-old shop sells silks of all ilks, both made into clothing and loose by the metre.

Vila Cini   Clothing, Accessories
(www.vilacini.com; 30-34 Th Charoenrat (Th Faham); ⊗9.30am-10.30pm) Set in an atmospheric teak house with marble floors and a narrow, rickety staircase, Vila Cini sells high-end, handmade silks and cotton textiles that are reminiscent of the Jim Thompson brand. There's a **branch** (www. vilacini.com; Th Chang Khlan, OP Place; ⊗11am-11pm) on Th Chang Khlan.

West of the Old City

Studio Naenna   Clothing, Homewares
(www.studio-naenna.com; 22 Soi 1, Th Nimmanhaemin; ⊗10am-6pm) The colours of the mountains have been woven into the naturally dyed silks and cottons here, part of a project to preserve traditional weaving and embroidery. You can see the whole production process at their **main workshop** (www.studio-naenna.com; 138/8 Soi Chang Khian; ⊗9am-5pm Mon-Fri, also 9am-5pm Sat Oct-Mar), north of Th Huay Kaew.

Srisanpanmai   Clothing, Accessories
(6 Soi 1, Th Nimmanhaemin; ⊗10am-6.30pm) The display cases here are like a library of Lanna textiles, with reams of silk and cotton shawls, scarves and hill-tribe costumes. You're guaranteed to find something to surprise the folks at home.

⊗ ENTERTAINMENT

Sudsanan   Live Music
(off Th Huay Kaew; ⊗6pm-midnight) A stroll down an unlit dirt track off Th Huay Kaew will take you to a creaky wooden house full of character and music. It's primarily a local hang-out, with Thais of all ages sipping whisky, chewing the fat and nodding appreciatively to performers playing

Artificial flowers at Sunday Walking Street (p121)

tear-jerking *pleng pêu·a chee·wít* (songs for life).

Look for the easy-to-miss signboard just west of Th Ratchaphuek.

Inter   Live Music
(271 Th Tha Phae; ⊙4pm-1am) This small wooden house packs in a lively line-up of local talent. It has that beach-shack vibe beloved by travellers everywhere and a popular pool table – though we recommend against challenging the multiple-trophy-winning lady who owns the place!

⊗ EATING
⊗ Old City
Angel's Secrets   International $
(Soi 1, Th Ratchadamnoen; mains 90-150B; ⊙7am-4pm Tue-Sun; 🛜🍴) True to its name, this sweet little restaurant is shielded by a fence of greenery from peeping appetites. Inside you'll find creative and wholesome Western breakfasts, including crusty home-made bread, crêpes and omelettes, and made-to-order vegetarian Thai food.

Dada Kafe   Vegetarian $
(Th Ratchamankha; mains 60-140B; ⊙9am-9pm, to 6pm May & Jun; 🍴) A tiny hole in the wall that does a busy trade in vitamin-rich, tasty vegetarian health food and smoothies. Wholesome ingredients like pollen and wheatgrass are whisked into fruit shakes and the food menu includes vegie burgers, omelettes, salads, sandwiches and curries with brown rice.

AUM Vegetarian
Food   Vegetarian $
(65 Th Moon Muang; mains 80-150B; ⊙10.30am-8.30pm; 🍴) One of the original health-food peddlers, AUM (pronounced 'om') attracts crowds of vegie travellers and a few vegie-curious carnivores. The menu runs from vegetable maki rolls to blue sticky rice and delicious *sôm·đam* (Isan-style pounded papaya salad) with cashews and carrot. They make their own mushroom-based stock.

Blue Diamond   Vegetarian $
(35/1 Soi 9, Th Moon Muang; mains 65-140B; ⊙7am-9pm Mon-Sat; 🍴) Packed with fresh

Sôm·đam (pounded papaya salad)

produce, pre-packaged spice and herb mixes and freshly baked treats, Blue Diamond feels a little like a wholefood store. The cafe offers an adventurous menu of sandwiches, salads, curries, stir-fries and curious fusion dishes such as *dôm yam* macaroni.

Good Morning Chiang Mai
International $

(29/5 Soi 6, Th Ratchamankha; breakfasts & mains 80-130B; ⊙8am-8pm) A favourite among expats, this guesthouse cafe near Wat Phra Jao Mengrai serves big, international breakfasts, from pancake towers to continental spreads and *dôm yam*– flavoured pasta. You can eat inside, in the movie-memorabilia-covered cafe, or in the garden by the pool.

Swan
Burmese $

(48 Th Chaiyaphum; mains 70-150B; ⊙11am-11pm) This worn-looking restaurant just east of the old city offers a trip across the border, with a menu of tasty Burmese dishes such asv (dry, sour pork curry with tamarind and peanuts). The backyard courtyard provides an escape from the moat traffic.

Huen Phen
Northern Thai $$

(☑053 277103; 112 Th Ratchamankha; lunch dishes 40-60B; evening mains 80-200B; ⊙8am-3pm & 5-10pm) This antique-cluttered restaurant cooks up some true northern magic. By day, meals are served in the canteen out front, but at night, the action moves back to the atmospheric dining room, where you can sample a full range of delicious, highly spiced jungle curries, stir-fries and regional variations on *nám prík* (chilli sauces with vegetables to dip).

Ruen Tamarind
Northern Thai $$$

(Tamarind Village, 50/1 Th Ratchadamnoen; mains 220-440B; ⊙11am-10.30pm; ☑) For a more sophisticated dinner, the restaurant at Tamarind Village serves superior Northern Thai food in sleek surrounds overlooking the hotel pool. Dishes such as *yum tawai gài* (spicy chicken salad with tamarind dressing) are presented

¶⊙¶ Cooking Courses

Chiang Mai is the most popular place in the country to learn Thai cooking. A few recommended schools include:

Asia Scenic Thai Cooking (☑053 418657; www.asiascenic.com; 31 Soi 5, Th Ratchadamnoen; half-/full-day courses from 800/1000B)

Chiang Mai Thai Cookery School (☑053 206388; www.thaicookeryschool.com; 47/2 Th Moon Muang; courses from 1450B)

Gap's Thai Culinary Art School (☑053 278140; www.gaps-house.com; 3 Soi 4, Th Ratchadamnoen; 1-/2-day course 900/1800B; ⊙Mon-Sat)

as works of art, and musicians serenade diners.

⊗ East of the Old City

La Fourchette
French $$

(Th Phra Pokklao; mains 250-580B; ⊙6-10.30pm) Decked out like a 1920s living room, La Fourchette is owned by a jazz-bass-loving, French-trained Thai chef who is putting his education to excellent use in Chiang Mai. Come for excellent steaks and funky fusion dishes such as red snapper fillet with mango.

Huan Soontaree
Northern Thai $$

(☑053 872707; 208 Th Patan; mains 110-200B; ⊙4-11pm Mon-Sat) Thai tourists eagerly make the pilgrimage out of town to this rustic restaurant in the hope of hearing the dulcet tones of its owner, the Thai chanteuse Soontaree Vechanont. She performs

Stimulating Brew

Chiang Mai adores coffee. Much of it is grown locally as a replacement crop for opium. Here are some top spots for a brew.

Akha Ama Cafe (www.akhaama.com; 9/1 Soi 3, Th Hutsadisawee, Mata Apartment; coffee from 50B; ⊙9am-9pm; 🛜) A cute local coffee shop founded by an enterprising Akha who was the first in his village to graduate from college. There's also a branch (p115) on Th Ratchadamnoen in the old city.

Wawee Coffee (www.waweecoffee.com; Th Ratchadamnoen, Kad Klang Wiang; drinks from 50B; ⊙8am-9pm Mon-Sat, to 11pm Sun; 🛜) Chiang Mai's local version of a Starbucks.

Café de Museum (Th Ratwithi, Lanna Folklife Museum; drinks from 40B; ⊙9am-6pm Mon-Fri, to 7pm Sat & Sun; 🛜) The perfect spot to refuel after touring the old city's museums.

Raming Tea House (Th Tha Phae; drinks 50-100B; ⊙8.30am-5.30pm) This elegant Victorian-era cafe serves Thai mountain tea.

LOVEISCHIANGRAI/GETTY IMAGES ©

The Service 1921
Southeast Asian $$$

(☎053 253333; Anantara Resort, 123 Th Charoen Prathet; mains 250-2000B; ⊙6am-11pm) The pan-Asian restaurant at the Anantara is elegance incarnate, with wait staff in full 1920s garb and interior decor resembling the secret offices of MI6 – appropriate as the gorgeous teak villa housing the restaurant used to be the British Consulate. The food is made with top-notch ingredients, though some dishes have the spice dialled down to appeal to international palates.

✖ West of the Old City

Pun Pun
Vegetarian $

(www.punpunthailand.org; Th Suthep, Wat Suan Dok; mains 40-75B; ⊙8am-4pm Thu-Tue; 🍴) 🌱 Tucked away at the back of Wat Suan Dok, this student-y cafe is a great place to sample Thai vegetarian food prepared using little-known herbs and vegetables and lots of healthy whole grains grown on its concept farm, which doubles as an education centre for sustainable living.

There's a branch called **Imm Aim Vegetarian Restaurant** (10 Th Santhitham; mains 40-75B; ⊙10am-9pm; 🍴) 🌱 near the International Hotel Chiangmai.

Palaad Tawanron
Central Thai $$$

(☎053 216039; off Th Suthep; mains 160-380B; ⊙11am-midnight) Set into a rocky ravine near Doi Suthep, this restaurant inhabits a magical spot overlooking a forest reservoir, with the city lights twinkling below. The ambience and the ride here through the forest are great, the food only so-so.

To get here, go to the end of the university compound on Th Suthep and follow the signs; if you reach the back entrance to the zoo, you're on the right track.

⊙ DRINKING & NIGHTLIFE

Zoe In Yellow
Bar

(40/12 Th Ratwithi; ⊙11am-2am) Part of a complex of open-air bars at the corner of Th Ratchaphakhinai and Th Ratwithi, Zoe is where backpackers come to sink pitchers of

at the restaurant from around 8pm Monday to Saturday. The menu is a pleasing blend of Northern, Northeastern and Central Thai specialities.

It is 8km north of town on the west side of the river, just south of Rte 11.

cold Chang, sip cocktails from buckets, rock out to cheesy dancefloor-fillers, canoodle and swap travel stories until the wee hours.

Writer's Club & Wine Bar   Bar
(141/3 Th Ratchadamnoen; ☺10am-midnight; ☎) Run by a former foreign correspondent, this bar and restaurant is popular with expats, and travellers looking for a more low-key drinking experience, with wine by the glass (from 140B).

UN Irish Pub   Pub
(24/1 Th Ratwithi; ☺11am-midnight) Chiang Mai's Irish pub offers the standard Emerald Isle package – draught Guinness, familiar pub grub, Thursday quiz nights, and international sports on the big screen.

Riverside Bar & Restaurant   Bar
(www.theriversidechiangmai.com; 9-11 Th Charoenrat (Th Faham); mains 130-370B; ☺10am-1am) Almost everyone ends up at Riverside at some point in their stay. Set in an old teak house, it feels like a boondocks reimagining of a Hard Rock Cafe, and bands play nightly until late. Stake out a claim on the riverside terrace or the upstairs balcony to catch the evening breezes on the Mae Ping river. They also serve good Thai and Western food, and there's a posher annexe across the road with a lounge-bar feel.

ℹ️ INFORMATION

Traffic is annoying; during rush hour, expect long waits at traffic lights. Take care when crossing busy roads; drivers don't give way. In March and April, smoky haze from farmers burning off their fields causes poor air quality. But, otherwise, compared to Bangkok, Chiang Mai is a breeze.

Chiang Mai Ram Hospital (☎053 920300; www.chiangmairam.com; 8 Th Bunreuangrit) The most modern hospital in town.

Main Post Office (☎053 241070; Th Charoen Muang; ☺8.30am-4.30pm Mon-Fri, 9am-noon Sat & Sun) Other convenient branches on Th Samlan, Th Prasaini, Th Phra Pokklao, and at the airport and university.

Tourism Authority of Thailand (TAT; ☎053 248604; www.tourismthailand.org; Th Chiang Mai-Lamphun; ☺8.30am-4.30pm) English-

Museum of World Insects & Natural Wonders (p130)

SAIKO3P/SHUTTERSTOCK ©

speaking staff provide maps, and advice on travel across Thailand.

Tourist Police (☏053 247318, 24hr emergency 1155; 608 Rimping Plaza, Th Charoenraj; ☺6am-midnight) Volunteer staff speak a variety of languages.

ⓘ GETTING THERE & AWAY

AIR

Domestic and international flights arrive and depart from **Chiang Mai International Airport** (☏053 270222; www.chiangmaiairportthai.com), 3km southwest of the old city. **Thai Airways** (THAI; ☏053 211044, 023 561111; www.thaiair.com; 240 Th Phra Pokklao; ☺8.30am-4.30pm Mon-Fri), **Thai Air Asia** (☏053 234645; www.airasia.com; 416 Th Tha Phae; ☺10am-8pm) and other budget airlines fly to Chiang Mai from domestic and some international destinations.

BUS

The **Arcade Bus Terminal** (Th Kaew Nawarat), about 3km from the old city, is Chiang Mai's long-distance station. A chartered *rót daang* will cost about 60B; a túk-túk will cost 80B to 100B. Destinations include Bangkok (605B to 810B, 9½ hours, frequent), Chiang Rai (135B to 265B, three to four hours, frequent) and Sukhothai (220B, five to six hours, frequent).

TRAIN

Run by the State Railway of Thailand, the **Chiang Mai Railway Station** (☏053 242094, 1690; www.railway.co.th; Th Charoen Muang; ☺ticket office 5am-10pm) is about 2.5km east of the old city on Th Charoen Muang. Trains run five times daily on the main line between Bangkok and Chiang Mai, but there have been derailments on this line, and with the growth of discount air travel in Thailand, the trains are mostly used by Thais. The train station has an ATM, a left-luggage room (5am to 8.45pm, 20B per item) and an advance-booking counter (you'll need your passport to book a ticket).

ⓘ GETTING AROUND

Cycling is a good way to get around. Bicycles can be rented for 50B to 300B per day. Motorcycles

⑪ Kôw Soy Sampler

Chiang Mai's unofficial dish is *kôw soy* (*khao soi*), a rich curry soup with crispy fried noodles and soft boiled noodles, coconut milk and plenty of turmeric and chilli, served with pickled vegetables. The dish originated with the Yunnanese traders.

Along Halal St, **Kao Soi Fueng Fah** (Soi 1, Th Charoen Phrathet; mains 40-60B; ☺7am-9pm) does a full-flavoured version. Foodies make the trek to the *kôw soy* 'ghetto' around Wat Faham on Th Charoenrat (Th Faham), north of the Th Ratanakosin bridge on the eastern bank of the Mae Ping. Our top pick is **Khao Soi Lam Duan Fah Ham** (352/22 Th Charoenrat (Th Faham); mains from 40B; ☺9am-4pm), but **Khao Soi Samoe Jai** (391 Th Charoenrat (Th Faham); mains 50-70B; ☺8am-5pm) is a close second. Another top slurp is **Khao Soi Prince** (105-109 Th Kaew Nawarat; mains 30-50B; ☺8am-3.30pm), close to the Prince Royal's College.

Kôw soy
FINALLAST/GETTY IMAGES ©

cost 150B to 500B to rent. **Thai Rent a Car** (☏053 904188; www.thairentacar.com; Chiang Mai International Airport) has a good reputation for car hire.

Rót daang (literally 'red trucks') operate as shared taxis and roam the streets picking up passengers heading in the same direction. Journeys start at 20B for a short trip and 40B for a longer trip. Túk túk and *rót daang* can be chartered. Negotiate a price beforehand.

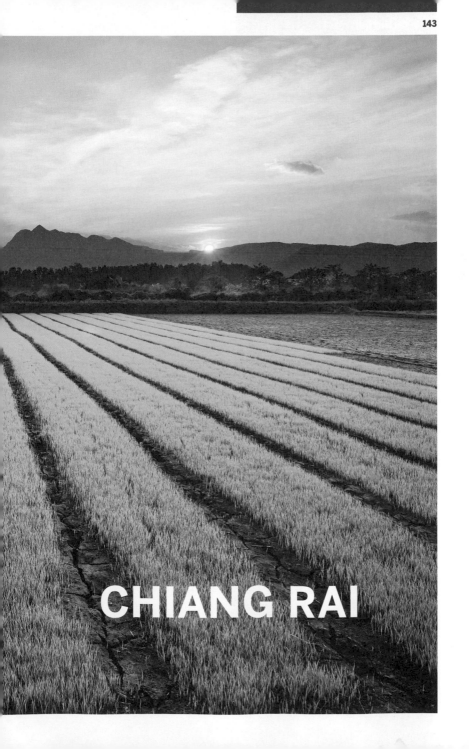

CHIANG RAI

Chiang Rai

Rising from the fertile plains to a rugged mountain range, Thailand's northernmost province, Chiang Rai, belts the border between Southeast Asia and China. The delightful provincial capital of Chiang Rai is used as a base to explore this intersection of cultures and dramatic mountain scenery. The province is home to many minority hill tribes, Shan and other Tai groups, and more recently Chinese immigrants, struggling to maintain their cultural identity and traditional lifestyle in the modern age.

Two Days in Chiang Rai

Experience the provincial charms of Chiang Rai town with a visit to **Wat Phra Kaew** (p150) and **Mae Fah Luang Art & Culture Park** (p152). Then take shelter from the heat at a local cafe. Devote the evening to shopping at the **Night Bazaar** (p154) or **Walking Street** (p153). The next day visit **Wat Rong Khun** (p148) and enjoy dinner at **Lung Eed** (p154).

Four Days in Chiang Rai

Head out of town for a **multiday trek**, the proceeds of which go to aid local hill-tribe villages with infrastructure and education projects. Or do an overnight trip to **Mae Salong** (p149), an ethnic Chinese village that balances on a mountain ridge cultivated with tea plantations.

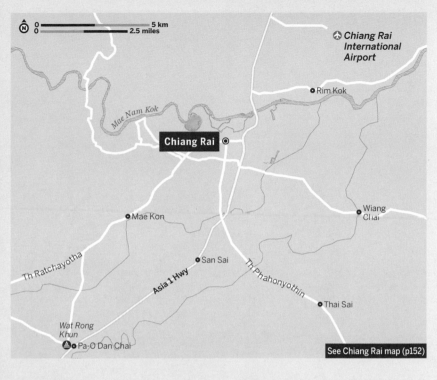

Chiang Rai International Airport

Rim Kok

Mae Nam Kok

Chiang Rai

Mae Kon

Wiang Chai

Th Ratchayotha

San Sai

Asia 1 Hwy

Th Phahonyothin

Thai Sai

Wat Rong Khun

Pa-O Dan Chai

See Chiang Rai map (p152)

Arriving in Chiang Rai

Chiang Rai International Airport
Located approximately 8km north of the city. Taxis run into town for 200B.

Bus station Frequent *sŏrng·tǎa·ou* link it with town from 6am to 5.30pm (15B, 15 minutes).

Interprovincial bus station Located in the centre of town.

Where to Stay

Chiang Rai has a great selection of places to stay, and price increases have been incremental over recent years, making accommodation in town good value. Most budget places are in the centre, clustered around Th Jetyod; the majority of midrange places are a brief walk from 'downtown.' Chiang Rai's upscale accommodation is generally located outside the centre of town in country-style resorts.

Akha women picking tea leaves

KAMONRATT/SHUTTERSTOCK ©

Minority Cultures

Thailand's ethnic minorities who inhabit the mountainous region of Chiang Rai province are often called 'hill tribes,' or chow kŏw (mountain people). Hill-tribe villages host trekking groups from the provincial capital to showcase their unique culture.

Great For...

☑ **Don't Miss**

Sharing a meal with a village family is a treasured cultural exchange.

Hill-Tribe History

Most of the hill-tribe communities are of semi-nomadic origin, having come from Tibet, Myanmar, China and Laos during the past 200 years or so. The Tribal Research Institute in Chiang Mai recognises 10 different hill tribes, but there may be up to 20. Hill tribes are increasingly integrating into the Thai mainstream and many of the old ways and traditional customs are disappearing.

Hilltribe Museum

This **museum** (พิพิธภัณฑ์และศูนย์การศึกษาชาว เขา; www.pdacr.org; 3rd fl, 620/25 Th Thanalai; admission 50B; 8.30am-6pm Mon-Fri, 10am-6pm Sat & Sun) and cultural centre is a good place to visit before undertaking any hill-tribe trek. Run by the nonprofit Population

○ Rai Pian Karuna (☑082 195 5645; www.facebook.com/raipiankaruna) A new, community-based enterprise conducting one- and multiday treks and homestays at Akha, Lahu and Lua villages in Mae Chan, north of Chiang Rai.

○ PDA Tours & Travel (☑053 740 088; www.pda.or.th/chiangrai/package_tour.htm; Hilltribe Museum & Education Center, 3rd fl, 620/25 Th Thanalai; ⊙8.30am-6pm Mon-Fri, 10am-6pm Sat & Sun) A well-established NGO offering one- to three-day treks. Profits go back into community projects such as HIV/AIDS education, mobile health clinics, education scholarships and the establishment of village-owned banks.

○ Mirror Foundation (☑053 737 616; www.thailandecotour.org) Higher rates than most but this NGO helps support the training of its local guides. Treks range from one to three days and traverse the Akha, Karen and Lahu villages of Mae Yao District, north of Chiang Rai.

& Community Development Association (PDA), the displays are a bit dated, but contain a wealth of information.

A visit begins with a 20-minute slide show on Thailand's hill tribes, followed by self-guided exploration through exhibits on traditional clothing, tools and implements, and other anthropological objects. The curator is passionate about his museum and, if present, will talk about the different hill tribes and the community projects that the museum funds. The PDA also runs highly recommended treks.

Trekking

Nearly every guesthouse and hotel in Chiang Rai offers hill-tribe hiking excursions. The following have a grassroots, sustainable or nonprofit emphasis.

Wat Rong Khun

GONZALO AZUMENDI/GETTY IMAGES ©

Day Trips from Chiang Rai

Dabble in the bizarre and the foreign with these day trips. Wat Rong Khun is an elaborate and fantastic hybrid of modern and religious art, while Mae Salong is a sleepy ethnic Chinese village perched on a mountain spine.

Great For...

☑ Don't Miss

Strawberries and other more familiar fruits can grow in the cooler, northern climate. Pick up a peck from roadside stands.

Wat Rong Khun

Looking like a supersized confection, **Wat Rong Khun** (White Temple, วัดร่องขุ่น; off Rte 1/AH2; ◷8am-5pm Mon-Fri, to 5.30pm Sat & Sun) **FREE** is Thailand's most eclectic and avant-garde temple. It was built in 1997 by noted Thai painter-turned-architect Chalermchai Kositpipat and mixes modern motifs and pop-culture references with traditional religious iconography.

The exterior of the temple is covered in whitewash and clear-mirrored chips. Walk over a bridge and sculpture of reaching arms (symbolising desire) to enter the sanctity of the wát where the artist has painted contemporary scenes representing *samsara* (the realm of rebirth and delusion). Images such as a plane smashing into the Twin Towers and, oddly enough,

Keanu Reeves as Neo from *The Matrix* dominate the one wall. If you like what you see, an adjacent gallery sells reproductions of Chalermchai Kositpipat's rather New Age–looking works.

The temple is 13km south of Chiang Rai. Take a regular bus bound for Chiang Mai or Phayao and ask to get off at Wat Rong (20B).

Mae Salong

For a taste of China without crossing any international borders, head to this hilltop village.

Mae Salong was originally settled by the 93rd Regiment of the Kuomintang (KMT), who had fled to Myanmar from China after the establishment of communist rule in 1949. The KMT were forced to leave Myanmar in 1961. Crossing into northern Thailand with their pony caravans, they settled into mountain villages and re-created a society like the one they had left behind in Yunnan.

Generations later, this unique community still persists and is a domestic tourist attraction. **Shin Sane Guest House** (⌨053 765026; www.maesalong-shinsane.blogspot.com; r 100B, bungalows 300B; @⊛) and **Little Home Guesthouse** (⌨053 765389; www.maesalonglittlehome.com; bungalows 800B; @⊛) both have free maps with hiking routes to hilltribe villages. Eating Yunnan-style dishes is a popular pastime for Thai tourists. Check out **Salema Restaurant** (mains 30-250B; ⊘7am-8pm) and **Sweet Maesalong** (mains 45-155B; ⊘8.30am-5pm; ⊛). If you decide to stay overnight, **Phu Chaisai Resort & Spa** (⌨053 910500; www.phu-chaisai.com; bungalows incl breakfast 3900-20,000B; ✳⊛⊠) is an exceptional resort.

To get to Mae Salong, take a bus to Mae Chan and transfer to a green *sŏrng·tăa·ou* to Mae Salong (60B, half-hourly from 7.30am to 4.30pm).

◉ SIGHTS

Wat Phra Kaew — Buddhist Temple

(วัดพระแก้ว; Th Trairat; ⊙temple 7am-7pm, museum 9am-5pm) FREE Originally called Wat Pa Yia (Bamboo Forest Monastery) in the local dialect, this is the city's most revered Buddhist temple. The main prayer hall is a medium-sized, well-preserved wooden structure. The octagonal *chedi* behind it dates from the late 14th century and is in typical Lanna style. The adjacent two-storey wooden building is a museum housing various Lanna artefacts.

Legend has it that in 1434 lightning struck the temple's *chedi*, which fell apart to reveal the Phra Kaew Morakot, or Emerald Buddha (actually made of jade). After a long journey that included a lengthy stopover in Vientiane, Laos, this national talisman is now ensconced in the temple of the same name in Bangkok.

In 1990, Chiang Rai commissioned a Chinese artist to sculpt a new image from Canadian jade. Named the Phra Yok Chiang Rai (Chiang Rai Jade Buddha), it was intentionally a very close but not exact replica of the Phra Kaew Morakot in Bangkok, with dimensions of 48.3cm across the base and 65.9cm in height, just 0.1cm shorter than the original. The image is housed in the impressive Haw Phra Yoke, the walls of which are decorated with beautiful modern murals, some depicting the journey of the original Phra Kaew Morakot, as well as the elaborate ceremony that saw the current image arrive at its new home in Chiang Rai.

Oub Kham Museum — Museum

(พิพิธภัณฑ์อูบคำ; www.oubkhammuseum.com; Th Nakhai; adult/child 300/100B; ⊙8am-5pm) This slightly zany museum houses an impressive collection of paraphernalia from virtually every corner of the former Lanna kingdom. The items, some of which truly are one of a kind, range from a monkey-bone food taster used by Lanna royalty to an impressive carved throne from Chiang Tung, Myanmar. It's located 2km west of the town centre and can be

Clockwise from top left: dishes at Lung Eed (p154);
Wat Phra Kaew; stall at the Night Bazaar (p154); Baan
Dum (p153)

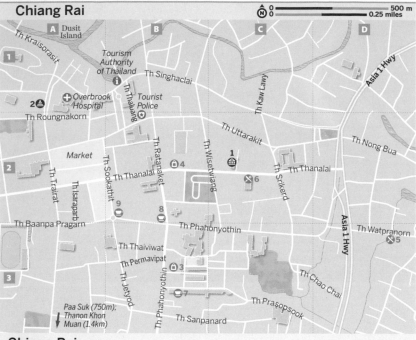

Chiang Rai

◎ Sights
1 Hilltribe Museum & Education Center...C2
2 Wat Phra Kaew...A1

◑ Activities, Courses & Tours
PDA Tours & Travel.............................(see 1)

◎ Shopping
3 Night Bazaar...B3
4 Walking Street...B2

◎ Eating
5 Lung Eed..D3
6 Phu Lae...C2

◎ Drinking & Nightlife
7 BaanChivitMai Bakery................................B3
8 Doi Chaang...B2
9 Pangkhon Coffee......................................B2

a bit tricky to find; túk-túk will go here for about 60B.

Guided tours (available in English) are obligatory and include a walk through a gilded artificial cave holding several Buddha statues, complete with disco lights and fake torches! The grounds of the museum are equally kitschy and include a huge golden *naga* statue (a mythical serpent-like being with magical powers), waterfalls and fountains. An equal parts bizarre and enlightening experience.

Mae Fah Luang Art & Culture Park   Museum

(ไร่แม่ฟ้าหลวง; www.maefahluang.org/rmfl; 313 Mu 7, Ban Pa Ngiw; adult/child 200B/ free; ☺8am-5pm Tue-Sun) In addition to a museum that houses one of Thailand's biggest collections of Lanna artefacts, this vast, meticulously landscaped compound includes antique and contemporary art, Buddhist temples and other structures. It's located about 4km west of the centre of

Chiang Rai; a túk-túk or taxi here will run around 100B.

Haw Kaew, the park's museum, has a permanent collection of mostly teak-based artefacts and art from across the former Lanna region, as well as a temporary exhibition room.

Haw Kham, a temple-like tower built in 1984 from the remains of 32 wooden houses, is arguably the park's centrepiece. The immense size of the structure – allegedly influenced by Lanna-era Wat Pongsanuk in Lampang – with its Buddha image seemingly hovering over white sand (the latter imported from Ko Samet), and sacred, candle-lit aura culminate in a vibe not unlike the place of worship of an indigenous cult.

You'll probably have to ask staff to open up **Haw Kham Noi**, a structure housing folksy but beautiful Buddhist murals taken from a dismantled teak temple in Phrae.

Baan Dum
Museum

(บ้านดำ, Black House; off Rte 1/AH2; ⊙9am-noon & 1-5pm) FREE The bizarre brainchild of Thai National Artist Thawan Duchanee, and a rather sinister counterpoint to Wat Rong Khun, Baan Dum unites several structures, most of which are stained black and ominously decked out with animal pelts and bones. It's located 13km north of Chiang Rai in Nang Lae; any Mae Sai–bound bus will drop you off here for around 20B.

The centrepiece is a black, cavernous temple-like building holding a long wooden dining table and chairs made from deer antlers – a virtual Satan's dining room. Other buildings include white, breast-shaped bedrooms, dark phallus-decked bathrooms, and a bone- and fur-lined 'chapel'. The structures have undeniably discernible northern Thai influences, but the dark tones, flagrant flourishes and all those dead animals coalesce in a way that is more fantasy than reality.

🟢 ACTIVITIES

Nearly every guesthouse and hotel in Chiang Rai offers hiking excursions in hill tribe country, some of which have grass-roots, sustainable or nonprofit emphasis.

In general, trek pricing depends on the type of activities and the number of days and participants. Rates, per person, for two people, for a two-night trek range from 2900B to 5800B. Generally everything from accommodation to transport and food is included in this price.

🅐 SHOPPING

Walking Street
Market

(Th Thanalai; ⊙4-10pm Sat) If you're in town on a Saturday evening be sure not to miss the open-air Walking Street, an expansive street market focusing on all things Chiang Rai, from handicrafts to local dishes. The market spans Th Thanalai from the Hilltribe Museum to the morning market.

Thanon Khon Muan
Market

(Th Sankhongnoi; ⊙6-9pm Sun) Come Sunday evening, the stretch of Th Sankhongnoi from Soi 2 heading west is closed to traffic, and in its place are vendors selling clothes, handicrafts and local food. Th Sankhongnoi is called Th Sathanpayabarn where

---

💬 Speaking Northern

Găm méuang, the northern Thai dialect, differs from standard Thai in that it has its own set of tones and specific vocabulary. Northern Thai also has its own written script that is sometimes used on signs for decorative purposes. Here are some local expressions.

An née tôw dai? How much is this?

Mee kôw nêung bòr? Do you have sticky rice?

Lám đáa đáa Delicious

Mâan lâ Yes/That's right

Yin dee nôe Thank you

Jôw A polite word used by women; equivalent to the central Thai *ka*.

it is nevertheless an OK place to find an assortment of handicrafts and touristy souvenirs.

✹ EATING

Lung Eed — Northern Thai $

(Th Watpranorn; mains 40-100B; ⊙11.30am-9pm Mon-Sat) One of Chiang Rai's most delicious dishes is available at this simple shophouse restaurant. There's an English-language menu on the wall, but don't miss the sublime *làhp gài* (minced chicken fried with local spices and topped with crispy deep-fried chicken skin, shallots and garlic). The restaurant is on Th Watpranorn about 150m east of Rte 1/AH2.

Paa Suk — Northern Thai $

(Th Sankhongnoi, no roman-script sign; mains 10-25B; ⊙8.30am-3pm) Paa Suk does big, rich bowls of *kà·nŏm jeen nám ngée·o* (a broth of pork or beef and tomatoes served over fresh rice noodles). The restaurant is between Soi 4 and Soi 5 of Th Sankhongnoi (the street is called Th Sathanpayabarn where it intersects with the southern end Th Phahonyothin); look for the yellow sign.

Phu Lae — Thai $

(673/1 Th Thanalai; mains 80-320B; ⊙11.30am-3pm & 5.30-11pm; ❄) This air-conditioned restaurant is popular with Thai tourists for its tasty but somewhat gentrified northern Thai fare. Recommended local dishes include the *gaang hang·lair* (pork belly in a rich Burmese-style curry) served with cloves of pickled garlic and *sâi òo·a* (herb-packed pork sausages).

ⓘ INFORMATION

There are several banks with foreign exchange and ATMs on both Th Phahonyothin and Th Thanalai.

Overbrook Hospital (☑053 711 366; www.overbrook-hospital.com; Th Singhaclai) English is spoken at this modern hospital.

Tourism Authority of Thailand (TAT; ☑053 744 674, nationwide 1672; tatchrai@tat.or.th; Th Sing-

Cafe Culture

For a relatively small town, Chiang Rai has an enviable spread of high-quality, Western-style cafes. This is largely due to the fact many of Thailand's best coffee beans are grown in the more remote corners of the province.

BaanChivitMai Bakery (www.baanchivitmai.com; Th Prasopsook; ⊙8am-7pm Mon-Fri, to 6pm Sat & Sun; ☎) In addition to a proper cup of joe made from local beans, you can snack on surprisingly authentic Swedish-style sweets and Western-style meals and sandwiches at this popular bakery. Profits go to BaanChivitMai, an organisation that runs homes and education projects for vulnerable, orphaned or AIDS-affected children.

Doi Chaang (542/2 Th Ratanaket; ⊙7am-10pm; ☎) Doi Chaang is the leading brand among Chiang Rai coffees, and its beans are now sold as far abroad as Canada and Europe.

Pangkhon Coffee (Th Sookathit; ⊙7am-10pm; ☎) Combine coffee brewed from local beans with views of Chiang Rai's gilded clock tower.

it intersects with the southern end Th Phahonyothin.

Night Bazaar — Market

(off Th Phahonyothin; ⊙6-11pm) Adjacent to the bus station off Th Phahonyothin is Chiang Rai's night market. On a much smaller scale than the one in Chiang Mai,

haclai; ⊙8.30am-4.30pm) English is limited, but staff here do their best to give advice and can provide a small selection of maps and brochures.

Tourist Police (☏053 740 249, nationwide 1155; Th Uttarakit; ⊙24hr) English is spoken and police are on stand-by around the clock.

ℹ GETTING THERE & AWAY

AIR

Chiang Rai International Airport (p308) is approximately 8km north of the city. Taxis run into town from the airport for 200B. From town, a metred trip with **Chiang Rai Taxi** (☏053 773477) will cost around 120B.

There are 12 daily flights to Bangkok's Don Muang International Airport (390B to 1090B, 1 hour 20 minutes) and seven to Bangkok's Suvarnabhumi International Airport (1090B to 1800B, one hour 20 minutes).

BUS

Buses bound for destinations within Chiang Rai Province depart from the **interprovincial bus station** (☏053 715952; Th Prasopsook) in the centre of town. If you're heading beyond Chiang Rai (or are in a hurry), you'll have to go to the **bus station** (☏053 773989), 5km south of town on Rte 1/AH2; frequent *sŏrng·tăa·ou* linking it and the interprovincial station run from 6am to 5.30pm (15B, 15 minutes). Destinations include:

○ **Bangkok** (495B to 935B, 11 to 12 hours, frequent 7am to 7pm)

○ **Chiang Mai** (140B to 280B, three to seven hours, hourly)

○ **Mar Chan** (transfer to Mae Salong; 25B, 45 minutes, frequent)

ℹ GETTING AROUND

Chiang Rai Taxi operates inexpensive metred taxis in and around town. A túk-túk ride anywhere within central Chiang Rai should cost around 60B. In addition to most guesthouses, several places along Th Jetyod hire motorcycles, with rates starting at 200B for 24 hours.

Stall at the Night Bazaar

SAN0P9/SHUTTERSTOCK ©

NONG KHAI

Nong Khai

Rest and relaxation are Nong Khai's claims to fame. It is a pleasant northeastern town perched on the banks of the muddy Mekong River, just across from Vientiane in Laos. As a border town it enjoys many Laos characteristics, including a friendly and laid-back disposition. Seduced by its dreamy pink sunsets and sluggish pace of life, many visitors who intend staying one night end up bedding down for many more.

Two Days in Nong Khai

Rent a bicycle and tour around the town enjoying the laid-back provincial lifestyle and fiery Isan cuisine. Visit **Sala Kaew Ku** (p160) and have dinner along the riverside promenade. The next day, visit **Tha Sadet Market** (p162) filled with shoppers and diners. Become a *sôm·dam* expert at **Saap Lah** (p165).

Four Days in Nong Khai

Treat yourself to a whole lot of nothing. Read a book, get a massage, pick up some handicraft souvenirs. Don't worry, the time will melt away. Join the great Thai tradition of near constant eating with at least three meals plus snacks in between.

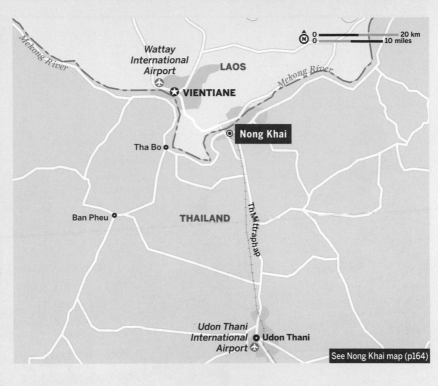

Arriving in Nong Khai

Udon Thani Airport Located 55km south of town. Udonkaew Tour runs minivans (150B per person) to/from the airport.

Nong Khai bus terminal Located in town.

Nong Khai train station Located 2km west of the city centre. Take a túk-túk for around 40B to 60B.

Where to Stay

Catering to the steady flow of backpackers, Nong Khai's budget lodging is the best in Isan. Most guesthouses are centered along the river.

Sala Kaew Ku

MARTIN RICHARDSON/GETTY IMAGES ©

Sala Kaew Ku

Tour the dream-like garden of Sala Kaew Ku, filled with larger-than-life figures from Hindu-Buddhist mythology. It is a surreal combination of art and religion that exemplifies the experimental aspects of Buddhist worship.

Great For...

☑ **Don't Miss**

The mummified body of the park's founder on the 3rd floor of the pavilion.

Built over a period of 20 years, the park features a weird and wonderful array of gigantic sculptures that merge Hindu and Buddhist imagery. The temple is locally known as Wat Kaek.

Mystic Visionary

The park's founder was a mystic shaman named Luang Pu Boun Leua Sourirat. As he tells his own story, Luang Pu tumbled into a hole as a child and met an ascetic named Kaewkoo, who introduced him to the manifold mysteries of the underworld and set him on course to become a Brahmanic-yogi-priest-shaman. Though he attracted followers, he had no formal training as a religious leader.

Shaking up his own unique blend of Hindu and Buddhist philosophy, mythology

Sculptures at Sala Kaew Ku

ANDREW WATSON/GETTY IMAGES ©

ⓘ Need to Know

Sala Kaew Ku (ศาลาแก้วกู่; admission 20B; ⊙8am-6pm) Chartered túk-túk cost 150B return with a one-hour wait, or you can get here by bike in about 30 minutes.

✕ Take a Break

Stop by Tha Sadet Market (p162) for a pre- or post-outing meal.

★ Top Tip

Mut Mee Garden Guest House (p162) distributes a map of the site with explanatory text.

Luang Pu's dreams and cast by workers under his direction. They crowd together like a who's who of religious celebrities. Other pieces depict stories and parables meant to teach the seekers how to gain enlightenment. Touring the grounds is a 3-D experience of Hindu-Buddhist symbols and tales.

Some of the sculptures are quite amusing. The serene elephant wading though a pack of anthropomorphic dogs teaches people to not be bothered by gossip.

The tallest sculpture, a Buddha seated on a coiled *naga* with a spectacular seven-headed hood, is 25m high. It is a classic Thai Buddhist motif but with Luang Pu's unique twist.

Also of interest is the Wheel of Life (the process of life and rebirth), which you enter through a giant mouth. The final scene is of a young man stepping across the installation to become a Buddha figure.

and iconography, Luang Pu developed a large following on both sides of the Mekong in this region. In fact, his original project was on the Lao side of the river where he had been living until the 1975 communist takeover in Laos. He died in 1996.

The main shrine building, almost as strange as the sculptures, is full of images of every description and provenance (guaranteed to throw even an art historian into a state of disorientation). There are also photos of Luang Pu at various ages and Luang Pu's corpse lying under a glass dome ringed by flashing lights.

Life-Sized Parables

The park is a smorgasbord of large and bizarre cement statues of Buddha, Shiva, Vishnu and other celestial deities born of

◎ SIGHTS

Tha Ṣadet Market   Market
(ตลาดท่าเสด็จ; Th Rimkhong; ⊘8.30am-6pm) It is
the most popular destination in town and
almost everyone loves a stroll through this
covered market. It offers the usual mix of
clothes, electronic equipment, food and
assorted bric-a-brac, most of it imported
from Laos and China, but there are also a
few shops selling quirky quality stuff.

✦ ACTIVITIES

Healthy Garden   Massage
(☑042 423323; Th Banthoengjit; Thai/foot
massage per hr 170/200B; ⊘8am-8pm) For the
most effective massage in Nong Khai, this
place has foot massage and traditional Thai
massage in air-conditioned rooms.

Pantrix Yoga   Yoga
(www.pantrix.net; Soi Mutmee) Pantrix offers
seven-day yoga courses through **Mut Mee
Garden Guesthouse** (☑042 460717; www.
mutmee.com; 1111/4 Th Kaew Worawut; s & d
without bathroom 200-300B, d 300-420B, d with
air-con 600-1400B; ❄️🛜) for serious students.
The courses start on the 1st and 15th day
of each month except May and December.
The one-week courses are run by qualified
yoga instructors who have been teaching
for many years, and cost 7700B (they are
not live-in courses).

ⓐ SHOPPING

Nong Khai
Walking Street Market   Market
(⊘4pm-10pm Sat) This street festival featuring music, handmade items and food takes
over the promenade every Saturday night.

Village Weaver
Handicrafts   Handicrafts
(1020 Th Prajak) This place sells high-quality,
handwoven fabrics and clothing (ready-
made or made to order) that help fund development projects around Nong Khai. The
mát·mèe cotton is particularly good here.

Clockwise from top left: relaxing in Nong Khai; dish of minced-shrimp on sugarcane at Daeng Namnuang (p164); rice steamers for sale; traditional coffee filters at Tha Sadet Market

Nong Khai

Nong Khai

◉ Sights

1 Tha Sadet Market..............................D1

◆ Activities, Courses & Tours

2 Healthy Garden.................................C2
3 Pantrix Yoga.....................................B2

🔒 Shopping

4 Hornbill Books..................................B2
5 Nong Khai Walking Street Market.............C1
6 Village Weaver Handicrafts.................C3
7 Village Weaver Workshop...................D3

✕ Eating

8 Café Thasadej..................................C1
9 Daeng Namnuang.............................C1
10 Dee Dee Pohchanah........................C3
11 Nagarina...B2
12 Saap Lah...A3

◉ Drinking & Nightlife

13 Gaia..B2

Village Weaver Workshop Handicrafts
(☏0 4241 1236; 1151 Soi Jittapanya; ⊙8am-5pm
Mon-Sat) This workshop, where some of the
nearby Village Weaver Handicrafts' products
are produced, has a somewhat different
inventory, with many more Lao designs.

Hornbill Books Books
(Soi Mut Mee; ⊙10am-7pm Mon-Sat) Buys, sells
and trades books in English, French and
other languages. Also sells coffee and has
internet access.

✕ EATING

Dee Dee Pohchanah Thai $
(Th Prajak; dishes 45-250B; ⊙10.30am-2am)
How good is Dee Dee? Just look at the din-
nertime crowds. Despite having a full house
every night, this simple place is a well-oiled
machine and you won't be waiting long.

Daeng Namnuang Vietnamese $
(Th Rimkhong; dishes 60-130B; ⊙8am-8pm;
ⓟ🛈) This massive river restaurant has

grown into an Isan institution, and hordes of out-of-towners head home with car boots and carry-on bags (there's an outlet at Udon Thani's airport) stuffed with *năam neu·ang* (pork spring rolls).

Saap Lah   Thai $
(Th Meechai; dishes 25-150B; ☺7am-8pm) For excellent *gài yâhng, sôm·đam* and other Isan foods, follow your nose to this no-frills shop.

Nagarina   Thai $$
(☏042 412211; Th Rimkhong; dishes around 100B, meals 200B; ☺10am-9pm; ☏☏) Mut Mee Garden Guesthouse's floating restaurant, which specialises in fish, turns out the real deal. There's a sunset cruise most nights (100B; at least 10 guests needed before the cruise will go ahead) around 5pm; order food at least 30 minutes before departure.

Café Thasadej   International $$
(Th Banthoengjit; dishes 60-375B; ☺8am-late) At this little restaurant both the menu and liquor list – the latter among the best in town – span the globe.

🍺 DRINKING & NIGHTLIFE
Gaia   Bar
(Th Rimkhong; ☺7pm-late) Much of the Mut Mee crowd, and many resident *fa·ràng*, fill this laid-back floating bar on the Mekong. There's a great drinks list, a chilled vibe and sometimes live music. It often hosts fundraisers for local charitable projects.

ℹ️ INFORMATION
Nongkhai Hospital (☏042 413461; Th Meechai) Has a 24-hour casualty department.

Tourist Police (☏042 460186; Th Prajak) Next to the *naga* fountain.

ℹ️ GETTING THERE & AWAY
AIR
The nearest airport is 55km south in Udon Thani. **Udonkaew Tour** (☏042 411530; Th Pranang

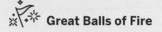
Great Balls of Fire

Since 1983 (or for ages, depending on who you ask) the sighting of the *bâng fai pá·yah·nâhk* (loosely translated as '*naga* fireworks') has been an annual event along the Mekong River. Sometime in the early evening, at the end of the Buddhist Lent (October), small reddish balls of fire shoot from the Mekong River and float into the air before vanishing.

Naga fireballs have become big business in Nong Khai Province, and curious Thais from across the country converge along the river banks for the annual show. The fireball experience is more than just watching a few small lights rise from the river; it's mostly about watching Thais (sometimes as many as 40,000 people) watching a few small lights rise from the river.

Cholpratan; ☺8.30am-5.30pm) runs minivans (150B per person) to/from the airport. Buy tickets in advance.

BUS
The **bus terminal** (☏042 412679) is just off Th Prajak, about 1.5km from the riverside guesthouses. Destinations include Bangkok (380B to 760B, 11 hours, frequent afternoon and evening departures) and Suvarnabhumi (Airport) bus station (495B, nine hours, 8pm).

TRAIN
Nong Khai's train station is located 2km west of the city centre. Three daily express trains connect to Bangkok (1117B to 1317B, 11½ hours).

ℹ️ GETTING AROUND
Nong Khai is a great place for cycling. A túk-túk hop costs 40B to 50B.

HUA HIN

Hua Hin

Hua Hin and the upper gulf have long been the favoured playground of the Thai elite. Following in the footsteps of the royal family, countless domestic tourists flock to this stretch of coast, an easy weekend escape from Bangkok, in pursuit of fun and fine seafood. A winning combination of outdoor activities and culture is on offer, with historic sites, long sandy beaches ideal for swimming, and the relaxed pace of provincial life. There's not much diving or snorkelling, but kiteboarders will be in paradise as this is the best place in Thailand to ride the wind.

Two Days in Hua Hin

Hang out on the beach and play in the waves. Explore **Hua Hin town** and the **night market** (p172) in the evening. The next day go beach-hopping to **Khao Takiab** (p171) and grab lunch from the nearby vendors.

Four Days in Hua Hin

Day-trip to **Phetchaburi** (p174) for its hillside royal palace and ballroom-sized caves. Pay homage to the Thai kings at the former palaces and monuments in **North Hua Hin** (p170). Join a **cycling tour** of the nearby countryside.

N
0 — 50 km
0 — 25 miles

Nakhon Pathom

BANGKOK

Chachoengsao

Samut Sakhon

Samut Prakan

Suvarnabhumi International Airport

Ratchaburi

Samut Songkhram

Chonburi

Phetchaburi

THAILAND

Si Racha

Rayong

Gulf of Thailand

Hua Hin

Khao Sam Roi Yot National Park

MYANMAR

Hua Hin Map (p177)

Arriving in Hua Hin

Night market Minivans from Bangkok's southern bus terminal and Victory Monument arrive in town near the night market.

Train station There are frequent trains running to/from Bangkok's Hualamphong station and other stations on the southern railway line. Charter a túk-túk (100B) or motorcycle (40B to 50B) to town.

Where to Stay

Most budget and midrange options are in the old shophouse district. It is an atmospheric setting with cheap tasty food nearby but you'll have to 'commute' to the beach, either by walking to northern Hat Hua Hin (best at low tide) or catching a *sŏrng·tăa·ou* a couple of kilometres to the southern end of Hat Hua Hin.

The top-end options are beachfront resorts sprawling south from the Sofitel.

Hua Hin beach

Hua Hin Beaches

Thailand's original beach resort is no palm-fringed castaway island, and arguably it is the better for it. Instead, it is a delightful mix of city and sea with a cosmopolitan ambience, long beaches and a fully functional infrastructure.

Great For...

☑ **Don't Miss**

Posing in front of the stone headlands for which Hua Hin ('Stone Head') is named.

North Hua Hin

The coast north from Hua Hin town is lined with genteel garden estates, bestowed with poetic names such as 'Listening to the Sea House.' The current palace, **Klai Kangwon Palace**, is 3km north of town; visitors are only allowed on the grounds (passport ID required).

A former summer palace, **Phra Ratchaniwet Mrigadayavan** (พระราชนิเวศน์ มฤคทายวัน; ☎032 508443; admission 50B; ⏲8.30am-4pm Thu-Tue) has a breezy seaside location, 12km north of Hua Hin. The palace was built in 1924 for Rama VI, who was suffering from rheumatoid arthritis. It is within the Camp Rama VI military base, and you may need to show passport ID. As this is a royal palace, dress modestly.

Beach dining

The newly erected **Seven Kings Monument**, in Ratchaphakdi Park, boasts seven bronze statues, standing 14m high and weighing in at 30 tonnes each. The statues depict the most famous Thai kings and was paid for by the Thai military, a powerful piece of propaganda. You'll need private transport to these attractions.

Hua Hin Beach

When viewed from the main public entrance, Hua Hin's beach is a pleasant stretch of sand punctuated by round, smooth boulders. This is where Thais come to photograph their friends wading ankle-deep in the sea and pony rides are offered to anyone standing still.

Continue south where the sand is a fine white powder and the sea a calm

grey-green, perfect for swimming and sunbathing. The 5km-long beach stretches past resort towers to a Buddha-adorned headland (Khao Takiab or Chopstick Mountain). Atop the mountain is **Wat Khao Lat**, a Thai-Chinese temple, with great sea views and untrustworthy monkeys.

South Hua Hin

Khao Tao (Turtle Mountain) oversees a barely inhabited beach south from Khao Takiab and about 13km south of Hua Hin town. There are no high-rises, no beach chairs, no sarong sellers and no horseback riders. The mountain has a sprawling temple dedicated to almost every imaginable deity: Buddha, Guan Yin (Chinese goddess of Mercy), Vishnu and even the Thai kings.

When to Go

The best time to visit is during the hot and dry season (February to June). From July to October (southwest monsoon) and October to January (northeast monsoon) there is occasional rain and strong winds, but the region tends to stay drier than the rest of the country because of a geographic anomaly.

During stormy periods, jellyfish are often carried close to shore, making swimming hazardous. Thais get around this by swimming fully clothed.

Night market

LEISA TYLER/GETTY IMAGES ©

Hua Hin Dining

Hua Hin may have a beach but Thais come for the dining. Evening meals are a festive affair unfolding in simple eateries and night markets packed to the rafters with patrons enjoying Thai-Chinese-style seafood dishes.

Great For...

☑ **Don't Miss**

Pàt pŏng gà·rèe þoo (crab curry) is a Thai-Chinese seafood celebrity.

Hua Hin Town

This old fishing village hosts a food orgy for both visiting Thai and foreign tourists.

○ **Night market** (Th Dechanuchit btwn Th Phetkasem & Th Sasong; dishes from 50B; ⊘5pm-midnight) Hua Hin's night market displays fresh seafood like fine jewels on a bed of ice. Lobsters and king prawns appeal to the big spenders but simple stir-fries are just as tasty. Try *pàt pŏng gà·rèe þoo* (crab curry), *gûng tôrt* (fried shrimp) and *hŏy tôrt* (fried mussel omelette).

○ **Hua Hin Koti** (☎032 511252; 16/1 Th Dechanuchit; dishes from 120B; ⊘noon-10pm) Across from the night market, this place is adored for its fried crab balls. Foreigners swoon over *đôm yam gûng* (shrimp soup with lemon grass). And everyone loves the spicy seafood salad (*yam tá-lair*) and deep-

clog the roadways heading north, obeying the pull of the upcoming work week.

Their presence is so pronounced that there is an irresistible urge to join them. And because of restaurant features on Thai TV or in food magazines, everyone goes to the same places. So don your designer sunglasses and elbow your way to a table at one of these popular spots in North Hua Hin:

○ **Eighteen Below Ice Cream** (Th Naebkehardt; ice cream from 55B; ⊙11am-5pm Wed-Mon) Gourmet ice-cream shop behind Baan Talay Chine hotel.

○ **Jae Siam** (Th Naebkehardt; dishes from 35B; ⊙9am-10pm) Simple noodle shop famous for *gŏo·ay dĕe·o mŏo dŭn* (stewed pork noodles) and *gŏo·ay dĕe·o gài dŭn* (stewed chicken noodles).

○ **Ratama** (12/10 Th Naebkehardt; dishes from 120B; ⊙10am-10pm) Spicy seafood curries in a breezy restaurant.

For more Eating options, see p178.

fried fish with ginger. Be prepared to wait for a table.

○ **Jek Pia Coffeeshop** (51/6 Th Dechanuchit; dishes from 50B; ⊙6.30am-1.20pm & 5.30-8.30pm) More than just a coffee shop, this 50-year-old culinary legend specialises in an extensive array of stir-fried seafood dishes. It's wildly popular with the locals. They stick rigidly to their serving hours here; arrive after 7.30pm and you won't be able to order.

Th Naebkehardt

On weekends, a different kind of tidal system occurs in Hua Hin. Bangkok professionals flow in, filling up hotels and restaurants on Th Naebkehardt, washing over the night market or crowding into nightclubs. And then come Sunday they

Tham Khao Luang

NOUMAE/GETTY IMAGES ©

Phetchaburi

A day trip from Hua Hin, Phetchaburi is a cultural traveller's stop with former royal palaces and cave shrines. The town itself is a sleepy provincial town more popular with school tour groups than with foreigners.

Great For...

☑ **Don't Miss**

Saying hello to the school children visiting Phetchaburi's famous sites yields giggles and glee.

Phra Nakhon Khiri Historical Park

This **palace** (อุทยานประวัติศาสตร์พระนครคีรี; ☎032 401006; admission 150B, tram return adult/child 50/15B; ☉park & tram 8.30am-4.30pm) sits atop Khao Wang (Palace Hill), surveying the city with subdued opulence. Rama IV (King Mongkut) built the palace, in a mix of European and Chinese styles, in 1859 as a retreat from Bangkok. The hilltop location allowed the king to pursue his interest in astronomy.

Cobblestone paths lead from the palace to three summits, each topped by a *chedi* (stupa). The white spire of Phra That Chom Phet skewers the sky and can be spotted from the city below.

There are two entrances to the site. The front entrance is across from Th Ratwithi

Phra That Chom Phet in Phra Nakhon Khiri Historical Park

COMZEAL/GETTY IMAGES ©

ⓘ Need to Know

Buses with air-con link Hua Hin to Phetch-aburi (1½ hours, frequent); the stop is outside of town at the Big C. *Sŏrng·tăa·ou* (500B) and motorcycles (200B to 300B) can be rented to tour the sites.

✗ Take a Break

Rabieng Rim Nam (☏032 425707; 1 Th Chisa-In; dishes 50-100B; ☺8am-midnight; ☜) has a pleasant riverside location and tourist information.

★ Top Tip

Keep a tight hold on bags and don't feed or interact with the local monkeys.

---

and involves a strenuous footpath. The back entrance has a tram.

Phra Ram Ratchaniwet

An incredible art nouveau creation, this elegant **summer palace** (พระรามราชนิเวศน์; ☏032 428083; Ban Peun Palace; admission 50B; ☺8.30am-4.30pm Mon-Fri) began construc-tion in 1910 at the behest of Rama V (who died just after the project was started). It was designed by German architects, who used the opportunity to showcase contem-porary design innovations: sun-drenched rooms decorated with glazed tiles, stained glass, parquet floors and wrought-iron details. The palace is on a military base 1km south of town; you may be required to show your passport.

Tham Khao Luang

About 4km north of town is **Tham Khao Luang** (ถ้ำเขาหลวง; ☺8am-6pm) **FREE**, a dramatic stalactite-stuffed chamber that's one of Thailand's most impressive cave shrines, and was a favourite of Rama IV. Accessed via steep stairs, its central Buddha figure is often illuminated with a heavenly glow when sunlight filters in through the heart-shaped skylight. At the opposite end of the chamber are a row of sitting Buddhas casting shadows on the undulating cavern wall.

Tham Khao Bandai-It

This hillside **cave** (ถ้ำเขาบันไดอิฐ; donation appreciated; ☺9am-4pm), 2km west of town, sprawls through several large caverns converted into shrines and meditation rooms. English-speaking guides (100B) lead tours, mainly as protection against the monkeys. One cavern contains a popu-lation of bats.

◎ SIGHTS

A former fishing village, Hua Hin town retains its roots with an old teak shophouse district bisected by narrow soi, pier houses that have been converted into restaurants or guesthouses and a busy fishing pier still in use today.

Hua Hin Train Station   Historic Site
(สถานีรถไฟหัวหิน; Th Liap Thang Rot Fai) An iconic piece of local architecture, the red-and-white pavilion that sits beside Hua Hin's train station once served as the royal waiting room during Rama VI's reign. By cutting the journey time from Bangkok to a mere four hours, it was the arrival of the railway that made Hua Hin a tourist destination for the Bangkok-based monarchy and the city's elite. One hundred years later even speeding minivan drivers fuelled by energy drinks can't do it much quicker.

Hua Hin Hills Vineyard   Vineyard
(ไร่องุ่นหัวหินฮิลล์ วินยาร์ด; ☑081 701 0222; www. huahinhillsvineyard.com; Th Hua Hin-Pa Lu-U; vineyard tour 1700-2400B, wine tasting 3 glasses 290B; ⊙9am-7pm) This vineyard is nestled in a scenic mountain valley 45km west of Hua Hin. The loamy sand and slate soil feeds Rhone grape varieties that are used in their Monsoon Valley wine label. There are daily **vineyard tours** from 1700B, including wine, an excellent three-course meal and return transport. Alternatively you can just do the **wine tasting**.

The most expensive tour includes the completely unnecessary option of an elephant ride. There's also a *pétanque* course, mountain biking and the picturesque Sala Wine Bar & Bistro.

A vineyard shuttle leaves the affiliated **Hua Hin Hills Wine Cellar store** (☑032 511497; 2F Villa Market, Th Phetkasem) at 10.30am and 3pm and returns at 1.30pm and 6pm; a return ticket is 300B.

Plearn Wan   Notable Building
(เพลินวาน; ☑032 520311; www.plearnwan.com; Th Phetkasem btwn Soi 38 & Soi 40; ⊙9am-9pm) As much an art installation as a commercial enterprise, Plearn Wan is a recreation of the old-fashioned shophouses that once occupied the Thai-Chinese neighbourhoods of Bangkok and Hua Hin. There's a pharmacy selling (well actually displaying) roots, powders and other concoctions that Thai grandmothers once used, as well as music and clothes stores.

✈ ACTIVITIES

Kiteboarding Asia   Kiteboarding
(☑081 591 4593; www.kiteboardingasia. com; 143/8 Soi 75/1, Th Phetkasem, South Hua Hin; 3-day beginner course 11,000B) This long-established company operates three beachside shops that rent kiteboarding equipment and offer lessons. The three-day introductory course teaches beginners the physical mechanics of the sport, and the instructor recommends newbies come when the winds are blowing from the southeast (January to March) and the sea is less choppy.

Thai Cooking Course Hua Hin   Cooking Course
(☑081 572 3805; www.thai-cookingcourse.com; 19/95 Th Phetkasem; courses 1500B) Aspiring chefs should sign up for a one-day cooking class here that includes a market visit and recipe book. The course runs only if there are a minimum of three people.

Thai Thai Massage   Massage
(20/1 Th Dechanuchit; massage from 250B; ⊙10am-11pm) There are luxury spas inside all the posh hotels, but if you want something less pricey but still a cut above the average, the trained and friendly masseuses at this respectable place get excellent feedback.

Hua Hin Golf Centre   Golf
(☑032 530476; www.huahingolf.com; Th Selakam; ⊙noon-9pm) The friendly staff at this pro shop can steer you to the most affordable, well-maintained courses where the monkeys won't try to run off with your balls. The company also organises golf tours and rents sets of clubs (500B to 700B per day).

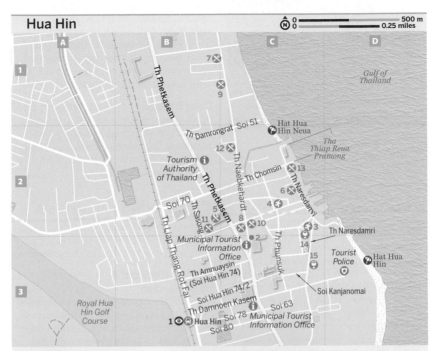

Hua Hin

◎ Sights
1 Hua Hin Train Station...................................B3

◉ Activities, Courses & Tours
2 Hua Hin Adventure Tour.............................C3
3 Hua Hin Golf Centre....................................C2
4 Thai Thai Massage......................................C2

✕ Eating
5 Chatchai Market B2
6 Cool Breeze C2
7 Eighteen Below Ice Cream B1

8 Hua Hin Koti..C2
9 Jae Siam..C1
10 Jek Pia Coffeeshop C2
11 Night Market...B2
12 Ratama...C2
13 Sang Thai Restaurant...............................C2

◉ Drinking & Nightlife
14 El Murphy's Mexican Grill &
   Steakhouse..C2
15 Mai Tai Cocktail & Beer Garden...............C3

⊙ TOURS

Hua Hin Bike Tours   Cycling
(☏081 173 4469; www.huahinbiketours.com;
15/120 Th Phetkasem btwn Soi 27 & 29; tours
from 2000B) A husband-and-wife team
operates this cycling company that leads
day-long and multiday tours to a variety of
attractions in and around Hua Hin. Pedal
to the Hua Hin Hills Vineyard for some
well-earned refreshment, tour the coastal
byways south of Hua Hin, or ride among the
limestone mountains of Khao Sam Roi Yot
National Park.

**Hua Hin
Adventure Tour**   Adventure Tour
(☏095 493 6942, 032 530314; www.huahin
adventuretour.com; 69/7 Th Naebkehardt) Hua
Hin Adventure Tour offers active excursions, including kayaking trips in the Khao
Sam Roi Yot National Park and mountain
biking in Kaeng Krachan National Park.

Khao Sam Roi Yot National Park

Towering limestone outcrops form a rocky jigsaw-puzzle landscape at this 98-sq-km **park** (☑032 821568; www.dnp. go.th; adult/child 200/100B), the name of which means Three Hundred Mountain Peaks. There are also caves, beaches and coastal marshlands to explore for outdoor enthusiasts and bird-watchers. With its proximity to Hua Hin, the park is well travelled by day-trippers and contains a mix of public conservation land and private shrimp farms, so don't come expecting remote virgin territory. Travel agencies in Hua Hin run day trips to the park. Hua Hin Bike Tours (p177) offers cycling and hiking tours.

Khao Sam Roi Yot National Park
NANUT BOVORN/GETTY IMAGES ©

⊗ EATING

Chatchai Market Market $
(Th Phetkasem; dishes from 35B; ⊘daylight hours) The city's day market resides in an historic building built in 1926 with a distinctive seven-eaved roof in honour of Rama VII. There are the usual market refreshments: morning vendors selling *pah·tôrng·gŏh* (Chinese-style doughnuts) and *gah·faa boh·rahn* (old-style coffee spiked with sweetened condensed milk), as well as all-day noodles with freshly made wontons, and the full assortment of fresh fruit.

Sang Thai Restaurant Seafood $$
(Th Naresdamri; dishes from 150B; ⊘10am-11pm) One of a number of long-established pier-

side restaurants, Sang Thai is a Hua Hin institution and a massive operation. There's a vast choice of seafood housed in giant tanks awaiting your decision. You can eat very well for not much, or spend lots if you want to feast on prime lobster.

Cool Breeze Mediterranean $$
(62 Th Naresdamri; tapas from 70B; ⊘11am-11pm; 🛜) Popular tapas joint spread over two floors. The daily set lunch (260B) is a good deal. Decent wine list and an amiable spot for a drink as well.

🍺 DRINKING & NIGHTLIFE

Drinking destinations in Hua Hin are stuck in a time warp of sports bars or hostess bars – and sometimes you can't tell the difference.

Mai Tai Cocktail & Beer Garden Bar
(33/12 Th Naresdamri; beers from 70B, cocktails from 129B; ⊘noon-1am; 🛜) Cheap and convivial and it always gets a crowd. Grab a table on the outdoor terrace for a pre-dinner drink and some serious people-watching.

El Murphy's Mexican Grill & Steakhouse Bar
(25 Soi Selakam, Th Phunsuk; beers from 90B, cocktails from 180B; ⊘7am-1.30am) Every sports bar needs a gimmick and this busy spot marries Mexico and Ireland. There's a big menu, live music and a pleasant vibe, although the beers aren't cheap.

ℹ️ INFORMATION

There are exchange booths and ATMs all over town.

Bangkok Hospital Hua Hin (☑032 616800; www.bangkokhospital.com/huahin; Th Phetkasem btwn Soi Hua Hin 94 & 106) An outpost of the well-regarded hospital chain; it's in South Hua Hin.

Municipal Tourist Information Office (☑032 511047; cnr Th Phetkasem & Th Damnoen Kasem; ⊘8.30am-4.30pm Mon-Fri) Provides maps and information about Hua Hin. There's another

branch (☎032 522797; Th Naebkehardt; ⊕9am-7.30pm Mon-Fri, 9.30am-5pm Sat & Sun) near the clock tower.

Tourism Authority of Thailand (TAT; ☎032 513885; 39/4 Th Phetkasem; ⊕8.30am-4.30pm) Staff here speak English and are quite helpful; the office is north of town near Soi Hua Hin 70.

Tourist Police (☎032 515995; Th Damnoen Kasem) At the eastern end of the street.

ⓘ GETTING THERE & AWAY

AIR

The airport is 6km north of town, but only has charter services.

BUS

Buses to Bangkok leave from a bus company's in-town **office** (Th Sasong), near the night market. Buses to Bangkok Suvarnabhumi International Airport leave from the long-distance bus station. Minivans go to Bangkok's southern bus terminal and Victory Monument. They leave from an office on the corner of Th Phetkasem and Th Chomsin.

Buses depart to Phetchaburi from north of the market on Th Phetkasem.

Lomprayah offers a bus-boat combination to Ko Samui (1400B, 10 hours, 8.30am).

TRAIN

There are frequent trains running to/from Bangkok's Hualamphong station and other stations on the southern railway line.

ⓘ GETTING AROUND

Green *sŏrng·tăa·ou* depart from the corner of Th Sasong and Th Dechanuchit, near the night market, and travel south on Th Phetkasem to Khao Takiab (20B).

Túk-túk fares in Hua Hin start at a whopping 100B. Motorcycle taxis are cheaper (40B to 50B) for short hops.

Motorcycles (200B to 300B) and bicycles (50B to 100B) can be hired from shops on Th Damnoen Kasem and Th Chomsin. **Thai Rent A Car** (☎02 737 8888; www.thairentacar.com) is a professional car-rental agency.

Hua Hin Train Station (p176)

AMNACHPHOTO/GETTY IMAGES ©

KO SAMUI

Ko Samui

Ko Samui is a small city by the sea, wearing a soft stole of white sand and adorned by modern conveniences. Curvaceous beaches, fast flights to Bangkok, high-end hotels, all-night parties and luxury spas cement Samui's reputation as Phuket's little sister. In places it is glitzy, brash and even slapdash, perfect for holidaymakers who prefer recreation over rest. Yet sleepy villages can still be found and beach hopping to quieter corners delivers solitude. Samui is everyone's version of an island idyll, you just have to know where to look.

Two Days in Ko Samui

Laze around the beach, eat, sleep, drink, repeat. Do a spa treatment at **Tamarind Springs** (p189). Have dinner at a local seafood spot, like **Bang Po Seafood** (p192) or **Ging Pagarang** (p192). Party with pros in Chaweng's beach bars and nightclubs.

Four Days in Ko Samui

Join a tour to **Ang Thong Marine National Park** (p186). Rent a motorcycle and tour the southern part of the island with stops at **Ban Hua Thanon** (p188), **Hin-Ta** and **Hin-Yai** (p188), and **Wat Khunaram** (p188). Enjoy your last night on the island with a splash-out dinner at **Dining on the Rocks** (p193).

Arriving in Ko Samui

Ko Samui Airport Located in the northeast of the island near Big Buddha Beach. Taxis charge around 500B for an airport transfer. Boats to nearby islands depart from various piers around Samui and pier transfer is usually included in the ticket price.

Where to Stay

Chaweng and Lamai have the largest range of accommodation but they are also the busiest. The north coast is quieter with pretty Choeng Mon, populated mainly by high-end hotels; Bo Phut, with artsy flash-pads; and low-key Mae Nam, which retains some backpacker spots.

For more information on which neighbourhood to stay in, see p195.

Lamai

JON ARNOLD/GETTY IMAGES ©

Ko Samui Beaches

East coast beaches are leggy and legendary, famed for their looks and their parties. The north coast gets quieter and more family-friendly. And the south-western beaches are perfect for a sundowner.

Great For...

☑ **Don't Miss**

Doing an around-the-island tour to discover your favorite stretch of sand.

Each beach on Samui has a different personality, ranging from uber-social to quiet recluse.

East Coast

Most of the beach development on Samui is on the east coast. **Chaweng** has the beach version of an hourglass figure: soft white sand that gently curves from Ko Matlang in the north to Chaweng Noi in the south. The wide centre swath is crowded. Bodies of various shapes and sizes, in various states of undress, lie prostrate before the tropical sun god, while jet skis roar over the waves. Music blares from the beach bars and vendors tirelessly trudge through the sand to deliver amusements.

Lamai is just as pretty but not as famous as flamboyant Chaweng. In fact, Lamai has an identity complex. It is the birthplace

of Samui's fasting culture thanks to Spa Samui's two Lamai branches, but visitors looking for enlightenment will find hedonism in Lamai's commercial strip of girly bars. The southern end of the beach has a more old-fashioned, castaway feel.

North Coast

Samui's alternative coast, the north coast, is more subdued. Near the northeastern tip, **Choeng Mon** is a scenic bay with shallow waters and a low-key bar scene that's popular with families. Locals consider Choeng Mon's crescent-shaped beach to be the best on the island. Next in line is **Big Buddha Beach** (Bang Rak), named after the huge golden Buddha. The beach's western half is by far the best, with an empty stretch of white sand, though uncomfortably close to the main road. **Bo Phut** and its **Fisher-**

man's Village represent the new generation of Thai beaches. Bo Phut's beach is pebbly and narrow but the village is the place to be for an evening dinner and stroll. The village retains the ambience of an old fishing town now occupied by design-minded restaurants and hotels. Rarely does commerce in Thailand dress up, preferring instead the drab uniform of concrete and neon. **Mae Nam** offers the right balance of beach distractions and enough Thai necessities to give it a sense of place. It is the practical person's beach. The northwestern peninsula is carved into a few stunning bays for luxury resorts but you can spend the day soaking up the views on **Ao Thong Sai**.

South & West Coasts

The south coast is good for exploring, cruising through little village lanes checking out different spits of land, nodding to a forlorn water buffalo. The coast is spotted with rocky headlands and smaller coves of pebble sand that are used more as parking lots for Thai fishing boats than for lounge chairs. With more Thai tourists, Samui's west coast has skinny beaches of grainy sand where the sunsets can be breathtaking, but they aren't good for swimming because of the proximity to the ferries. The west coast also has views out to the Five Islands and the shadowy greens of the mainland are beguiling. It's a welcome escape from the often draining east-side bustle.

PAVINEEC/GETTY IMAGES ©

Ang Thong Marine National Park

The 40-some jagged jungle islands of Ang Thong Marine National Park stretch across the cerulean sea like a shattered emerald necklace.

Great For...

☑ **Don't Miss**

The islands' full-time residents are monkeys, birds, bats and crustaceans.

This virgin territory is best explored on a guided tour from Samui. After an hour's boat journey from Samui, you start to see a looming landmass on the horizon. Slipping closer, the jumbled shadow separates into distinct islands, seemingly moored together. Limestone outcroppings jut skyward like ship masts creating the illusion of anchored shapes in the sapphire-coloured water. Closer still and an internal geometry is revealed: primordial figures woven together by a watery maze. The powerful ocean has whittled dramatic arches and hidden caves into the malleable rock.

Birth of a Park

Designated a park in 1980, Ang Thong (Golden Bowl) is 35km west of Samui. The parks covers a total area of 102 sq km with

land comprising only 18 sq km. It used to be a training ground for the Royal Thai Navy. The rugged islands are devoid of human inhabitants except day-trippers. This dynamic landscape hosted the fictionalised commune in the other backpacker bible, *The Beach,* by Alex Garland.

Ko Mae

The myth-maker is Ko Mae (Mother Island) and its inner lagoon. The exterior of the island is a jagged shell of limestone and grizzled vegetation, but a steep climb up to the top reveals a sink hole filled with a gleaming gem-coloured lake filled by underwater channels. You can look but you can't touch: the lagoon is strictly off-limits to the unclean human body.

Ko Wua Talap

Ko Wua Talap (Sleeping Cow Island) is the largest island in the chain and hosts the national park office and visitor bungalows. The island has a stunning mountain-top viewpoint, a necessary reward after clawing your way to the summit of the 450m trail, booby-trapped with sharp, jagged rocks. A second trail leads to **Tham Bua Bok**, a cavern with lotus-shaped stalagmites and stalactites. There is a small sandy beach on the sunrise side of the island and a castaway's tranquillity.

Other Islands

The naturally occurring stone arches on **Ko Samsao** and **Ko Tai Plao** are visible during seasonal tides and certain weather conditions. Because the sea is quite shallow around the island chain, reaching a maximum depth of 10m, extensive coral reefs have not developed except in a few protected pockets on the southwest and northeast sides. There is also some diving, though the park is not as spectacular as other nearby spots. Soft powder beaches line Ko Tai Plao, **Ko Wuakantang** and **Ko Hintap**.

Offering at Wat Khunaram

⊙ SIGHTS

Ban Hua Thanon   Area
Just beyond Hat Lamai, Hua Thanon is
home to a vibrant Muslim community, and
its anchorage of high-bowed fishing vessels
by the almost deserted beach is a veritable
gallery of intricate designs.

Hin-Ta & Hin-Yai   Landmark
At the south end of **Hat Lamai**, the island's
second-largest beach, you'll find these
infamous genitalia-shaped stone formations (also known as Grandfather and
Grandmother Rocks) that provide endless
mirth for giggling Thai tourists.

Wat Khunaram   Buddhist Temple
(⊙dawn-dusk) FREE Several temples have
the mummified remains of pious monks,
including Wak Khunaram, which is south
of Rte 4169 between Th Ban Thurian and
Th Ban Hua. Its monk, Luang Phaw Daeng,
has been dead for over two decades but his
corpse is preserved sitting in a meditative
pose and sporting a pair of sunglasses.

✪ ACTIVITIES

Spa Resort   Bungalow
(☏077 230855; www.spasamui.com; Lamai
North) Programs at this friendly, practical
and simple spa include colonics, massage, aqua detox, hypnotherapy and yoga,
just to name a few. With rattan furniture,
traditional wall art and balconies, rooms
are comfortable and excellent value, but
book up quickly. Nonguests are welcome to
partake in the spa programs and dine at the
excellent (and healthy) open-air restaurant
by the beach.

Anantara   Resort
(☏077 428300; www.samui.anantara.com)
Anantara's stunning palanquin entrance
satisfies fantasies of a far-flung oriental
kingdom. Clay and copper statues of
grimacing jungle creatures abound on the
property's wild acreage, while guests savour wild teas in an open-air pagoda, swim
in the lagoon-like infinity-edged swimming
pool or indulge in relaxing treatments amid
the lush tropical foliage of the beautiful spa.

Samahita Retreat   Yoga, Spa

(✆077 920090; www.samahitaretreat.com; Laem Saw Beach; retreats around €840) Secreted away along the southern shores, Samahita Retreat has state-of-the-art facilities and a dedicated team of trainers for the growing band of therapeutic holidaymakers, wellness seekers and detoxers. Accommodation is in a comfy apartment block up the street while yoga studios, wellness centres and a health food restaurant sit calmly along the shore.

Tamarind Springs   Spa

(✆077 424221; www.tamarindsprings.com; spa treatments 1500-8500B; ⊙10am-8pm) More like a spa journey than a day spa, Tamarind Springs incorporates an exploration of the natural world into its steam baths and spa treatments. Follow the path to the steam room carved into towering boulders, plunge into the pool dappled in sunlight and then pad softly to the massage pavilion serenaded by bird song.

⊗ EATING

The most fun dining experiences on Ko Samui are on 'Walking Streets,' where hawker stalls and craft vendors set up along the village's main drag. Check with your accommodation about the current schedule.

⊗ Chaweng

Laem Din Market   Market $

(dishes from 35B; ⊙4am-6pm, night market 6pm-2am) A busy day market, Laem Din is packed with stalls that sell fresh fruits, vegetables and meats and stock local Thai kitchens. Pick up a kilo of sweet green oranges or wander the stalls trying to spot the ingredients in last night's curry. For dinner, come to the adjacent night market and sample the tasty southern-style fried chicken and curries.

Stacked   Steak $$

(www.stacked-samui.com; mains from 295B; ⊙noon-midnight; 🛜) All sharp lines, open

🍽 Salt and Spice in Southern Thai Cuisine

Don't say we didn't warn you: southern Thai cooking is undoubtedly the spiciest regional cooking style in a land of spicy regional cuisines. The food of Thailand's southern provinces also tends to be very salty, and seafood, not surprisingly, plays an important role, ranging from fresh fish that is grilled or added to soups, to pickled or fermented fish or served as sauces or condiments. Two of the principal crops in the south are coconuts and cashews, both of which find their way into a variety of dishes. In addition to these, southern Thais love their greens, and nearly every meal is accompanied by a platter of fresh herbs and vegies, and a spicy 'dip' of shrimp paste, chillies, garlic and lime.

Dishes you are likely to come across in southern Thailand include the following:

Gaang đai þlah – An intensely spicy and salty curry that includes *đai þlah* (salted fish stomach); much tastier than it sounds.

Gaang sôm – Known as *gaang lĕu·ang* (yellow curry) in central Thailand, this sour/spicy soup gets its hue from the liberal use of turmeric, a root commonly used in southern Thai cooking.

Gài tôrt hàht yài – The famous deep-fried chicken from the town of Hat Yai gets its rich flavour from a marinade containing dried spices.

Kà·nŏm jeen nám yah – This dish of thin rice noodles served with a fiery currylike sauce is always accompanied by a tray of fresh vegetables and herbs.

Kôo·a glîng – Minced meat fried with a fiery curry paste is a southern staple.

Pàt sà·đor – This popular stir-fry of 'stink beans' with shrimp, garlic, chillies and shrimp paste is both pungent and spicy.

Motorbike Rental Scams

Even if you escape unscathed from a motorbike riding experience, some shops will claim that you damaged your rental and will try to extort some serious cash. The best way to avoid this is to take copious photos of your vehicle (cars included) at the time of rental, making sure the person renting you the vehicle sees you do it (they will be less likely to make false claims against you if they know you have photos). If they still make a claim against you, keep your cool. Losing your temper won't help you win the argument and could significantly escalate the problem. The situation is just as bad on Ko Pha-Ngan, a bit less so on Ko Tao.

If things get really bad call the **tourist police** (☏077 421281, emergency 1155), not the regular police.

kitchen/grill, a team of busy and super-efficient staff plus a cracker of a menu, this awesome burger restaurant is a visual and culinary feast. Burgers and steaks – bursting with flavour – are served up on slate slabs in generous portions. Go with a sizeable hunger as the inclination is to simply keep on ordering.

Pepenero Italian $$

(www.pepenerosamui.com; mains from 250B; ⊙5.30-10.30pm Mon & Wed-Sat, 6-10.30pm Sun) Pepenero has caused quite a stir on Ko Samui. What this excellent and neatly designed Italian restaurant lacks in views, is more than made up for by a terrific menu

(including cutting boards with cheese and cold cuts) and the care and attention displayed to customers by the very sociable, hard-working hosts. Put this one in your planner.

Larder European $$$

(www.thelardersamui.com; mains 300-900B; ⊙noon-11pm; 🖥) This restaurant/bar/gastropub pulls out the stops in an invigorating menu of classic fare in a relaxing and tasteful setting, supported by a strong selection of wines and zesty cocktails. It's a winning formula, with dishes ranging from slow cooked lamb spare ribs to beer battered snow fish and warm falafel with feta cucumber and chilli salad.

✖ Lamai

Hua Thanon Market Market $

(dishes from 30B; ⊙6am-6pm) Slip into the rhythm of this village market slightly south of Lamai; it's a window into the food ways of southern Thailand. Vendors shoo away the flies from the freshly butchered meat and housewives load bundles of vegetables into their baby-filled motorcycle baskets. Follow the market road to the row of food shops delivering edible Muslim culture: chicken *biryani,* fiery curries or toasted rice with coconut, bean sprouts, lemon grass and dried shrimp.

Lamai Day Market Market $

(dishes from 30B; ⊙6am-8pm) Lamai's market is a hive of activity, selling food necessities and takeaway food. Visit the covered area to pick up fresh fruit or to see vendors shredding coconuts to make coconut milk. Or hunt down the ice-cream seller for homemade coconut ice cream. It's next door to a petrol station.

Pad Thai Thai $

(www.manathai.com/samui/phad-thai; mains from 70B; ⊙11am-11pm) On the corner of the huge Manathai hotel, this highly affordable, semi al fresco and smart restaurant is a fantastic choice for stir-fried and soup noodles, rounded off with a coconut ice cream.

Clockwise from top: Hin-Ta & Hin-Yai (p188); market food stalls in Lamai; Chaweng beach (p184)

Dining on the beach at Lamai

La Fabrique — Bakery $$

(set breakfasts from 120B; ⏱6.30am-10.30pm; 📶) Ceiling fans chop the air and service is snappy and helpful at this roomy French-styled boulangerie/patisserie away from the main drag, near Wat Lamai on Rte 4169. Choose from fresh bread, croissants, gratins, baguettes, meringues, yoghurts, pastries or unusually good set breakfasts that include fresh fruit and well-cooked eggs. Wash down with a selection of coffees or teas.

There's a smaller and noisier branch in Chaweng.

✖ North Coast

Fish Restaurant — International $

(mains from 50B; ⏱noon-10pm) With elegant Thai tablecloths and a well-priced, tasty menu of Thai seafood and pan-Asian dishes and international appetisers, this popular concrete-floor eatery pulls in a regular stream of diners, although portions are a bit on the teeny side and the relaxing music edges into muzak territory. There's a book-swap library here as well.

Ging Pagarang — Seafood $

(Thong Tanote; meals from 50B; ⏱11.30am-8pm) Locals know this is one of the island's best beachside places to sample authentic Samui-style seafood. It's simple and family-run, but the food and views are extraordinary. Try the sea algae salad with crab, fried dried octopus with coconut or the spectacular fried fish or prawns with lemon grass.

69 — Thai Fusion $$

(mains from 149B; ⏱1-10pm; 📶) The simply roaring roadside setting puts it on the wrong side of the tracks and the dated, eclectic decor is looking rather limp and tired; that said, almost unanimous rave reviews for its creative twists on Thai favourites make this a really popular choice.

Bang Po Seafood — Seafood $$

(Bang Po; dishes from 100B; ⏱dinner) A meal at Bang Po Seafood is a test for the taste buds. It's one of the only restaurants that serves traditional Ko Samui fare: recipes call for ingredients such as raw sea urchin roe, baby octopus, sea water, coconut and local turmeric.

Dining on the Rocks
Asian Fusion $$$

(☑077 245678; reservations-samui@sixsenses. com; Choeng Mon; menus from 2200B; ⊘5-10pm) Samui's ultimate dining experience takes place on nine cantilevered verandahs of weathered teak and bamboo that yawn over the gulf. After sunset (and wine), guests feel like they're dining on a barge set adrift on a starlit sea. Each dish on the six-course setmenu is the brainchild of the cooks who regularly experiment with taste, texture and temperature.

Chez François
French $$$

(www.facebook.com/chezporte; 33/2 Moo 1 Fisherman's Village; set meal 1700B; ⊘6-11pm Tue-Sat) With no à la carte menu, but a reputation for outstanding cuisine that has sent waves across the culinary map of Ko Samui, Chez Francois serves a three-course surprise meal. Book ahead using the Facebook page and if you're only on Ko Samui for a few days, book early to get a table. It's tiny (and cash only).

Chez Francois is hidden away behind a wooden door near a pharmacy.

🍸 DRINKING & NIGHTLIFE

Ark Bar
Bar

(☑7am-2am; www.ark-bar.com; Hat Chaweng) Drinks are dispensed from the multicoloured bar to an effusive crowd, guests recline on loungers on the beach, and the party is on day and night.

Bar Solo
Bar

(Hat Chaweng) Bar Solo's bubbly party mood, decent DJs and evening drink specials lure in front-loaders preparing for a late, late night at the dance clubs on Soi Solo and Soi Green Mango.

Green Mango
Bar

(ww.thegreenmangoclub.com; Hat Chaweng) This place is so popular it has an entire soi named after it. Samui's favourite power drinking house is very big, very loud and

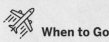

✈ When to Go

○ February to April celebrates endless sunshine after the monsoon rains have cleared.

○ June to August, conveniently coinciding with the Northern Hemisphere's summer holidays, are among the most inviting months, with relatively short drizzle spells.

○ October to December is when torrential monsoon rains rattle hut-tin roofs, and room rates drop significantly to lure optimistic beach goers.

very *fa·ràng*. Green Mango has blazing lights, expensive drinks and masses of sweaty bodies swaying to dance music.

Reggae Pub
Bar

(Hat Chaweng; ⊘6pm-3am) This fortress of fun sports an open-air dance floor with music spun by foreign DJs. It's a towering two-storey affair with long bars, pool tables and a live-music stage. The whole place doubles as a shrine to Bob Marley; it's often empty early in the evening, getting going around midnight. The long road up to Reggae Pub is ladyboy central.

Beach Republic
Bar

(www.beachrepublic.com; 176/34 Mu 4, Hat Lamai; ⊘7am-11pm) Recognised by its yawning thatch-patched awnings, Beach Republic could be the poster child of a made-for-TV, beachside, booze swilling holiday. There's a wading pool, comfy lounge chairs, an endless cocktail list and even a hotel if you never, ever want to leave the party. The Sunday brunches here are legendary.

ℹ INFORMATION

Always wear a helmet and drive carefully on a motorcycle; traffic fatalities are high.

Ko Samui airport

Bangkok Samui Hospital (☑077 429500, emergency 077 429555) Your best bet for just about any medical problem.

Tourism Authority of Thailand (TAT; ☑077 420504; Na Thon; ⊗8.30am-4.30pm)

Tourist Police (☑077 421281, emergency 1155) Based at the south of Na Thon.

❶ GETTING THERE & AWAY

AIR

Ko Samui's airport is in the northeast of the island. Bangkok Airways flies to Bangkok's Suvarnabhumi International Airport (50 minutes, frequent), Phuket and Chiang Mai. **Firefly** (www.fireflyz.com.my) goes to Malaysia. During the high season, make reservations in advance.

BOAT

There are a dozen daily departures from Ko Samui to Ko Pha-Ngan (200B to 300B, 20 minutes to one hour). There are also special services during Ko Pha-Ngan's Full Moon parties.

To reach the mainland, take the high-speed **Lomprayah** (☑077 4277 656; www.lomprayah.com; 450B). Agencies sell boat/bus combinations for overlanding to Bangkok (1400B to 1500B, 14 hours).

❶ GETTING AROUND

You can rent motorcycles (and bicycles) on the island for 150B to 200B per day. *Sŏrng·tăa·ou* (pick-up trucks) run regular routes around the island during daylight hours. It's about 50B to travel between beaches. These vehicles can also be chartered for private transport. Taxis now have high but standardised prices.

Where to Stay

The most famous beaches, Chaweng and Lamai, are crowded in the central area but calm on the periphery. Families opt for Choeng Mon, Bo Phut and Mae Nam.

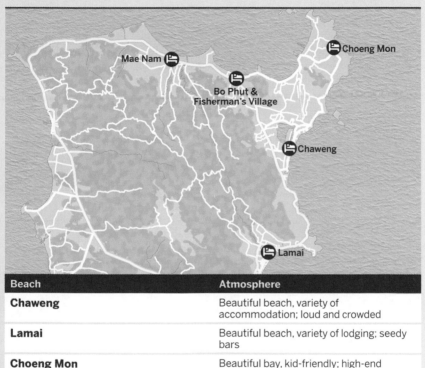

Beach	Atmosphere
Chaweng	Beautiful beach, variety of accommodation; loud and crowded
Lamai	Beautiful beach, variety of lodging; seedy bars
Choeng Mon	Beautiful bay, kid-friendly; high-end lodging
Bo Phut & Fisherman's Village	Small, coarse-sand beach, atmospheric village; artsy midrange lodging
Mae Nam	Pretty and quiet beach; backpacker and midrange lodging

KO PHA-NGAN

Ko Pha-Ngan

Hippie-at-heart Ko Pha-Ngan has become so synonymous with the wild Full Moon party that the rest of the island gets eclipsed. After the werewolves of the Full Moon leave, Ko Pha-Ngan returns to its hammock hanging. The island is carved into sandy coves with offshore reefs and a thick jungle crown in the interior. The gentle coral-fringed bays make it perfect for families. And a diversity of accommodation – from cheapish bungalows on party beaches to sophisticated resorts on the remote east coast – makes this tropical island a well-rounded holiday companion.

Two Days in Ko Pha-Ngan

Savour the great diversity of the ocean's blues and greens from one of Ko Pha-Ngan's many beautiful **beaches**. Go for a beach **snorkel** or **dive**. Check out the punters on **Hat Rin** for a sundowner, or more.

Four Days in Ko Pha-Ngan

Start day three exploring the western side of the island for castaway fantasies. Then do a full-day **dive tour** (p202) of the Gulf's famous dive spots. Lounge around and do nothing on your last day.

Gulf of Thailand

Ko Tao (40km)

Ao Hat Thong Lang
Ko Ma
Hat Thong Lang
Ao Mae Hat
Ban Mae
Ao Hat Salad
Hat
Ao Chalok Lam
Khao Kin Non
Ban Wang Ta Khian
Ban Chalok Lam
Ban Fai Mai
Khao Ra
Ao Thong Nai Pan Noi
Ao Thong Nai Pan Yai
Ban Thong Nai Pan
Ko Kong
Than Sadet
Ban Si Thanu
Sri Thanu
Khao Ta Luang
Ban Hin Kong
Ban Thong Nang
Ao Thong Reng
Ao Hin Kong
Ban Madeua Wan
Ao Wok Tum
Ban Wok Tum
Ban Nam Tok
Ko Tae Nok
Ko Tae Nai
Ao Nai Wok
Thong Sala
Ao Bang Charu
Wat Pho
Ban Nok
Hat Thian
Ban Tai
Ao Bang Tai
Ban Khai
Ao Ban Khai
Pang Bon
Hat Yuan
Surat Thani (50km)
Ao Hin Lor
Hat Rin Nai
Hat Rin Nok

Ko Samui (25km); Na Thon (25km)

5 km / 2.5 miles

Arriving in Ko Pha-Ngan

Thong Sala Boats for Ko Samui (200B to 300B, 20 minutes to one hour) and the mainland towns of Chumphon (800B to 1000B, 2½ hours) and Surat Thani (350B to 400B, 4½ to 7 hours) arrive here. *Sŏrng·tăa·ou* meet passengers for hotel transfers (100B to 200B).

Where to Stay

Hat Rin is the busy party beach with a huge selection of accommodation. The west coast is a nice hybrid, with enough amenities to avoid feeling stranded and a diverse range of accommodation. There's limited lodging and transport is expensive at the north coast beaches but there's also dramatic scenery and secluded beaches. The east coast beaches are deliciously secluded and have minimal development; transport is limited.

Drink buckets for sale at Hat Rin

ALEX ROBINSON/GETTY IMAGES ©

Ko Pha-Ngan Party Scene

Throngs of whisky bucket-sippers and fire twirlers gather on the legendary Sunrise Beach (Hat Rin Nok) for the infamous Full Moon parties. Full-on debauchery rages until the sun replaces the moon in the sky.

Great For...

☑ **Don't Miss**

Transforming yourself into a walking day-glo stick – it is *the* thing to do.

No one knows exactly when or how these crazy parties started – most believe they began in 1988, but accounts of the first party range from an Australian backpacker's going-away bash to a group of hippies escaping Samui's 'electric parties.' None of that is relevant now: today thousands of bodies converge for an epic trance-a-thon. Crowds can swell to an outrageous 40,000 partiers during high season, while the low season still sees a respectable 5000 pilgrims.

Party Tips

If your trip doesn't coincide with a full moon, fear not. Enterprising locals have organised a slew of other reasons to get sloshed. There are Black Moon Parties,

Body painting during a Full Moon party, Hat Rin

STEPHEN J BOITANO/GETTY IMAGES ©

❶ Need to Know

Party dates vary so check ahead. A 100B fee is charged for post-party cleanup. Check **Backpackers Information Centre** (☏077 375535; www.back packersthailand.com; Hat Rin; ⏱11am-8pm).

✕ Take a Break

Chicken corner is a popular street stall area to load up for party stamina.

★ Top Tip

Make reservations in advance as accommodation books up fast.

Party Places

The Full Moon party unfolds on the soft sands of Hat Rin. Surrounding bars also have their own periphery parties.

○ Rock Superb views of the party from the elevated terrace on the far southern side of the beach are matched by the best cocktails in town.

○ Drop-In Bar A dance shack blasting all the chart toppers that we secretly or unabashedly love. This is one of the liveliest places on Full Moon nights.

○ Sunrise Claims a spot on the sand where trance beats shake the graffitied walls, with drum 'n' bass coming into its own at Full Moon.

○ Tommy Hat Rin's largest venue with blaring Full Moon trance music. Drinks are dispensed from a large ark-like bar.

Half Moon Parties and Moon-set Parties to name a few. Some critics claim the party has lost its carefree flavour after increasing violence (assaults, thefts and injuries). Precautions should be followed to ensure personal and property safety.

○ Secure all valuables, especially when staying in budget bungalows.

○ Wear protective shoes during the sandy celebration, unless thou wants a tetanus shot.

○ Don't sample the drug buffet, nor a swim in the ocean under the influence of alcohol.

○ Stay in a group of two or more people, especially if you're a woman, and especially when returning home at the end of the evening.

Ko Ma

SKUNTEVSKI/GETTY IMAGES ©

Diving

Everyone will tell you to go to nearby Ko Tao to learn to dive. But Ko Pha-Ngan enjoys a much quieter, more laid-back diving scene focused on fun diving.

Great For...

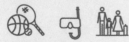

☑ **Don't Miss**

Wake up and hit the near-shore snorkelling spots – better than a cup of coffee.

Dive Sites

A major perk of diving from Ko Pha-Ngan is the proximity to Sail Rock (Hin Bai) and Chumphon Pinnacle, the premier dive sites in the Gulf of Thailand.

Chumphon Pinnacle (36m maximum depth) has a colourful assortment of sea anemones along the four interconnected pinnacles. The site plays host to schools of giant trevally, tuna and large grey reef sharks. Whale sharks are known to pop up once in a while.

Sail Rock (40m maximum depth) features a massive rock chimney with a vertical swim-through, and large pelagics like barracuda and kingfish. This is one of the top spots in Southeast Asia to see whale sharks; in the past few years they

Pink anemonefish

PETER FRANK/GETTY IMAGES ©

have been seen year-round, so there's no clear season. An abundance of corals and large tropical fish can be seen at depths of 10m to 30m.

Like the other islands in the Samui Archipelago, Pha-Ngan has several small reefs dispersed around the island. The clear favourite is **Ko Ma**, a small island in the northwest connected to Ko Pha-Ngan by a sandbar. There are also some rock reefs of interest on the eastern side of the island.

Hiking and snorkelling day trips to **Ang Thong Marine National Park** generally depart from Ko Samui, but recently tour operators are starting to shuttle tourists from Ko Pha-Ngan as well. Ask at your accommodation for details about boat trips as companies often come and go due to unstable petrol prices.

Dive Companies

Group sizes tend to be smaller on Ko Pha-Ngan than on Ko Tao since the island has fewer divers in general. But be warned that demand goes up before and after the Full Moon parties because there are more tourists.

The most popular trips departing from Ko Pha-Ngan are three-site day trips, stopping at Chumphon Pinnacle, Sail Rock and one of the other premier sites in the area. These trips cost from around 3650B to 4000B and include a full lunch. Two-dive trips to Sail Rock will set you back around 2500B to 2800B:

Lotus Diving (☑077 374142; www.lotusdiv ing.com) and **Haad Yao Divers** (☑086 279 3085; www.haadyaodivers.com; Hat Yao) are the main operators on the island with a solid reputation.

◎ SIGHTS

Nam Tok Than Sadet — Waterfall

These falls feature boulders carved with the royal insignia of Rama V, Rama VII and Rama IX. King Rama V enjoyed this hidden spot so much that he returned over a dozen times between 1888 and 1909. The river waters of Khlong Than Sadet are now considered sacred and used in royal ceremonies. Also near the eastern coast, **Than Prawet** is a series of chutes that snake inland for approximately 2km.

Nam Tok Phaeng — Waterfall

Nam Tok Phaeng is protected by a national park; this waterfall is a pleasant reward after a short, but rough, hike. After the wa-

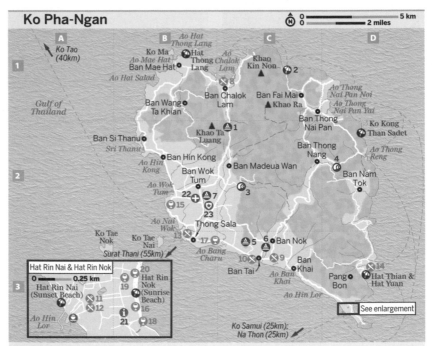

Ko Pha-Ngan

terfall (dry out of season), it's a further ex-hilarating 15-minute climb up a root-choked path (along the Phaeng-Domsila Nature Trail) to the fantastic Domsila Viewpoint, with ranging views. The two- to three-hour trail then continues on through the jungle in a loop, past other waterfalls before bringing you back. Take water and good shoes.

It's possible to continue up to Khao Ra, the highest mountain on the island at 625m. Those with eagle-eyes will spot wild crocodiles, monkeys, snakes, deer and boar along the way, and the viewpoint from the top is spectacular – on a clear day you can see Ko Tao. Although the trek isn't arduous, it is very easy to lose one's way, so consider finding a guide.

Guanyin Temple Buddhist Temple

(40B; ⊘7am-6pm) Signposted as the 'Goddess of Mercy Shrine Joss House', this fascinating Chinese temple is dedicated to the bodhisattva Guanyin, the Buddhist Goddess of Mercy. The temple's Chinese name (普岳山) on the entrance gate refers to the island in China that is the legendary home of the goddess. The main hall – the Great Treasure Hall – is a highly colourful confection, containing several bodhisattvas, including Puxian (seated on an elephant) and Wenshu (sitting on a lion).

Look out for the statue of a 1000-hand Guanyin, housed in the Guanyin Palace.

Hat Khuat Beach

Also called Bottle Beach, Hat Khuat is a good choice for a relaxing day of swimming and snorkelling, and some opt to stay the night at one of the several bungalow operations along the beach.

Wat Phu Khao Noi Buddhist Temple

(⊘dawn-dusk) **FREE** The oldest temple on the island is Wat Phu Khao Noi, near the hospital in Thong Sala. While the site is open to visitors throughout the day, the monks are only around in the morning.

Ko Pha-Ngan's Tallest Yang Na Yai Tree Tree

Near Wat Pho, Ko Pha-Ngan's tallest Yang Na Yai (dipterocarpus alatus; ยางนา) is an astonishing sight as you veer round the bend for the diminutive Wat Nok temple, a small shrine tucked away in the greenery. These colossal giants grow to over 50m in height and, for tree lovers, are real beauties. This imposing specimen is often garlanded with colourful ribbons.

Wat Pho Buddhist Temple

(⊘herbal sauna 1-7pm) **FREE** With a dazzling gateway and extensive temple grounds, Wat Pho, near Ban Tai, has a **herbal sauna** (admission 50B) accented with natural lemon grass. When we last visited, a new temple hall was under construction.

Wat Khao Tham Buddhist Temple

(www.kowtahm.com; ⊘dawn-dusk) **FREE** With resident female monks, Wat Khao Tham, near Ban Tai, sits among the trees high on a hill. A bulletin board details a meditation retreat at the temple; see the website for details. Don't miss the temple hall at the top of the steps with the colourful glass, housing a sleeping Buddha.

⊙ TOURS

This large island has many jungle attractions in addition to its spectacular beaches. **Eco Nature Tour** (☏084 850 6273) offers day trips for island 'safaris'. Explore the isolated beaches on the east coast: **Than Sadet, Hat Yuan, Hat Thian** and the teeny **Ao Thong Reng**. Note that most of the waterfalls slow to a trickle during the dry season, so aim to visit from October to January.

✖ EATING

✖ Hat Rin

Lazy House International $$

(Hat Rin Nai; dishes 90-270B; ⊘lunch & dinner) Back in the day, this joint was the owner's apartment – everyone liked his cooking so much that he decided to turn the place into a restaurant and hang-out spot. Today, Lazy House is easily one of Hat Rin's best places to veg out in front of a movie with a scrumptious shepherd's pie.

🏝️ Lay of the Land on Ko Pha-Ngan

Ko Pha-Ngan's legendary history of laid-back revelry has solidified its reputation as *the* stomping ground for the gritty backpacker lifestyle. Even so, many local mainstays have recently collapsed their bamboo huts and constructed newer, sleeker accommodation aimed at the ever-growing legion of 'flashpackers'.

On other parts of the island, new tracts of land are being cleared for Samui-esque five-star resorts. But backpackers fear not – it will still be a while before the cast-away lifestyle goes the way of the dodo. For now, Ko Pha-Ngan can revel in having excellent choices to suit every budget. Pha-Ngan also caters to a subculture of seclusion-seekers who crave a deserted slice of sand – the northern and eastern coasts offer just that.

The accommodation along the southern coast is the best bang for your baht on Ko Pha-Ngan, while the west coast is seeing a lot of development. The atmosphere here is a pleasant mix of quiet seclusion and a sociable vibe, although some of the beaches, particularly towards the south, aren't as picturesque as other parts of the island. Price tags are also higher than north or south of here.

Stretching from Chalok Lam to Thong Nai Pan, the dramatic northern coast is a wild jungle with several stunning and secluded beaches – it's the most scenic coast on the island.

The east coast is the ultimate hermit hang-out. For many of these refuges, you'll have to hire a boat from Thong Sala, Chalok Lam and Hat Rin and 4WD taxis from Thong Sala are an option for those that have dirt roads. The *Thong Nai Pan Express* boat runs daily at noon from Hat Mae Nam on Ko Samui stopping at Hat Rin and the east coast beaches as far as Thong Nai Pan Noi. The boat is a casual, rickety fishing-style vessel and won't run in rough weather.

Clockwise from top: Guanyin Temple (p205); Hat Yuan (p205); visitor relaxing in a hammock

Monna Lisa
Italian $$

(Hat Rin Nai; pizza & pasta from 200B; ⊘1-11pm) Travellers rave about the pizza here, and the pasta gets a thumbs-up as well. It's run by a team of friendly Italians and has a basic, open-air atmosphere.

🌀 Southern Beaches

On Saturday evenings from 4pm to 10pm, Thong Sala hosts a Walking Street.

Night Market
Market $

(Thong Sala; dishes 25-180B; ⊘2-11pm) A heady mix of steam and snacking locals, Thong Sala's night market is a must for those looking for doses of culture while nibbling on low-priced snacks. Wander the stalls for a galaxy of Thai street food, from vegetable curry puffs to corn on the cob, spicy sausages, kebabs, spring rolls and coconut cake.

Fisherman's Restaurant
Seafood $$

(📱084 454 7240; Ban Tai; dishes 50-600B; ⊘1-10pm) Sit in a long-tail boat looking out over the sunset and a rocky pier. Lit up at night, it's one of the island's nicest settings and the food, from the addictive yellow curry crab to the massive seafood platter to share, is as wonderful as the ambience. Reserve ahead, especially during party time.

Fabio's
Italian $$

(📱083 389 5732; Ban Khai; dishes 150-400B; ⊘5-10pm Mon-Sat) An intimate, authentic and truly delicious Italian place with golden walls, cream linens and bamboo furniture. There are only seven tables, so reserve in advance. House-made delicacies like seafood risotto, pizzas and iced limoncello are as artfully presented as they are fresh and delicious.

🌀 Other Beaches

Cucina Italiana
Italian $$

(Jenny's; Chalok Lam; pizzas 180-200B; ⊘5-10pm) If it weren't for the sand between your toes and the long-tail boats whizzing by, you might think you had been transported to the Italian countryside. The friendly Italian chef is passionate about his food, and creates everything from his pasta to his tiramisu daily, from scratch. The rustic, thin-crust pizzas are out-of-this-world good.

Sanctuary
Health Food $$

(www.thesanctuarythailand.com; Hat Thian; mains from 130B; 📶) The Sanctuary's restaurant proves that wholesome food (vegetarian and seafood) can also be delicious. Enjoy a tasty parade of plates – from massaman curry to crunchy Vietnamese spring rolls. Don't forget to wash it all down with a blackberry, soya milk and honey immune booster. No credit cards.

🍸 DRINKING & NIGHTLIFE

Amsterdam
Bar

(Ao Plaay Laem) Near Ao Wok Tum on the west coast, Amsterdam attracts tourists and locals from all over the island, who are looking for a chill spot to watch the sunset.

Outlaws Saloon
Bar

(⊘4pm-2am) With its buffalo skulls, US flags, sounds from the King (Elvis, not the Thai monarch) and other American icons, this fun ranch-style saloon is quite a sight on a lively night. There's a meaty menu, excellent Sunday roast dinners and imported beers and ciders.

It's on the north side of the road between Thong Sala and Ban Tai.

🩺 Medical Services

Medical services can be a little crooked in Ko Pha-Ngan – expect unstable prices and underqualified doctors. Many clinics charge a 3000B entrance fee before treatment. Serious medical issues should be dealt with on nearby Ko Samui.

Beachside dining

ℹ INFORMATION

Main Police Station (☏077 377114) Located 2km north of Thong Sala.

Ko Pha-Ngan Hospital (☏077 377034; ◷24hr) Located 2.5km north of Thong Sala.

ℹ GETTING THERE & AWAY

AIR

Ko Pha-Ngan's airport was under construction at the time of writing; it's opening date has not been released.

BUS

Rough waves cancel ferries during the monsoon (October and December). Boats connect to Ko Samui (200B to 300B, 20 minutes to one hour, 12 daily) and the mainland at Chumphon (800B to 1000B, 2½ hours) and Surat Thani (350B to 400B, 4½ to seven hours). Bus-boat combinations provide overland transport to Bangkok (from around 1300B, 17 hours).

ℹ GETTING AROUND

You can rent motorcycles all over the island for 150B to 250B per day. Ko Pha-Ngan has many motorcycle accidents; always wear a helmet.

Sŏrng·tăa·ou chug along the island's major roads and the riding rates double after sunset.

Long-tail boats connect the southern piers (Thong Sala and Hat Rin) to the north and east coast beaches (Chalok Lam and Hat Khuat). Short trips start at 50B and go up to 300B for a lengthier journey.

PHUKET

Phuket

Branded the 'pearl of the Andaman,' Phuket doesn't feel like an island at all. It's so huge (49km long, the biggest in Thailand) that the sea feels secondary to the city accoutrements that have made Phuket the country's premier international resort and expat retirement destination. The beach town of Patong is the ultimate gong show of beachaholics and go-go bars. Other beaches are more refined and luxury hotels, restaurants and spas dominate the island's attractions.

Two Days in Phuket

Pop into Phuket in a hurry and then take it slow in professional resorts and intimate boutique hotels. Break up the beach routine with a visit to the old **Sino-Portuguese architecture** (p234) and Chinese shrines of Phuket Town. Enjoy fabulous fusion cuisine at **Suay** (p219). Party hard in Patong with a stop at good old **Nicky's Handlebar** (p233). Or drink up the view and cocktails at **Baba Nest** (p233).

Four Days in Phuket

Devote one day to **Ao Phang-Nga Marine National Park** (p222), a protected bay cluttered with more than 40 peaked karst islands. Spend the night on **Ko Yao** (p223) for a small sip of backwater island living.

0 — 200 km
0 — 100 miles

THAILAND

BANGKOK ⊗ ⊙ Suvarnabhumi
International
Airport

Phetchaburi ⊙

Rayong ⊙

CAMBODIA

Myeik ⊙

Trat ⊙

MYANMAR ⊙ Prachuap
Khiri Khan

*Andaman
Sea*

⊙Chumphon

*Gulf of
Thailand*

Ranong ⊙

Ao Phang-Nga

⊙Surat
Thani

Phuket
International
Airport ✈ ⊙Phang-Nga ⊙ Nakhon Si
Thammarat

⊙Krabi

Phuket ⊙

See Phuket map (p228)

Arriving in Phuket

Phuket International Airport Located 30km northwest of Phuket Town, it takes 45 minutes to an hour to reach the southern beaches from here. Most airport transfers cost about 700B.

Phuket Bus Terminal 2 Located 4km north of Phuket Town. Taxis or túk-túk do the run from Phuket Town for 300B.

Tha Rassada The main pier for boats to Ko Phi-Phi, Krabi (Railay) 3km southeast of Phuket Town.

Where to Stay

Phuket is where you splash out for lodging. The island is packed with fashionable resorts and boutique hotels. Save your penny-pinching for other locations. Book hotels well in advance during the busy high season (November to April) and hunt the online booking sites for hotel discounts.

For local recommendations see p235.

Hat Karon

Phuket Beaches

Phuket's beaches are stunning stretches of sand with emerald waters. Like a big family, each beach has its own personality. And the island's modern roads make it easy to explore the island.

Great For...

☑ **Don't Miss**

Sampling the beaches until you've found a favourite – it's a Phuket tradition.

Patong

Patong is *not* the poster child of sophistication. In fact it makes its bread and butter from the whims of the everyman: knock-off T-shirts, girly bars for those in midlife crisis, and slapdash commercialism of mediocre quality but immense quantity. If you aren't a sex tourist or a Russian package tourist, you'll likely end up in Patong for the nightlife: a neon-filled affair with a port town seediness.

But past the brash beach village is a breathtaking crescent bay. In Thailand, the pretty beaches get all of the attention, for better or worse.

Karon

The next beach south of Patong is Hat Karon, which is a spillover for Patong's hyperactive commercialism. The beach village is a harmless mess of local food, Russian

Traveller on a long-tail boat

JORDAN SIEMENS/GETTY IMAGES ©

signage, low-key girly bars, T-shirt vendors and pretty Karon Park, with its artificial lake and mountain backdrop. Southern Karon takes on more sophistication.

Karon has a broad golden beach that culminates at the northernmost edge (accessible from a rutted road past the roundabout) with glass-like turquoise waters. Megaresorts dominate the beach and there's still more sand space per capita here than at Patong or Kata.

Kata

The classiest of the popular west coast beaches, Kata attracts travellers of all ages and walks of life. While you won't bag a secluded strip of sand, you'll still find lots to do.

Kata has surfing in the shoulder and wet seasons (a rarity in Thailand), terrific day

spas, fantastic food, and a top-notch yoga studio. The gold-sand beach is carved in two by a rocky headland. **Hat Kata Yai** (Map p228) lies on the northern side; more secluded **Hat Kata Noi** (Map p228) unfurls to the south. The road between them is home to Phuket's original millionaire's row.

Rawai

Now this is a place to live, which is exactly why Phuket's rapidly developing south coast is teeming with retirees, artists, Thai and expat entrepreneurs, and a service sector that, for the most part, moved here from somewhere else.

The region is defined not just by its beaches but also by its lush coastal hills that rise steeply and tumble into the Andaman Sea, forming **Laem Phromthep** (Map p228; Rte 4233), Phuket's beautiful southernmost point. For a more secluded sunset spot, seek out the **secret viewpoint** (Map p228; Rte 4233) 1.5km north. These hills are home to neighbourhoods knitted together by just a few roads – though more are being carved into the hills each year and you can almost envision real-estate money chasing away all the seafood grills and tiki bars. Even with the growth you can still feel nature, especially when you hit the beach.

Ask a Phuket local or expat about their favourite beach and everyone's answer is **Hat Nai Han**, one of Rawai's great swimming spots (be careful of rips in low season).

Kamala

A chilled-out beach hybrid, Kamala lures in a mix of long-term, low-key visitors, families and young couples. The bay is magnificent and serene. Palms and pines mingle on the rocky northern end, where the water is a rich emerald green and the snorkelling around the rock reef is halfway decent. Flashy new resorts are carved into the southern bluffs and jet skis make an appearance, but Kamala is quiet and laid-back, by Phuket standards.

Laem Singh, 1km north of Kamala, conceals one of the island's most beautiful beaches. Park on the headland and clamber down a steep jungle-frilled path, or charter a long-tail (1000B) from Hat Kamala. It gets crowded.

Surin

With a wide, blonde beach, water that blends from pale turquoise in the shallows to a deep blue on the horizon, and lush, boulder-strewn headlands, Surin could easily attract visitors on looks alone. Day passes are available at **Catch Beach Club** (Map p228; ☑076 316567; www.catchbeach club.com; Hat Surin; day pass low/high season 1000/2000B; ⊙9am-2am), one of Surin's swishest resorts.

Ao Bang Thao

Stunning, and we mean 'stunning', 8km-long, white-sand Bang Thao is the glue that binds this area's disparate elements. The southern

Kamala

half of the region is dotted with three-star bungalow resorts, plus the swanky Bliss Beach Club (p229). Further inland is an old fishing village laced with canals, upstart villa subdivisions and some stellar restaurants. If you see a herd of water buffalo grazing beside a gigantic construction site...well, that's how fast Bang Thao has developed.

Smack in the centre of it all is the somewhat bizarre Laguna Phuket complex, a network of five four- and five-star resorts tied together by an artificial lake (patrolled by tourist shuttle boats) and a paved nature trail. At the northern end, Mother Nature reasserts herself, and a lonely stretch of powder-white sand and tropical blue sea extends past the bustle into the peaceful bliss you originally had in mind.

SUPPALAKKLABDEE/GETTY IMAGES ©

Sirinat National Park

Comprising the exceptional beaches of Nai Thon, Nai Yang and Mai Khao, along with the former Nai Yang National Park and Mai Khao wildlife reserve, **Sirinat National Park** (อุทยานแห่งชาติสิรินาถ; Map p228; ☑076 327152, 076 328226; www.dnp.go.th; adult/child 200/100B; ☉8.30am-4pm) encompasses 22 sq km of coastline and 68 sq km of sea, stretching from the northern end of Ao Bang Thao to Phuket's northernmost tip. This is one of the sweetest slices of the island. The whole area is 15 minutes from Phuket International Airport.

The Big Phuket Beach Clean-Up

As of Thailand's 2014 military takeover, the governing Thai junta has been tackling Phuket's widespread corruption. Most noticeably, this has involved a firm crackdown on illegal construction and consumer activity on the island's overcrowded beaches.

Initially, all rental sunbeds, deckchairs and umbrellas were banned. Vendors, masseuses and restaurants on the sand were ordered off the beach. Illegally encroaching buildings were bulldozed, including well-established beach clubs and restaurants, and others dramatically reduced in size.

At the time of writing, beach mats and umbrellas are still available to rent, in limited numbers and in '10%' allocated areas; sunbeds remain banned. Tourists may pitch their own umbrellas and chairs within the '10%' zone. Of course, people aren't necessarily following these new regulations. For now, you'll be enjoying Phuket's beautiful beaches in refreshingly tidier, less-hassle versions, albeit with more limited amenities. Some businesses have defied close-down orders and popped back up elsewhere.

Did You Know?

Jet skis, which were banned by the junta, are still very much operating on Patong and Kamala.

JAN TEPASS/GETTY IMAGES ©

Market food stall

Phuket Dining

A melange of cultures come together in the cuisine of this internationally spiced island. Southern Thai food hangs out in the markets, while the high-end resorts do international gastronomy.

Great For...

☑ **Don't Miss**

You don't need fancy decor to have a fabulous meal. Be sure to check out the street stalls and markets.

Phuket Town

The cultural centre of the island provides authentic dining experiences, from simple market meals to formal dining.

For more Eating options see p230.

○ **Walking Street** (Th Thalang; ⊙4-10pm Sun) Unfolds along Th Thalang for southern Thai food.

○ **Weekend Market** (Map p228; off Th Chao Fa West; ⊙4-10pm Sat & Sun) A massive market for cheap eats and cheap souvenirs.

○ **Thanon Ranong Day Market** (Th Ranong; ⊙5am-noon) Traces its history back to the port-town days.

○ **Blue Elephant** (☑076 354355; www.blue elephant.com; 96 Th Krabi; mains 670-1000B, set menus 1350-2400B; ⊙11.30am-2.30pm

Fresh seafood

THANATHAM PIRIYAKARNJANAKUL/EYEEM/GETTY IMAGES ©

Home Kitchen (Map p228; ☎093 764 6753; www.facebook.com/HOME.kitchen.bar.bed; 314 Th Phra Barami, Hat Kalim; mains 300-800B; ⊙5am-1am; ☎) A quirky-chic restaurant-bar with creative Thai-Mediterranean food.

Boathouse Wine & Grill (Map p228; ☎076 330015; www.boathousephuket.com; 182 Th Koktanod, Hat Kata; mains 470-1750B, tasting menu 1800-2200B; ⊙11am-10.30pm) Old-school ambience and top-notch Thai and Mediterranean.

Rum Jungle (Map p228; ☎076 388153; www.facebook.com/Rum-Jungle-Cafe-Rawai-Phuket-173738946050909; 69/8 Mu 1, Th Sai Yuan; mains 240-620B; ⊙11.30am-2pm & 6-10.30pm; ☎) A family affair spearheaded by a terrific Aussie chef.

Bampot (Map p228; ☎093 586 9828; www.bampot.co; 19/1 Mu 1, Th Laguna; mains 500-600B; ⊙6pm-midnight Tue-Fri, noon-3pm & 6pm-midnight Sat & Sun) A modern, urban edge for ambitious European-inspired meals (lobster mac and cheese, sea bass ceviche).

& 6.30-10.30pm; ☎✎) Excels in Royal Thai cuisine presented in a sumptuous mansion.

The Cook (☎076 258375; 101 Th Phang-Nga; mains 65-240B; ⊙8am-9.30pm Tue-Sun) Creative fusion of Thai and Italian.

Suay (☎081 797 4135; www.suayrestaurant.com; 50/2 Th Takua Pa; mains 15-400B; ⊙5pm-midnight) Prepares fabulous fusion at this converted house, just south of old town.

Beaches

The restaurants on the west coast include a side order of sea view.

Baan Rim Pa (Map p228; ☎076 340789; www.baanrimpa.com; 223 Th Phra Barami; mains 290-750B; ⊙noon-10pm) A Patong institution, serving refined Thai fare.

Diving at Ko Raya Noi

PAUL KENNEDY/GETTY IMAGES ©

Phuket Water Sports

Ride the waves, the winds or the underwater currents in Phuket's ocean playground. The island has access to some of the Andaman's most famous dive sites. Monsoon weather turns surfing and kite-boarding into adrenalin sports.

Great For...

☑ Don't Miss

Take this opportunity to learn a new sport, if you've never mastered the waves.

Diving

Phuket enjoys an enviable central location to the Andaman's top diving destinations.

Most Phuket operators take divers to the nine decent sites, including **Ko Raya Noi** and **Ko Raya Yai** (Ko Racha Noi and Ko Racha Yai), but these spots rank lower on the wow-o-meter. The reef off the southern tip of Raya Noi is the best spot, with soft corals and pelagic fish species, though it's usually reserved for experienced divers. Manta and marble rays are frequently glimpsed here and occasionally a whale shark. Snorkelling here is better than elsewhere on the island.

From Phuket, you can join a huge range of live-aboard diving expeditions to the Similan Islands and Myanmar's Mergui

Archipelago. Recommended dive schools include the following:

- **Sea Fun Divers** (Map p228; ☑076 340480; www.seafundivers.com; 29 Soi Karon Nui; 2/3 dives 4100/4500B, Open Water certification 18,400B; ⊙9am-6pm)

- **Rumblefish Adventure** (Map p228; ☑095 441 8665; www.rumblefishadventure.com; 98/79 Beach Centre, Th Kata, Hat Kata; 2/3 dives 2900/3700B; ⊙10am-7pm)

- **Sunrise Divers** (Map p228; ☑084 626 4646, 076 398040; www.sunrise-divers.com; 269/24 Th Patak East, Hat Karon; 2/3 dives 3200/3800B; live-aboards from 12,900B; ⊙9am-5pm)

Kitesurfing

The best kitesurfing spots are Hat Nai Yang from April to October and Rawai from mid-October to March. **Kite Zone** (Map p228; ☑083 395 2005; www.kitesurfthailand. com; Hat Friendship; 1hr lesson 1100B, 3-day course 10,000-15,000B) has all the gear and classes to get you started.

Surfing

With the monsoon's mid-year swell, glassy seas fold into barrels. **Phuket Surf** (Map p228; ☑087 889 7308; www.phuketsurfing.com; Hat Kata Yai; lesson 1500B, board rental per hr/day 150/500B; ⊙8am-7pm Apr-late Oct) is a good spot for break information and gear rental.

Kata Yai and Hat Nai Han both have surf spots but beware of the vicious undertows. Hat Kalim is sheltered and has a consistent 3m break, considered one of the best breaks on the island. Other spots can be found at Hat Kamala and Laem Singh. Hat Nai Yang has a consistent (if soft) wave that breaks more than 200m offshore. Hat Nai Thon gets better shape.

Ko Khao Phing Kan

STARCEVIC/GETTY IMAGES ©

Ao Phang-Nga

Between turquoise bays peppered with craggy limestone towers, brilliant-white beaches and tumbledown fishing villages, Ao Phang-Nga is one of the Andaman's most spectacular landscapes.

Great For

☑ Don't Miss

Keep an eye out for the monitor lizard, a smaller dinosaur lookalike.

Ao Phang-Nga National Park

Established in 1981, 400-sq-km Ao Phang-Nga National Park is famous for its classic karst scenery. Huge vertical cliffs frame 42 islands, some with caves accessible only at low tide and leading into hidden *hôrng* (semi-submerged island caves). The bay is composed of large and small tidal channels, which run north to south through vast mangroves functioning as aquatic highways for fisherfolk and island inhabitants. These are Thailand's largest remaining primary mangrove forests.

In high season (November to April), the bay becomes a clogged package-tourist superhighway. But if you explore in the early morning (ideally from the Ko Yao Islands) or stay out later, you'll have more opportunity to enjoy the curious formations and natural splendour.

❶ Need to Know

Ao Phang-Nga National Park (อุทยาน แห่งชาติอ่าวพังงา; ✆076 481188; www.dnp. go.th; adult/child 300/100B; ⊙8am-4pm)

✕ Take a Break

If you're headed to Ko Yao, the pier at Bang Rong has vendors for quick snacks. Just watch out for the monkeys.

★ Top Tip

The best way to explore the bay is by kayak.

Ko Khao Phing Kan ('Leaning on Itself Island') is the bay's top tourist draw. The Thai name efficiently describes the massive rock formation surrounded by a small spit of sand but it is Hollywood that made it famous. In the James Bond film *The Man with the Golden Gun,* this rocky island starred as Scaramanga's hidden lair. Most tour guides refer to the island as 'James Bond Island' and photo-snapping visitors and souvenir-hawking vendors have turned the impressive natural feature into something of a circus.

A stilted Muslim village clings to **Ko Panyi**, a popular lunch stop for tour groups. It's busy, but several Phang-Nga town tours enable you to stay overnight and soak up the scenery without the crowds.

Keep an eye out in the mangroves for Ao Phang-Nga's marine animals including monitor lizards, two-banded monitors (reminiscent of crocodiles when swimming), flying lizards, banded sea snakes, shore pit vipers and Malayan pit vipers. Mammals include serows, crab-eating macaques, white-handed gibbons and dusky langurs.

Although it's nice to create your own Ao Phang-Nga itinerary by chartering a boat, it's easier (and cheaper) to join a tour from either Phuket or Ko Yao. From Phuket, John Gray's Seacanoe (p229) is the top choice for kayakers.

Ko Yao

Soak up island living with a quick escape from Phuket to the Yao Islands. With mountainous backbones, unspoilt shorelines, varied bird life and a population of friendly Muslim fisherfolk, Ko Yao (Ko Yao Yai and Ko Yao Noi) are laid-back vantage points for soaking up Ao Phang-Nga's beautiful karst scenery. The islands are part of Ao Phang-Nga National Park, but most easily accessed from Phuket (30km away).

The relative pipsqueak, **Ko Yao Noi** is the main population centre, with fishing, coconut farming and tourism sustaining its small, year-round population. Most resorts occupy the bays on the east coast that recede to mud flats at low tides, but the views of the otherworldly rock formations are incredible.

Scenic beaches include gorgeous Hat Pasai, on the southeast coast, and Hat Paradise, on the northeast coast. Hat Tha Khao, on the east coast, has its own dishevelled charm. Hat Khlong Jark is a beautiful sweep of sand with good sleeping options.

Ko Yao Yai is wilder, more remote and less developed; it's twice the size of Yao Noi with a fraction of the infrastructure. The most accessible beaches are slightly developed Hat Lo Pared, on the southwest coast, and powder-white Hat Chonglard on the northeast coast.

Ko Yao can be reached from Phuket's Tha Bang Rong (200B, 30 minutes, nine daily departures). Taxis to the pier cost 600B to 800B; *sŏrng·tăa·ou* (50B) leave from Phuket Town.

Activities

Touring around the sandy trails is a great way to get to know the island. You can rent bicycles from resorts and guesthouses. And if you don't have time to overnight here, Amazing Bike Tours (p229) runs popular small-group day trips to Ko Yao Noi from Phuket. And you can tackle the water with a kayak, widely available on Ko Yao Noi.

There are over 150 rock-climbing routes in the area. **Mountain Shop Adventures** (☏083 969 2023; www.themountainshop.org; Tha Khao; half-day 3200B) arranges beginner

Jetty on Ko Yao Noi

to advanced outings that involve boat travel to remote limestone cliffs.

Ko Yao is so serene, you will want to harness that energy with a yoga class. **Island Yoga** (☑089 290 0233; www.thailandyoga retreats.com; 4/10 Mu 4, Hat Tha Khao, Ko Yao Noi; class 600B; ☺classes 7.30am & 4.30pm) has popular drop-in classes.

Eating

There are several options in Ao Phang-Nga that combine accommodation with restaurants. Some of the best include:

○ **Suntisook** (mains 70-140B; ☺7.30am-9pm; 🛜) Run by a sweet English-speaking Thai family, this is a good, authentic

> **Top Tip**
> Respect local beliefs and dress modestly away from the beaches.

ILONABUDZBON/GETTY IMAGES ©

restaurant that dishes up green, red and massaman curries, cashew and ginger stir fries, lemongrass-fried prawns and chilli-steamed fish, plus delightful Thai and European breakfasts, in a relaxed semi-open setting overlooking beautiful gardens teeming with butterflies.

○ **Sabai Corner Restaurant** (mains 85-260B; ☺8am-10pm) This chilled-out waterside restaurant is a bubbly place to hang out over cocktails, and the Thai and Italian dishes are good (if small) too.

○ **Ko Yao Island Resort** (☑076 597474; www. koyao.com; 24/2 Mu 5, Hat Khlong Jark; villa 6500-21,600B; ❄@🛜☲) There's a snazzy bar-restaurant area and service is stellar.

○ **Chaba Café** (www.facebook.com/Chaba-Café-and-Gallery-481886365211171; Hat Khlong Jark; mains 90-120B; ☺9am-5pm Mon-Sat; 🖊) Rustic-cute with pastel-painted prettiness, driftwood walls, mellow music and a small gallery. Organic-oriented offerings include juices, shakes, tea and home-baked paninis, cookies and cakes, and Thai dishes. It's just beyond northern Hat Khlong Jark.

Rock Art in Ao Phang-Nga

Many of Ao Phang-Nga's limestone islands have prehistoric rock art painted on or carved into cave walls and ceilings, rock shelters, cliffs and rock massifs. You can see rock art at Khao Khian, Ko Panyi, Ko Raya, Tham Nak and Ko Phra At Thao. Images at **Khao Khian** (the most visited cave-art site) contain human figures, fish, crabs, prawns, bats, birds, and elephants, as well as boats, weapons and fishing equipment, seemingly referencing some communal effort tied to the all-important sea harvest. Most rock paintings are monochrome, though some have been traced in orange-yellow, blue, grey and black.

> **Did You Know**
> The Ao Phang-Nga National Park can be visited on two- to three-hour tours (1000B).

◎ SIGHTS

◎ PHUKET TOWN

Phuket Town is an atmospheric stroll through the past.

Phuket Thaihua Museum
Museum

(พิพิธภัณฑ์ภูเก็ตไทยหัว; ☎076 211224; 28 Th Krabi; admission 200B; ☺9am-5pm) Formerly a Chinese language school, this flashy museum is filled with photos and English-language exhibits on Phuket's history, from the Chinese migration (many influential Phuketian families are of Chinese origin) and the tin-mining era to local cuisine, fashion and literature. There's an overview of the building's history, which is a stunning combination of Chinese and European architectural styles, including art deco, Palladianism and a Chinese gable roof and stucco.

Shrine of the Serene Light
Chinese Shrine

(ศาลเจ้าแสงธรรม, Saan Jao Sang Tham; Th Phang-Nga; ☺8.30am-noon & 1.30-5.30pm) **FREE** A handful of Chinese temples pump colour into Phuket Town, but this restored shrine, tucked away up a 50m alley, is particularly atmospheric, with its Taoist etchings on the walls and the vaulted ceiling stained from incense plumes. The altar is always fresh with flowers and burning candles. The shrine is said to have been built by a local family in the 1890s.

◎ AROUND PHUKET

Big Buddha
Statue

Visible from half of the island, the 45m-high **Big Buddha** (พระใหญ่; Map p228; www.mingmongkolphuket.com; off Rte 4021; ☺6am-7pm; **P**) **FREE** sits grandly on Phuket's finest viewpoint. Though it's a tad touristy, tinkling bells and flapping flags give this space an energetic pulse. Pay your respects at the tented golden shrine, then step up to Big Buddha's glorious plateau, where you can peer into Kata's bay, the shimmering Karon strand and, to the southeast, the pebble-sized channel islands of Chalong Bay.

Construction began on Big Buddha in 2007. Phuketians refer to the Big Buddha

Big Buddha

Phuket Town

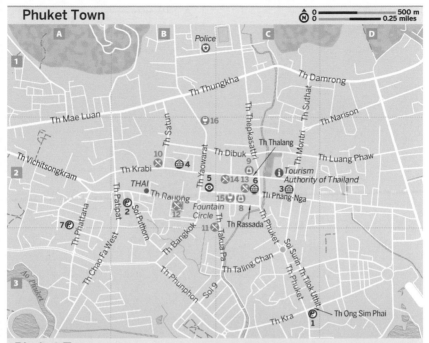

Phuket Town

as Phuket's most important project in the last 100 years, which means a lot considering that construction on Phuket didn't really start until the 1960s.

From Rte 4021, follow signs 1km north of Chalong circle to wind 6km west up a steep country road, passing terraces of banana groves and tangles of jungle.

✪ ACTIVITIES

Suay
Cooking School   Cooking Course

(☏081 797 4135; www.suayrestaurant.com; 50/2 Th Takua Pa; per person 1800B) Learn from one of Phuket's top chefs at the most laid-back, soulful and fun cooking school around. Noy Tammasak will lead you through the local market and teach you how to make three

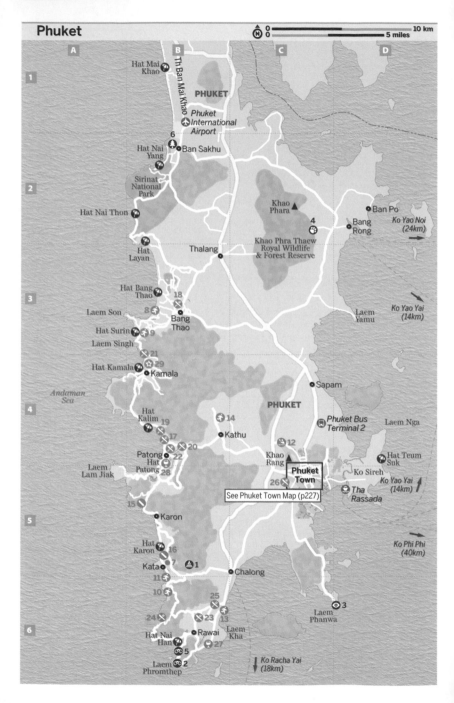

Phuket

Hat Mai Khao

Th Ban Mai Khao

PHUKET

Phuket International Airport

6 Ban Sakhu

Hat Nai Yang

Sirinat National Park

Hat Nai Thon

Khao Phara

Thalang

4

Bang Rong

Ban Po

Ko Yao Noi (24km)

Khao Phra Thaew Royal Wildlife & Forest Reserve

Hat Layan

Laem Yamu

Ko Yao Yai (14km)

Hat Bang Thao

18

Laem Son 8

Bang Thao

Hat Surin 9

Laem Singh

21

Hat Kamala 29

Kamala

Sapam

Andaman Sea

PHUKET

Hat Kalim 19

14

Phuket Bus Terminal 2

Laem Nga

Kathu

17

12

Hat Teum Suk

Patong 20

Hat Patong 22

28

Khao Rang

Ko Sireh

Ko Yao Yai (14km)

Laem Lam Jiak

Phuket Town

26

See Phuket Town Map (p227)

Tha Rassada

15

Karon

Ko Phi Phi (40km)

Hat Karon 16

7

1

Kata

11

Chalong

10

25

3

24

23 13

Laem Phanwa

Hat Nai Han

Laem Kha

27

5

Rawai

Ko Racha Yai (18km)

Laem Phromthep 2

10 km
5 miles

Phuket

⊙ **Sights**
1 Big Buddha... B5
2 Laem Phromthep.................................... B6
3 Phuket Aquarium................................... D6
4 Phuket Gibbon Rehabilitation
    Project.. C2
5 Secret Viewpoint B6
6 Sirinat National Park B2

⊕ **Activities, Courses & Tours**
7 Amazing Bike Tours B5
8 Bliss Beach Club B3
9 Catch Beach Club B3
10 Hat Kata Noi... B6
11 Hat Kata Yai B6
12 John Gray's Seacanoe C1
13 Kite Zone B6
    Phuket Surf .... (see 11)
14 Phuket Wake Park B4
    Rumblefish Adventure .... (see 7)
15 Sea Fun Divers B5
16 Sunrise Divers....................................... B5

✕ **Eating**
17 Baan Rim Pa... B4
18 Bampot.. B3

Boathouse Wine & Grill.....................(see 11)
19 Home Kitchen... B4
20 Kaab Gluay... B4
    Mama Noi's....................................(see 16)
21 Meena Restaurant.................................. B3
    Pad Thai Shop ....(see 7)
22 Patong Food Park B4
23 Rum Jungle B6
24 Sabai Corner.. B6
25 Som Tum Lanna B6
    Twin Brothers ....(see 9)
26 Weekend Market C5

⊙ **Drinking & Nightlife**
    After Beach Bar...............................(see 10)
    Daba Nest ....(see 3)
    Nicky's Handlebar .... (see 22)
27 Nikita's B6
28 Seduction... B4
    Ska Bar..(see 11)

⊕ **Entertainment**
29 Phuket Fantasea B4

ⓘ **Information**
    Bangkok Hospital Phuket................(see 12)

dishes, before cracking open a bottle of wine to enjoy with your culinary creations. Highly recommended; minimum three people.

Bliss Beach Club Beach Club
(Map p228; ☎076 510150; www.blissbeach club.com; 202/88 Mu 2, Hat Bang Thao; day pass 300B; ⊙11am-late; ⚐) As if Hat Bang Thao wasn't stunning enough, Bliss offers the ultimate super-swish Phuket beach experience. Mellow tunes beat in the background, guests lounge around reading, sipping cocktails on the shady sea-facing terrace and watching the kids splash around the pool. Admission covers a sun lounger, a towel and use of the facilities. On Sundays, it's Soundwave party time (from 2pm).

⊕ **TOURS**

John Gray's Seacanoe Kayaking
(Map p228; ☎076 254505; www.johngray-sea canoe.com; 86 Soi 2/3, Th Yaowarat; adult/child

from 3950/1975B) ⚐ The original, the most reputable and by far the most ecologically sensitive kayaking company on Phuket. The Hong by Starlight trip dodges the crowds, involves sunset paddling and will introduce you to Ao Phang-Nga's famed after-dark bioluminescence. Like any good brand in Thailand, John Gray's 'Seacanoe' name and itineraries have been frequently copied. He's 3.5km north of Phuket Town.

Amazing Bike Tours Cycling
(Map p228; ☎087 263 2031; www.amazingbike toursthailand.asia; 191 Th Patak East, Hat Kata; day trip adult/child 2900/2500B) This highly popular Kata-based adventure outfitter leads small groups on half-day bicycle tours through Khao Phra Thaew Royal Wildlife & Forest Reserve. It also runs terrific day trips around Ko Yao Noi and more challenging three-day adventures rides around Khao Sok National Park (14,900B) and Krabi Province (15,900B). Prices include bikes, helmets, meals, water and national park entry fees.

 Phuket for Children

There's plenty for kids to do on Phuket. **Phuket Aquarium** (สถานแสดงพันธุ์สัตว์ น้ำภูเก็ต; Map p228; 076 391126; www. phuketaquarium.org; 51 Th Sakdidej; adult/ child 180/100B; 8.30am-4.30pm; P) and a visit to the tiny **Phuket Gibbon Rehabilitation Project** (โครงการคืนชะนีสู่ป่า; Map p228; 076 260492; www.gibbonpro ject.org; off Rte 4027; admission by donation; 9am-4.30pm, to 3pm Thu; P) are terrific animal-themed activities that are sure to please. The main family-flogged feature of **Phuket Fantasea** (Map p228) is a pricey extravaganza of animals, costumes, song, special effects, pyrotechnics, and a lousy dinner. It also doesn't adhere to modern standards of animal welfare.

The newest attractions for kids of all ages, but especially for tweens and above, is the **Phuket Wake Park** (Map p228; 089 873 0187; www.phuket wakepark.com; 86/3 Mu 6, Th Vichitsong-kram, Kathu; adult/child 2hr 650/350B, day pass 1150/550B; 7.30am-11pm;), where you can learn to wake board by buzzing a lake nestled in the mountains of Kathu.

Phuket Aquarium
LONELY PLANET/GETTY IMAGES ©

🅐 SHOPPING

These shops are in Phuket Town.

Ranida Antiques, Fashion
(119 Th Thalang; 10.30am-7.30pm Mon-Sat) An elegant antique gallery and boutique featuring Buddha statues and sculpture, organic textiles, and ambitious, exquisite high-fashion women's clothing that is inspired by vintage Thai garments and fabrics.

Drawing Room Arts
(isara380@hotmail.com; 56 Th Phang-Nga; 10am-9pm) With a street-art vibe reminiscent of pre-boom Brooklyn or East London, this wide-open cooperative is by far the stand-out gallery in a town full of them. Canvases might be vibrant abstract squiggles or comical pen-and-ink cartoons. Metallic furniture and bicycles line concrete floors. House music thumps at low levels.

✖ EATING

For Phuket highlights, see the Phuket Dining Top Experience (p218). Other noteworthy spots include:

Patong Food Park Thai $
(Map p228; Th Rat Uthit; dishes 50-200B; 4.30pm-midnight) Extending two blocks is this cheap, local foodie's dream world. There are all kinds of fresh fish, crab, lobster, roasted pork leg, steamed chicken, satay and sôm·đam (green papaya salad), and sticky rice with mango for dessert. All delicious.

Kaab Gluay Thai $
(Map p228; 076 346832; 58/3 Th Phra Barami; dishes 60-165B; 11am-2am;) It's hardly Patong's most peaceful spot, but this easygoing roadside eatery is a hit for its authentic, affordable Thai food, with switched-on staff and well-spelt (!) menus to match. Unpretentious dining happens under a huge tin roof. Expect red-curry prawns, chicken satay, sweet-and-sour fish, deep-fried honeyed chicken, classic noodles and stir-fries, and 30-plus takes on spicy Thai salads.

Pad Thai Shop Thai $
(Map p228; Th Patak East, Hat Karon; dishes 50B; 9am-6pm) This glorified roadside

Clockwise from top: Phuket Town; bells at Big Buddha (p226); Laem Phromthep (p215)

food shack does rich, savoury chicken stew and absurdly good *kôw pàt þoo* (crab fried rice), *pàt see·éw* (fried noodles) and noodle soup. It also serves up some of the best *pàt tai* we've ever tasted: spicy and sweet, packed with tofu, egg and peanuts, and plated with a side of spring onions, beansprouts and lime. Don't miss the house-made chilli sauces.

Mama Noi's   Thai, Italian $

(Map p228; Karon Plaza, Hat Karon; mains 90-185B; ☺9am-10pm; 🛜) This simple tile-floored cafe with faded Italy photos, a good local vibe and dangling pot-plants has been feeding the expat masses for a generation. They do fantastic versions of all the Thai dishes plus a huge list of popular pastas – anyone for red-curry spaghetti? Cheap, tasty and friendly.

Som Tum Lanna   Thai $

(Map p228; 📞081 597 0569; 3/7 Th Sai Yuan, Hat Rawai; mains 80-150B; ☺9am-5pm Tue-Sun) When it comes to *sôm·đam*, order it mild – it'll still bring some serious heat. And while

the fish at this Isan soul food shack is good, its equal exists elsewhere. The chicken on the other hand is outstanding.

Meena Restaurant   Thai $

(Map p228; Hat Kamala; mains 80-150B; ☺9am-5pm) This family-run beachside shack with rainbow-striped and leopard-print sarongs for tablecloths is a real find. The owners couldn't be more welcoming. The tasty, authentic Thai food is exceptional and so are the fresh fruit shakes. The rustic setting is exactly what you (most likely) came to Kamala for. It's at the north end of the beach.

Twin Brothers   Thai $$

(Map p228; Hat Surin; mains 120-350B; ☺11am-10pm) By day, one brother mans the wok, stirring up decent seafood-focused Thai food at (almost) local prices. At night, the other fires up a fresh seafood grill. It's more down to earth than Hat Surin's other options.

Patong (p214)

🍸 DRINKING & NIGHTLIFE

🍺 Phuket Town

Comics   Bar

(www.facebook.com/Comics-Cafe-Bar-358086 567609208; 44 Th Phang-Nga; ⊙6pm-midnight) A youthful all-Thai clientele crams into this bubbly, blue-lit, comic-covered space for mellow live music enjoyed with Thai and international beers, ciders, wines and cocktails.

Timber Hut   Club

(☑076 211839; 118/1 Th Yaowarat; ⊙6pm-2am) Thai and expat locals have been packing out this two-floor pub-club nightly for 25 years, swilling whisky and swaying to live bands that swing from hard rock to pure pop to hip-hop. No cover charge.

Baba Nest   Cocktail Bar

(Map p228; Sri Panwa, 88 Mu 8, Th Sakdidej; ⊙5-9pm) Sri Panwa's elegant rooftop Baba Nest lounge-bar, engulfed in unimaginably beautiful ocean-and-island views, is magical. It's perfectly positioned for sunsets on the southernmost tip of Laem Phanwa, 12km south of Phuket Town.

🍺 Patong

Seduction   Club

(Map p228; www.facebook.com/seductiondisco; 70/3 Th Bangla; ⊙10pm-5am) International DJs, professional-grade sound system and forever the best dance party on Phuket, without question.

Nicky's Handlebar   Bar

(Map p228; ☑076 343211; www.nickyhandle bars.com; 41 Th Rat Uthit; ⊙7.30am-1am; 🛜) This fun biker bar welcomes all, wheels or no wheels. Once a bit of a dive, Nicky's has never looked better. Ashtrays crafted from bike parts rest on the metal bar and weighty menus are made from hubcaps and heavy disk brakes. You can get your own wheels here by asking about Harley tours and hire (from 4800B).

👍 Vegetarian Festival

Deafening popping sounds fill the streets, the air is thick with smoke, and people pierce their cheeks with skewers and knives. Blood streams from their self-inflicted wounds. No, this isn't a war zone, this is the **Vegetarian Festival** (www.phuketvegetarian.com), one of Phuket's most important celebrations.

The festival takes place during the first nine days of the ninth lunar month of the Chinese calendar and celebrates the beginning of 'Taoist Lent'.

Those participating as mediums bring the nine deities to earth by entering a trance state and performing self-mortification. The temporarily possessed mediums (primarily men) stop at shopfront altars to pick up offerings.

Phuket Town's festival focuses on several Chinese temples, including **Jui Tui Shrine** (Map p227), off Th Ranong; **Bang Niew Shrine** (Map p227); and **Sui Boon Tong Shrine** (Map p227).

Oddly enough, there is no record of these acts of devotion associated with Taoist Lent in China. Local Chinese claim the festival was started in 1825 in Kathu, by a theatre troupe from China who performed a nine-day penance of self-piercing, meditation and vegetarianism after becoming seriously ill for failing to propitiate the nine emperor gods of Taoism.

Phuket's Tourism Authority of Thailand (p234) prints festival schedules.

Celebrations during the Vegetarian Festival
NATTHAWAT/GETTY IMAGES ©

 ### Sino-Portuguese Architecture

Stroll along Ths Thalang, Dibuk, Yaowarat, Ranong, Phang-Nga, Rassada and Krabi for a glimpse of Phuket Town's Sino-Portuguese architectural treasures.

The most magnificent examples are the **Standard Chartered Bank** (Th Phang-Nga), Thailand's oldest foreign bank; the **THAI office** (076 360444; www.thaiairways.com; 78/1 Th Ranong, Phuket Town; 8am-4.30pm); and the old post office building, which now houses the **Phuket Philatelic Museum** (Th Montri; 10am-5pm Mon-Sat) FREE. Some of the most colourfully revamped buildings line Soi Romanee, off Th Thalang, once home to brothels, gamblers and opium dens.

Phuket Town (p226)
DAVID HENLEY/GETTY IMAGES ©

Kata
Ska Bar   Bar

(Map p228; www.skabar-phuket.com; 186/12 Th Koktanod; noon-late) Tucked into rocks on the southernmost curl of Hat Kata Yai and seemingly intertwined with the trunk of a grand old banyan tree, Ska is our choice for seaside sundowners. The Thai bartenders add to the laid-back Rasta vibe, and buoys, paper lanterns and flags dangle from the canopy. Hang around if there's a fire show.

After Beach Bar   Bar

(Map p228; 081 894 3750; Rte 4233; 9am-10.30pm) It's impossible to overstate how glorious the 180-degree views are from this stilted, thatched reggae bar clinging to a cliff above Kata: rippling sea, rocky

peninsulas and palm-dappled hills. Now wack on the Bob Marley and you've got the perfect sunset-watching spot. When the fireball finally drops, lights from fishing boats blanket the horizon. It also does some flavour-bursting *pàt tai*.

ⓘ INFORMATION

Bangkok Hospital Phuket (Map p228; 076 254425; www.phukethospital.com; Th Hongyok Uthit) Reputedly the favourite among locals, 3km north of Phuket Town.

Police (076 212046, 191; Th Chumphon)

Tourism Authority of Thailand (TAT; 076 211036; www.tourismthailand.org/Phuket; 191 Th Thalang; 8.30am-4.30pm) Has maps, brochures, transport advice and info on boat trips to nearby islands.

ⓘ GETTING THERE & AWAY
AIR

Phuket International Airport (www.phuketairportthai.com) is 30km northwest of Phuket Town. A number of carriers serve domestic destinations, including Bangkok (from 1400B), Chiang Mai (1900B) and Ko Samui (3200B), as well as regional centres.

BUS & MINIVAN

Interprovincial buses depart from **Phuket Bus Terminal 2** (Th Thepkrasattri), 4km north of Phuket Town. Air-con minivans go to popular tourist destinations; tickets can be bought from travel agents.

BOAT

Tha Rassada, 3km southeast of Phuket Town, is the main pier for boats to Ko Phi-Phi, Krabi (Railay).

ⓘ GETTING AROUND

Large *sŏrng·tǎa·ou* run regularly from Phuket Town's Th Ranong near the day market to the beaches (25B to 40B, 30 minutes to 1½ hours, 7am to 6pm). Chartered túk-túk to the beaches costs 400B (Rawai, Kata and Ao Bang Thao), 500B (Patong, Karon and Surin) or 600B (Kamala).

Where to Stay

The beaches at the southern and northern ends of the west coast feel like escapes from the real world. Patong and Karon are very hyperactive.

Place	Atmosphere
Phuket Town	Quirky, affordable lodging; commute to the beach
Patong	Lots of nightlife and dining; noisy, crowded and seedy
Karon	Lively beach, mix of budget lodging; slightly seedy
Kata	Lively beach, mainly high-end resorts
Rawai	Quiet beach, high-end resorts, local eats
Kamala	Relaxed beach, boutique resorts
Surin	Low-key beach, classy resorts
Ao Bang Thao	Luxury resort complex
Sirinat National Park	Natural beach, a mix of accommodation; far from dining and nightlife

RAILAY

Railay

The Andaman's fairy-tale limestone crags come to a dramatic climax at Railay (also spelt Rai Leh), a mountainous peninsula of Krabi Province that is only reached by boat, giving the illusion of being a far-flung island. Rock climbers scramble up huge limestone towers for amazing clifftop views while kayakers and snorkellers take an amphibious assault on the landscape. The wind-down scene has a Thai-Rasta vibe that enthusiastically toasts the sunsets and welcomes new acolytes.

Two Days in Railay

Take a two-day rock-climbing course to master the vertical cliffs and embrace endless sea views. Carbo load for your day at **Mama's Chicken** (p242), a favourite for healthy eats.

Four Days in Railay

Find a cosy patch of sand and nap through the day. Break up the routine with a sweaty hike to Sa Phra Nang and Tham Phra Nang; remember your bug spray. Reward breaking a sweat with a cocktail at **Last Bar** (p242) and dinner at **Sunset Restaurant** (p242).

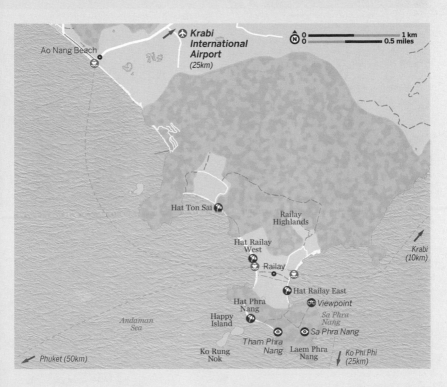

Arriving in Railay

Long-tails run from Krabi's Tha Khong Kha (150B, 45 minutes). Chartering the boat costs 1200B. There's also a year-round ferry from Phuket (700B, 2¼ hours). All boats arrive/depart at Hat Railay West.

Where to Stay

There aren't a lot of lodging options on Railay because it so small but the options do cover the budget spectrum. Railay Highlands and Hat Ton Sai favour backpackers while Railay East and Railay West have midrange and top-end options. Book in advance in December and January as vacancies become slim.

Rock climbing at Hat Railay East

EMANUELE SIRACUSA/GETTY IMAGES ©

Rock Climbing

Railay is one of Southeast Asia's top climbing spots and continues to gain in popularity. The routes are varied in their technical challenges and have rewarding sea views.

Great For...

☑ Don't Miss

If you're just a beginner, stick with it until you reach the summit. It is worth it.

With over 700 bolted routes, ranging from beginner to advanced, all with unparalleled clifftop vistas, you could spend months climbing and exploring. Deep-water solo-ing, where free-climbers scramble up ledges over deep water, is incredibly popular. If you fall you'll probably just get wet, so even beginners can try.

Climbing Routes

Most climbers start off at Muay Thai Wall and One, Two, Three Wall, at the southern end of Hat Railay East, where there are at least 40 routes graded from 4b to 8b on the French system. The mighty Thaiwand Wall sits at the southern end of Hat Railay West, offering a sheer limestone cliff with some of the most challenging climbing routes, graded from 6a to 7c+.

ℹ Need to Know

Climbing courses cost 800B to 1000B for a half-day and 1500B to 2000B for a full day.

✕ Take a Break

Talk bolts and ropes at **Highland Rock Climbing** (📞084 443 9539; Railay Highlands; ⊘8am-8pm), a popular climbing school hangout.

★ Top Tip

Chalk is super handy for avoiding sweaty palms in this tropical climate.

around 1000B per day (quality varies); the standard set consists of a 60m rope, two climbing harnesses and climbing shoes. If climbing independently, you're best off bringing your own gear, including nuts and cams as backup for thinly protected routes. Some climbing schools sell a limited range of imported gear.

Climbing Outfitters

Recommended companies include the following:

◉ Basecamp Tonsai (📞081 149 9745; www. tonsaibasecamp.com; Hat Ton Sai; half/full day 800/1500B, 3-day course 6000B; ⊘8am-5pm & 7-9pm)

◉ Hot Rock (📞085 641 9842; www.railay adventure.com; Hat Railay East; half/full day 1000/2000B, 3-day course 6000B; ⊘9am-8pm)

◉ King Climbers (📞081 797 8923; www.railay. com; Walking St; half/full day 1000/1800B, 3-day course 6000B; ⊘8.30am-9pm Mon-Fri, to 6pm Sat & Sun)

Other top climbs include Hidden World, with its classic intermediate routes; Wee's Present Wall, an overlooked 7c+ winner; Diamond Cave, a busy beginner-to-intermediate favourite; and Ao Nang Tower, a three-pitch climbing wall reached only by boat.

There's excellent climbing information at www.railay.com. *Rock Climbing in Thailand and Laos* (2014; Elke Schmitz) is an up-to-date guide to the area.

Courses & Gear

Beginners can start with a half- or full-day session. Private sessions are also available. Three-day courses involve lead climbing, where you clip into bolts on the rock face. Experienced climbers can rent gear sets for two people from the climbing schools for

◉ SIGHTS

Sa Phra Nang   Lagoon
(Holy Princess Pool) Halfway along the trail linking Hat Railay East to Hat Tham Phra Nang, a
sharp 'path' leads up the jungle-cloaked cliff
wall to this hidden lagoon. The first section
is a steep 10-minute uphill climb (with ropes
for assistance). Fork right for the lagoon,
reached by sheer downhill climbing. If you
fork left, you'll quickly reach a dramatic
cliff-side viewpoint; this is a strenuous but
generally manageable, brief hike.

Tham Phra Nang   Cave
(ถ้ำพระนาง, Princess Cave; Hat Tham Phra Nang)
At the eastern end of the beach, this is an
important shrine for local fishermen (Muslim
and Buddhist), who make offerings of carved
wooden phalluses in the hope that the inhab-
iting spirit of a drowned Indian princess will
provide a good catch. According to legend, a
royal barge carrying the princess foundered
here in a storm during the 3rd century
BC. Her spirit took over the cave, granting
favours to all who paid their respects.

❸ ACTIVITIES

Dive operations in Railay run trips out
to local dive sites, including Ko Poda. Two
dives cost 2500B; an Open Water dive
course is 13,500B. There are also dive trips
to Ko Phi-Phi (4000B) and King Cruiser
Wreck (4500B). Most dive operators in Ao
Nang, where there's more choice, will pick
up from Railay.

Full-day, multi-island **snorkelling trips**
(450B to 1400B) to Ko Poda, Ko Hong, Ko Kai
and beyond can be arranged through resorts

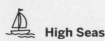

⛵ High Seas

During exceptionally high seas, boats
from Ao Nang and Krabi stop running;
you may still be able to get from Hat
Railay East to Ao Nam Mao (100B,
15 minutes), where you can pick up a
sŏrng·tăa·ou to Krabi or Ao Nang.

and agencies, or you can charter a long-tail
(half-/full day 1800/2800B) from Hat Railay
West. One-day snorkelling tours to Ko Phi-Phi
cost 1400B to 2000B. If you're just snorkelling off Railay, most resorts rent mask sets
and fins for around 150B each.

Rent **kayaks** on Hat Railay West or Hat
Ton Sai (per hour/day 200/800B).

❌ EATING

Mama's Chicken   Thai $
(Hat Ton Sai; 70-100B; ⊙7am-10pm; 🍴) Relocated to the jungle path leading inland to
Hat Railay East and West, Mama's remains
one of Ton Sai's favourite food stops for its
international breakfasts, fruit smoothies
and extensive range of cheap Thai dishes,
including a rare massaman tofu and other
vegetarian-friendly adaptations.

Sunset Restaurant   Seafood, Thai $$
(Hat Railay West; mains 180-400B; ⊙11am-9pm;
🛜) At the recommended beachfront of
Sand Sea Resort (📞075 819463; www.krabi
sandsea.com; Hat Railay West; bungalows incl
breakfast 3990-6800B; ❋@🛜🏊) red-shirted
waiters take seafood-grill and Thai-curry
orders on iPads.

❷ DRINKING & NIGHTLIFE

Last Bar   Bar
(Hat Railay East; ⊙11am-late) A reliably
packed-out multi-level tiki bar that rambles
to the edge of the mangroves, with bunting,
balloons and cushioned seats on one deck,
candlelit dining tables on another, live
music at the back and waterside fire shows.

❶ GETTING THERE & AROUND

Long-tails run from Krabi (150B, 45 minutes,
7.45am to 6pm) when full (eight people);
chartering the boat costs 1200B. A *sŏrng·tăa·ou*
leaves Krabi for Ao Nang where you can catch a
long-tail (100B to 150B, 15 minutes); chartering
costs 800B. A year-round ferry runs from Railay
to Ko Phi-Phi (400B, 1¼ hours, 9.45am) and
Phuket (700B, 2¼ hours).

Clockwise from top: Railay beach; phallus offering at Tham Phra Nang; Sa Phra Nang

KO PHI-PHI

Ko Phi-Phi

With its curvy, bleach-blonde beaches and bodacious jungles, it's no wonder Phi-Phi has become the darling of the Andaman coast. And like any good starlet, this island can party hard all night and still look great the next morning. Ko Phi-Phi is actually two islands: Ko Phi-Phi Don is a car-less island crisscrossed by footpaths leading to small-scale bungalows and resorts, while uninhabited Ko Phi-Phi Leh is a protected park only allowed visitors on day trips.

Two Days in Ko Phi-Phi

Bliss out on the beaches. Party till late at **Sunflower Bar** (p254), **Ibiza** (p254) or **Carlito's** (p254). Grab breakfast the next day at **Unni's** (p254). Do a climbing or cooking course if you've had your fill of navel gazing. But we won't judge you if you prefer a nap in the shade.

Four Days in Ko Phi-Phi

Dive and snorkel the spectacular underwater gardens of Ko Phi-Phi. Take a tour of Phi-Phi Don's virgin sister, **Phi-Phi Leh** (p250). Enjoy dinner at **Le Grand Bleu** (p254). Or do a dinner or cocktail cruise to Phi-Phi Leh if you prefer scenery with an adult beverage.

Phuket (50km)

Laem Thong

Tha Laem Thong

Chong Kiu • Hat Laem Thong

2 km
1 miles

Ao Lo Lana

Ao Lo Bakao

Andaman Sea

Ko Phi-Phi Marine National Park

Hat Phak Nam

Ao Lo Dalam

Hat Rantee

Phi-Phi Viewpoint

Ao Toh Ko

Krabi Town (35km)

Ton Sai Village

Tha Ao Ton Sai

Ao Ton Sai

Hat Hin Khom

Ao Lo Mu Di

Ko Nok

Laem Hin

Ko Nok

Laem Phaw

Ao Wang Long

Hat Yao

Phuket (50km)

Ko Lanta (30km)

Arriving in Ko Phi-Phi

Most boats from Phuket and Railay moor at Ao Ton Sai on Phi-Phi Don. There are no roads. Transport is by foot, or long-tail boat charter (100B to 1200B).

Where to Stay

Phi-Phi's reputation as a party island makes it very difficult to sleep peacefully. The island's small size also means that room shortages are a problem during the high season and rates increase excessively. Budget options huddle around the village of Ton Sai and Ao Lo Dalam. The island gets quieter on the east coast where there are top-end resorts and low-key bungalows.

Exploring a coral reef, Ko Phi-Phi

BORUT FURLAN/GETTY IMAGES ©

Ko Phi-Phi Diving & Snorkelling

Crystalline water and abundant marine life make the perfect recipe for top-notch diving. Leopard sharks and hawksbill turtles are common on Ko Phi-Phi's dive sites.

Great For...

☑ Don't Miss

Ko Mai Phai is a popular shallow snorkelling spot where you may see small sharks.

Dive Sites

Popular dive spots include **Anemone Reef**, which is a hard coral reef with plentiful anemones and clownfish at a depth of 17m to 26m. **Hin Bida Phi-Phi** is a submerged pinnacle with hard coral, turtles, leopard sharks and occasional mantas and whale sharks, at 5m to 30m. **King Cruiser Wreck** is a 1997 sunken passenger ferry; underwater creatures to keep an eye out for include snappers, leopard sharks, barracudas, scorpionfish, lionfish and turtles.

Kledkaeo Wreck is a decommissioned Thai navy ship that was deliberately sunk as an artificial dive site in March 2014. Underwater inhabitants include lionfish, snappers, groupers and barracudas.

Ko Bida Nok is a karst massif with gorgonians, leopard sharks, barracudas and occasional whale sharks and mantas (18m to 22m).

Ko Phi-Phi Leh is rimmed with coral and swim-throughs visited by moray eels, octopi and seahorses.

Snorkelling Sites

Ko Mai Phai, 6km north of Phi-Phi Don, is a popular shallow snorkelling spot where you may see small sharks. There's good snorkelling along the east coast of **Ko Nok**, along the east coast of **Ko Nai**, and off **Hat Yao**. Most resorts rent out snorkel, mask and fins sets (per day 200B).

Snorkelling trips cost 700B to 2500B, depending on whether you travel by long-

❶ Need to Know

Phi-Phi has fixed island-wide dive prices. Open Water certification costs 13,800B; standard two-dive trips cost 2500B to 3500B; and Discover Scuba costs 3400B.

✕ Take a Break

Lunch is usually provided on full-day dive trips.

★ Top Tip

November to February boasts the best visibility. Whale sharks sometimes make cameo appearances in February and March.

tail or motorboat. You can tag along with dive trips, and many dive operators also offer specialised snorkelling tours. Those with the Adventure Club come highly recommended.

Dive Companies

Recommended dive companies include the following:

○ **Adventure Club** (☏081 895 1334; www.diving-in-thailand.net; Ton Sai Village; 2 dives 2500B, Open Water certification 13,800B; ◷8am-10pm) ⚓

○ **Blue View Divers** (☏075 819 395; www.blueviewdivers.com; Phi Phi Viewpoint Resort, Ao Lo Dalam; 2 dives 2500B; ◷10am-8pm) ⚓

○ **Sea Frog Diving** (☏087 920 0680, 075 601073; www.ppseafrog.com; Ton Sai Village; 2 dives 2500B; ◷7am-10pm)

Ao Pileh

TAEHARDY/GETTY IMAGES ©

Ko Phi-Phi Leh

Rugged Phi-Phi Leh is the smaller of the two Phi-Phi Islands, protected on all sides by soaring, jagged cliffs. Coral reefs crawling with marine life under the crystal-clear waters are hugely popular with day-trippers.

Great For...

☑ **Don't Miss**

Kayaking around the bay gives a glimpse into the remarkable marine life that resides at the high-water mark.

Ever since Leo (DiCaprio) smoked a spliff in the film rendition of Alex Garland's *The Beach,* Phi-Phi Leh has been something of a pilgrimage site. Aside from long-tail boat trips to Phi-Phi Leh, tour agencies organise sunset tours around the island that include Monkey Bay and the beach at Wang Long.

Viking Cave

On the northeastern tip of the island, Viking Cave is a major collection point for valuable swifts' nests, the key components of Chinese speciality bird's-nest soup. Nimble collectors scamper up fragile bamboo scaffolding to the roof of the cave to gather the nests. Before ascending, they pray and make offerings of tobacco, incense and liquor. The cave gets its misleading moniker from the 400-year-old boat graffiti created by crews of passing Chinese fishing junks.

At research time, visitors were not allowed inside the cave, but most tour boats slow down for a good glimpse.

Ao Pileh

Of the two gorgeous emerald lagoons that await in Phi-Phi Leh's interior, Pileh lies on the east coast. It's predictably busy, but the thrill of kayaking between these towering limestone walls never gets old.

Ao Maya

Dramatically flanked by green-clad cliffs, majestic Ao Maya sits on Phi-Phi Leh's western shoreline. In 1999, its beautiful sands were controversially used as a set for *The Beach,* based on Alex Garland's cult novel. Natural sand dunes were flattened and extra palm trees planted to increase the paradisaical backdrop and, although the production's team restored things, many claim the damage to the ecosystem has been permanent. The level of boat traffic here nowadays somewhat detracts from the serenity, but the setting is still spectacular.

Tour Operators

You'll have to join a tour to gain access to Ko Phi-Phi Leh's territory.

○ **PP Original Sunset Tour** (Ton Sai Village; per person 900B; ☺tour 1pm) A sensational sunset cruise with snorkelling and kayaking, followed by dinner.

○ **Maya Bay Sleepaboard** (www.maya baytours.com; per person 3000B) Camping is no longer allowed in Maya Bay so this sleepaboard is the next best thing.

○ **Captain Bob's Booze Cruise** (☑084 848 6970; www.phiphiboozecruise.com; women/men 2500/3000B; ☺tour 1pm) Cruise the sea with an adult beverage in hand.

◎ SIGHTS

Phi-Phi Viewpoint   Viewpoint
(จุดชมวิวเกาะพีพีดอน; admission 30B) The
strenuous Phi-Phi viewpoint climb is a
steep, rewarding 20- to 30-minute hike
up hundreds of steps and narrow twisting
paths. Follow the signs on the road heading
northeast from Ton Sai Village; most people
will need to stop for a break (don't forget
your water bottle). The views from the
top are exquisite: Phi-Phi's lush mountain
butterfly brilliance in full bloom.

✈ ACTIVITIES

**Ibex Climbing &
Tours**   Rock Climbing
(☏075 601370, 084 309 0445; www.ibexclimbing
andtours.com; Ton Sai Village; half/full day
1100/1950B) One of Phi-Phi's newest and
best rock-climbing operators. Rates include
instruction and gear.

**Pum Restaurant &
Cooking School**   Cooking Course
(☏081 521 8904; www.pumthaifoodchain.com;
125/40 Mu 7, Ton Sai Village; per person 500-
4000B; ⊗classes 11am, 4pm & 6pm) Thai-food
fans can take highly recommended cooking
courses ranging from half-hour, one-dish
sessions to five-hour 'healthy lifestyle' ex-
travaganzas. You'll learn the secrets behind
some of the excellent dishes served in their
Ton Sai Village restaurant and go home with
a cookbook.

✖ EATING

Local Food Market   Market, Thai $
(Ton Sai Village; meals 60-80B; ⊗7am-10pm)
Phi-Phi's cheapest, most authentic eats are
at the market (which was being renovated
at research time), on the narrowest sliver of
the isthmus. A handful of enthusiastic local
stalls serve up scrumptious *pàt tai*, fried
rice, *sôm·dam* and smoked catfish.

Papaya Restaurant   Thai $
(☏087 280 1719; Ton Sai Village; dishes 100-
350B; ⊗10am-10.30pm) Cheap, tasty and

Clockwise from top left: Ko Bida Nok (p249); Viking Cave (p250); Ao Maya (p251); aerial view of Ko Phi-Phi

spicy. Here's some real-deal Thai food served in heaping portions. It has your basil and chilli, all the curries, *sôm·đam* and *đôm yam,* too. There's a second branch, **Papaya 2** (📞087 280 1719; Ton Sai Village; dishes 100-350B; ⏰10am-10pm), a block away.

Unni's   International $$

(📞081 979 2865; Ton Sai Village; mains 200-350B; ⏰8am-midnight; 🛜) Swing by this local expat fave for homemade breakfast bagels topped with everything from smoked salmon to meatballs or specials like avocado-and-feta toast. Other excellent global treats include massive Greek salads, pastas, burritos, nachos, burgers, tapas, cocktails and more. It's a chic cafe-lounge–style place with contemporary mood music.

Le Grand Bleu   Thai, French $$

(📞081 979 9739; 137 Mu 7, Ton Sai Village; mains 160-360B; ⏰6.30-11pm) Thai–French fusion in a charming wooden house with a trickling fountain, wall art and a colourful concrete bar, just off the main pier. Here you can get duck oven-roasted with honey, shrimp as ravioli, king prawns cooked in pesto and creamy mushroom tagliatelle, plus a selection of southern Thai specialities, accompanied by international wines.

🍸 DRINKING & NIGHTLIFE

Sunflower Bar   Bar

(Ao Lo Dalam; ⏰11am-2am; 🛜) Poetically ramshackle, this driftwood gem is still Phi-Phi's most chilled-out bar. Destroyed in the 2004 tsunami, it was rebuilt with reclaimed wood. The long-tail booths are named for the four loved ones the owner lost in the deluge.

Ibiza   Club

(Ao Lo Dalam; ⏰9pm-2am) Another of Dalam's beach dens of inebriation and iniquity (but, you know, in a good way). Relax on beachside cushions and marvel at expert fire twirlers and drunken daredevils as they jump through fiery hoops and limbo beneath a fiery cane, while everyone else dances and fist-pumps to bone-rattling bass.

Carlito's   Bar

(www.carlitosbar.net; Ao Ton Sai; ⏰11am-1am) For a (slightly) toned-down take on Dalam's fire-twirling madness, pull up a plastic chair on the sand at this fairy-light-lit beachside bar, which puts on fun fire shows and attracts beer- and cocktail-seeking *fa·ràng* (Westerners). It can get rowdy on party nights.

ℹ️ INFORMATION

ATMs are spread throughout the Tourist Village but not on the eastern beaches. Wi-fi is everywhere.

Break-ins are a problem: lock the door while you sleep and close all windows when you go out.

Phi Phi Island Hospital (📞075 622 151; Ao Ton Sai) Emergency care, at the west end of Ao Ton Sai. For anything truly serious, you're on the first boat to Krabi or Phuket.

Post Office (Ton Sai Village; ⏰9am-5pm Mon-Fri & 9am-1pm Sat)

ℹ️ GETTING THERE & AWAY

Ko Phi-Phi can be reached by boat from Phuket (250B to 300B, 1¼ to three hours, three daily departures) and Railay (350B to 400B, 1¼ hours, one daily departure). Most boats moor at Ao Ton Sai.

ℹ️ GETTING AROUND

There are no roads on Ko Phi-Phi Don. Transport is mostly by foot and chartered long-tails (100B to 1200B, depending on the beach).

Where to Stay

Noise pollution on Phi-Phi can be extreme. Expect serious room shortages and extortionate rates at peak holiday times.

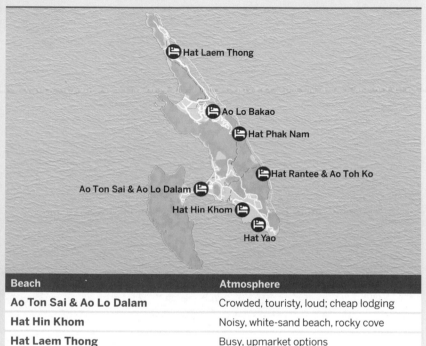

Beach	Atmosphere
Ao Ton Sai & Ao Lo Dalam	Crowded, touristy, loud; cheap lodging
Hat Hin Khom	Noisy, white-sand beach, rocky cove
Hat Laem Thong	Busy, upmarket options
Hat Phak Nam	Beautiful, low-key beach
Hat Rantee & Ao Toh Ko	Low-key, remote; family bungalows
Hat Yao	Great swimming; less busy than Ao Ton Sai
Ao Lo Bakao	Beautiful beach; upmarket lodging

Phraya Nakhon cave, Khao Sam Roi Yot National Park (p178)

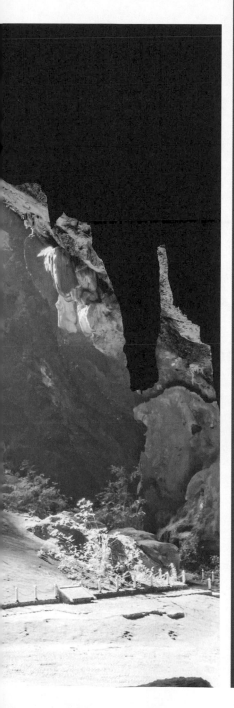

In Focus

Democracy Monument (p280), Bangkok

Thailand Today

After more than a decade, the country remains divided politically. The military has been in control of the country since May 2014 and the return of democratic elections is dependent on the passage of a constitution, fraught with political pressure.

Another Day, Another Coup

On 22 May 2014, the Thai military under General Prayuth Chan-o-cha overthrew the elected Puea Thai government led by Yingluck Shinawatra. It was the 13th coup in Thailand since 1932 and brought to an end months of anti-government protests. While the coup was hailed by the urban middle classes and elites, who accuse the Shinawatras of corruption, the rural poor and working classes regard Thaksin as a populist saviour.

Since taking power, the National Council for Peace and Order (NCPO) has muzzled the media, detained and imprisoned political opponents, and repealed the 2007 constitution and ordered a new one – Thailand's 20th since 1932 – to be drafted. An announcement was made in February 2016 that a general election would proceed the following year even if the constitution had not passed a referendum vote. Several draft constitutions

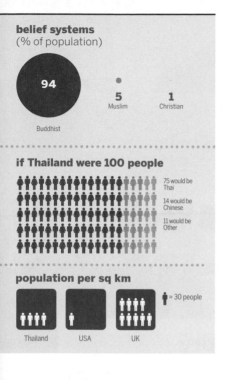

belief systems
(% of population)

94 Buddhist

5 Muslim

1 Christian

if Thailand were 100 people

75 would be Thai

14 would be Chinese

11 would be Other

population per sq km

♦ ≈ 30 people

Thailand   USA   UK

have been rejected because they severely limited the democratic process in selecting the legislature. With foreign investment down since the coup, the NCPO is also under increasing pressure for its failure to address Thailand's slumping economy and much-needed infrastructure upgrades.

Speak No Evil

With martial law in place, domestic newspapers and TV stations were told not to publish or broadcast any stories critical of the coup. Some 15 TV and radio stations were taken off the air altogether, 100 websites were blocked (including Facebook temporarily) and internet providers blocked any content that violated the junta's orders. In March 2015 Prayuth told journalists that he would 'execute' those who did not toe the official line. The domestic media now self-censors their stories to ensure they don't get into trouble. Accompanying the assault on press freedom has been a general crackdown on dissent. More than 1000 people – opposition politicians, academics, journalists, bloggers and students – have been detained, tried by military courts, or had their passports taken away.

There has also been a notable rise in the number of people being prosecuted under Thailand's lese-majesty laws. They are some of the strictest in the world and critics have accused the army of using them to silence political opponents. Recent cases have seen two university students imprisoned for appearing in a play said to have defamed the monarchy, while in August 2015 one man received a 30-year prison sentence for insulting the monarchy on his Facebook page.

The Next Chapter

After more than 70 years in power, the current king has spent close to a decade in the hospital with very few public appearances. In recent years the Crown Prince has performed most of the royal ceremonies: presiding over the Royal Ploughing Ceremony, changing the attire on the Emerald Buddha and handing out degrees at university commencements.

Concerns over succession have been a political undercurrent since the rise of former prime minister, self-exiled Thaksin Shinawatra. The anti-Thaksin, pro-royalist movement originally dressed in the royal colour of yellow and claimed to be protecting the king. Meanwhile the pro-Thaksin camp dressed in red and viewed themselves as the protectors of democracy. It is often theorised that the adoration that the average Thai once had for the king has been transferred to Thaksin. Exactly how the nation will react is unknown (and open discussion of the king's death is highly taboo), but the event will likely usher in a period of intense mourning.

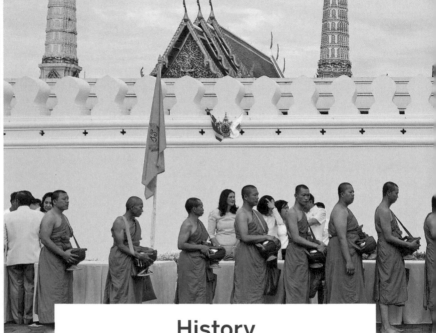

History

Thai history has all the dramatic elements to inspire the imagination: palace intrigue, wars waged with spears and elephants, popular protest movements and a penchant for 'smooth-as-silk' coups.

4000–2500 BC
Prehistoric inhabitants of northeastern Thailand develop agriculture and tool-making.

6th–11th centuries AD
The Mon Dvaravati thrive in central Thailand.

10th century
Tai peoples arrive in Thailand.

Monks walk towards the Grand Palace (p39)

From the Beginning

Though there is evidence of prehistoric peoples, most scholars start the story of Thai nationhood at the arrival of the 'Tai' people during the first millennium AD. The Tai people migrated from southern China and spoke Tai-Kadai, a family of tonal languages said to be the most significant ethno-linguistic group in Southeast Asia. The language group branched off into Laos (the Lao people) and Myanmar (the Shan).

Most of these new arrivals were farmers and hunters who lived in loosely organised villages, usually near a river source, with no central government or organised military. The indigenous Mon people are often recognised as assembling an early confederation (often referred to as Mon Dvaravati) in central and northeastern Thailand from the 6th to 9th centuries. Little is known about this period, but scholars believe that the Mon Dvaravati had a centre in Nakhon Pathom, outside of Bangkok, with outposts in parts of northern Thailand.

1351
The legendary kingdom of Ayuthaya is founded.

1511
Portuguese found foreign mission in Ayuthaya, followed by other European nations.

1767
Ayuthaya falls at the hands of the Burmese.

★ **Historical Sites & Museums**

Sukhothai Historical Park (p98)

Ayuthaya Historical Park (p84)

Chiang Mai City Arts & Cultural Centre (p118)

Wat Chai Wattanaram (p85), Ayuthaya

PRASIT PHOTO/GETTY IMAGES ©

The ancient superpower of the region was the Khmer empire, based in Angkor (in present-day Cambodia), which expanded across the western frontier into present-day northeastern and central Thailand starting in the 11th century. Sukhothai and Phimai were regional administrative centres connected by roads with way-station temples that made travel easier and were a visible symbol of imperial power. The Khmer monuments started out as Hindu but were later converted into Buddhist temples after the regime converted. Though their power would eventually decline, the Khmer imparted to the evolving Thai nation an artistic, bureaucratic and even monarchical legacy.

Thai history is usually told from the perspective of the central region, where the current capital is. But the southern region has a separate historical narrative that didn't merge with the centre until the modern era. Between the 8th and 13th centuries, southern Thailand was controlled by the maritime empire of Srivijaya, based in southern Sumatra (Indonesia), and controlled trade between the Straits of Malacca.

The Rise of the Thai Kingdoms

While the regional empires were declining in the 12th to 16th centuries, Tai peoples in the hinterlands established new states that would eventually unite the country.

Lanna

In the northern region, the Lanna kingdom, founded by King Mengrai, built Chiang Mai (meaning 'new city') in 1292 and proceeded to unify the northern communities into one cultural identity. For a time Chiang Mai was something of a religious centre for the region. However, Lanna was plagued by dynastic intrigues, fell to the Burmese in 1556 and was later eclipsed by Sukhothai and Ayuthaya as the progenitor of the modern Thai state.

Sukhothai

Then just a frontier town on the edge of the ailing Khmer empire, Sukhothai expelled the distant power in the mid-13th century and crowned the local chief as the first king. But

---

1768–82
King Taksin rules from the new capital of Thonburi.

1782
Chakri dynasty is founded, and the capital is moved to Bangkok.

1826
Thailand allies with Britain during the first Anglo-Burmese War.

it was his son Ramkhamhaeng who led the city-state to become a regional power with dependencies in modern-day Laos and southern Thailand. The city-state's local dialect (known as Siamese Tai) became the language of the ruling elite and the king is credited for inventing an early version of the script used today. Sukhothai replaced Chiang Mai as a centre of Theravada Buddhism on mainland Southeast Asia. The monuments built during this era helped define a distinctive architectural style. After his death, Ramkhamhaeng's empire disintegrated. In 1378 Sukhothai became a tributary of Ayuthaya.

Ayuthaya

Close to the Gulf of Thailand, the city-state of Ayuthaya grew rich and powerful from the international sea trade. The legendary founder was King U Thong, one of 36 kings and five dynasties that steered Ayuthaya through a 416-year lifespan. Ayuthaya presided over an age of commerce in Southeast Asia. Its main exports were rice and forest products, and many commercial and diplomatic foreign missions set up headquarters outside the royal city. Ayuthaya adopted Khmer court customs, honorific language and ideas of kingship. The monarch styled himself as a Khmer *devaraja* (divine king) instead of the Sukhothai ideal of *dhammaraja* (righteous king).

Ayuthaya paid tribute to the Chinese emperor, who rewarded this ritualistic submission with generous gifts and commercial privileges. Ayuthaya's reign was constantly under threat from expansionist Burma. The city was occupied in 1569 but later liberated by King Naresuan. In 1767 Burmese troops successfully sacked the capital and dispersed the Thai leadership into the hinterlands. The destruction of Ayuthaya remains a vivid historical event for the nation, and the tales of court life are as evocative as the stories of King Arthur.

The Bangkok Era

The Revival

With Ayuthaya in ruins and the dynasty destroyed, a general named Taksin filled the power vacuum and established a new capital in 1768 in Thonburi, across the river from modern-day Bangkok. King Taksin was deposed and executed in 1782 by subordinate generals. One of the leaders of the coup, Chao Phraya Chakri, was crowned King Buddha Yot Fa (Rama I), the founder of the current Chakri dynasty. He moved the capital across the river to the Ko Ratanakosin district of present-day Bangkok. The new kingdom was viewed as a revival of Ayuthaya and its leaders attempted to replicate the former kingdom's laws, government practices and cultural achievements. They also built a powerful military that avenged Burmese aggression, kicking them out of Chiang Mai. The Bangkok rulers continued courting Chinese commercial trade.

1868–1910	1932	1939
King Chulalongkorn (Rama V) reigns; it's a time of modernisation and European imperialism.	A bloodless revolution ends absolute monarchy.	The country's English name is officially changed from Siam to Thailand.

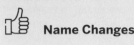

Name Changes

The country known today as Thailand has had several monikers. The Khmers are credited for naming this area 'Siam.' In 1939 the name of the country was changed from Siam (Prathet Syam) to Thailand (Prathet Thai).

The Reform

The Siamese elite had long admired China, but by the 1800s the West dominated international trade and geopolitics.

King Mongkut (Rama IV; r 1851–68), often credited with modernising the kingdom, spent 27 years prior to assuming the crown as a monk in the Thammayut sect, a reform movement he founded to restore scholarship to the faith. During his reign the country was integrated into the prevailing market system that broke up royal monopolies and granted more rights to foreign powers.

Mongkut's son, King Chulalongkorn (Rama V; r 1873–1910) took greater steps in replacing the old political order. He abolished slavery and introduced the creation of a salaried bureaucracy, a police force and a standing army. His reforms brought uniformity to the legal code, law courts and revenue offices. Schools were established along European models. Universal conscription and poll taxes made all men the king's men. Many of the king's advisors were British, and they ushered in a remodelling of the old Ayuthaya-based system. Distant sub-regions were brought under central command and railways were built to link them to population centres. Pressured by French and British colonies on all sides, the modern boundaries of Siam came into shape by ceding territory.

Democracy vs Dictator

The 1932 Revolution

During a period of growing independence movements in the region, a group of foreign-educated military officers and bureaucrats led a successful (and bloodless) coup against absolute monarchy in 1932. The pro-democracy party soon splintered and, by 1938, General Phibul Songkhram, one of the original democracy supporters, had seized control of the country. During WWII, Phibul, who was staunchly anti-royalist, strongly nationalistic and pro-Japanese, allowed that country to occupy Thailand as a base for assaults on British colonies in Southeast Asia. In the post-WWII era, Phibul positioned Thailand as an ally of the US in its war on communism.

The Cold War

During the Cold War and the US conflict in Vietnam, the military leaders of Thailand gained legitimacy and economic support from the US in exchange for the use of military installations in Thailand. By the 1970s a new political consciousness bubbled up from the

1941
Japanese forces enter Thailand during WWII.

1945
WWII ends; Thailand cedes territory seized from Laos, Cambodia and Malaysia.

1946
King Bhumibol Adulyadej (Rama IX) ascends the throne; Thailand joins the UN.

universities. In 1973 more than half a million people – intellectuals, students, peasants and workers – demonstrated in Bangkok and major provincial towns, demanding a constitution from the military government. The bloody dispersal of the Bangkok demonstration on 14 October led to the collapse of the regime and the creation of an elected constitutional government. This lasted only three years until another protest movement was brutally squashed and the military returned to restore civil order.

By the 1980s the so-called political soldier General Prem Tinsulanonda forged a period of political and economic stability that led to the 1988 election of a civilian government. Prem is still involved in politics today as the president of the palace's privy council, a powerful position that joins the interests of the monarchy with the military.

The Business Era

The new civilian government was composed of former business executives, many of whom represented provincial commercial interests, instead of Bangkok-based military officials, signalling a shift in the country's political dynamics. Though the country was doing well economically, the government was accused of corruption and vote-buying and the military moved to protect its privileged position with a 1991 coup. Elected leadership was restored shortly after the coup, and the Democrat Party, with the support of business and the urban middle class, dominated the parliament.

The 1997 Asian currency crisis derailed the surging economy and the government was criticised for its ineffective response. That same year, the parliament passed the watershed 'people's constitution,' which enshrined human rights and freedom of expression and granted more power to a civil society to counter corruption. (The 1997 constitution was thrown out during the 2006 coup.)

By the turn of the millennium, the economy had recovered and business interests had succeeded the military as the dominant force in politics. The telecommunications billionaire and former police officer Thaksin Shinawatra ushered in the era of the elected CEO. He was a capitalist with a populist message and garnered support from the rural and urban poor and the working class. From 2001 to 2005 Thaksin and his Thai Rak Thai party transformed national politics into one-party rule.

The Thaksin Era

Though Thaksin enjoyed massive popular support, his regime was viewed by urban intellectuals as a kleptocracy, with the most egregious example of corruption being the tax-free sale of his family's Shin Corporation stock to the Singaporean government in 2006, a windfall of 73 billion baht (US$1.88 billion) that was engineered by special legislation. This enraged the upper and middle classes and led to street protests in Bangkok. On 19 September 2006 the military staged a bloodless coup, the first in 15 years, which brought an end to the country's longest stretch of democratic rule. The military dissolved the constitution that had sought to ensure a civilian government and introduced a new

1957	**1968**	**1973**
A successful coup by Sarit Thanarat starts a period of military rule that lasts until 1973.	Thailand is a founding member state of the Association of Southeast Asian Nations.	Civilian demonstrators overthrow the military dictatorship; a democratic government is installed.

Yingluck Shinawatra during a press conference in July 2011

constitution that limited the resurgence of one-party rule by interests unsympathetic to the military and the aristocrats.

The Coup Decade

Following Thaksin's ouster a cycle of elections-protests-coups followed. Thaksin's allies would win an election, followed by massive protests by anti-Thaksin factions, then a military coup backed by the Constitutional Court and the palace. The final scene in the political ping-pong game came in 2011 when Thaksin's politically allied Puea Thai party won a parliamentary majority and Thaksin's sister Yingluck Shinawatra was elected as prime minister. Yingluck Shinawatra became both the first female prime minister of Thailand and the country's youngest-ever premier. The belief that the Yingluck government was a Thaksin administration in all but name ensured she faced bitter opposition.

The most disastrous misstep was a proposed bill granting amnesty for Thaksin, which would have allowed him to return to the country. Street demonstrations began in October 2013 with sporadic violence between Yingluck's supporters and opponents. Yingluck and nine of her ministers stepped down on 7 May. The military seized control 15 days later.

1997
The Asian economic crisis hits; 'people's constitution' is passed in parliament.

2004
A tsunami kills 5000 people and damages tourism and fishing on the Andaman Coast.

2006
Prime Minister Thaksin Shinawatra is ousted by a military coup.

The Modern Monarchy

The country's last absolute monarch was King Prajadhipok (Rama VII), who accepted the 1932 constitution, abdicated the throne and went into exile. By 1935 the new democratic government reinstated the monarchy, appointing the abdicated king's 10-year-old nephew, Ananda Mahidol (Rama VIII), who was living in Europe at the time. In 1946, after the king came of age, he was shot dead under mysterious circumstances. His younger brother was crowned King Bhumibol (Rama IX) and remains monarch today.

At the beginning of his reign King Bhumibol was primarily a figurehead of national unity. The military dictator General Sarit (1958–63) supported the expansion of the king's role as a symbol of modern Thailand. The attractive royal couple, King Bhumibol and Queen Sirikit, met Elvis and were portrayed in photographs in the same way as the US president John F Kennedy and his wife: fashionable models of the postwar generation.

Through rural development projects the king became regarded as the champion of the poor. The Royal Project Foundation was created in 1969 and is credited with helping to eradicate opium cultivation among the northern hill tribes. During the 1970s protest movements, the king came to be a mediating voice, calling for peace between the military and the pro-democracy factions. During another political crisis in 1992, the king summoned the leaders of the political factions to the palace in an effort to quell street protests.

2011

Yingluck Shinawatra becomes the first female prime minister; destructive floods hit the country.

2014

Yingluck Shinawatra and nine members of her cabinet guilty of abuse of power. The Thai military assumes control of the country.

2015

Terrorist bomb explosion in popular Bangkok Erawan shrine kills 20 people.

Traditional gong

MEDIAVN/GETTY IMAGES ©

Culture & Customs

It is easy to love Thailand: the pace of life is unhurried and the people are friendly and kind-hearted. A smile is a universal key in most social situations, a cheerful disposition will be met in kind, and friendships are spontaneous, requiring little more than curiosity and humour. Though Thais don't expect foreigners to know much about their country, they are delighted and grateful if they do.

The Monarchy

Thailand expresses deep reverence for the reigning monarch, King Bhumibol Adulyadej (phoo-mi-pone a-dun-ya-det). Pictures of the king are enshrined in nearly every household and business, and life-size billboards of the monarchs line Th Ratchadamnoen Klang, Bangkok's royal avenue. The king's image, which is printed on money, is regarded as sacred, and criticising the king or the monarchy is a criminal offence. The monarch's relationship to the people is intertwined with religion; it is deeply spiritual and personal. Most Thais view the king with great reverence, as an exalted father figure (his birthday is recognised as national Father's Day) and as a protector of the good of the country.

The National Psyche

In most social situations, establishing harmony is often a priority and Thais take personal pride in making others feel at ease.

Sà·nùk

Thais place a high value on having *sà·nùk* (fun). It is the underlying measure of a worthwhile activity and the reason why the country ranks so highly as a tourist destination. Thais are always up for a party, be it of their own invention or an import. Case in point: Thais celebrate three new years – the eve of the resetting of the international calendar, the Chinese lunar New Year and Songkran (the Southeast Asian Buddhist new year).

This doesn't mean that Thais are averse to work. Most offices are typically open six, and sometimes seven, days a week, and most Thais have side jobs to provide extra income. But every chore has a social aspect that lightens the mood and keeps it from being too 'serious' (a grave insult). Whether it's the backbreaking work of rice farming, the tedium of long-distance bus driving or the dangers of a construction site, Thais often mix their work tasks with socialising.

Thais in the tourism industry extend this attitude towards their guests and will often describe foreign visitors as needing a rest after a year of hard work. This cultural mindset reflects the agricultural calendar in which a farmer works from dawn to dusk during the rice-planting and harvesting season then rests until the next year's rains. That rest period involves a lot of hanging out, going to festivals and funerals (which are more party than pity) and loading up family and friends into the back of a pick-up truck for a *têe·o* (trip).

👍 **Dos & Don'ts**

- Always stand for the royal and national anthems.
- Don't show anger or frustration in public.
- Remove shoes before entering homes or temples; step over the threshold.
- Keep your feet off furniture.
- In temples, sit in the 'mermaid' position (with your feet tucked behind you).
- Pass and receive things with your right hand.
- Use your spoon like a fork, held with the right hand, and hold the fork in the left hand.

Status

Though Thai culture is famously non-confrontational and fun-loving, it isn't a social free-for-all. Thais are very conscious of status and the implicit rights and responsibilities. Buddhism defines the social strata, with the heads of the family, religion and monarchy sitting at the top of various tiers. Gauging where you fit into this system is a convenient ice-breaker. Thais will often ask a laundry list of questions: where are you from, how old are you, are you married, do you have children? They are sizing you up in the social strata.

In most cases, you'll get the best of both worlds: Thais will care for you as if you are a child and honour you as if you are a *pôo yài* (literally 'big person', or elder). When sharing a meal, don't be surprised if a Thai host puts the tastiest piece of fish on your plate.

Thais regard each other as part of an extended family and will use familial prefixes such as *pêe* (elder sibling) and *nórng* (younger sibling) when addressing friends as well as blood relations. When translated into English, this often leads foreigners to think that their Thai friends have large immediate families. Thais might also use *bâh* (aunt) or *lung* (uncle) to refer to an older person. Rarely do foreigners get embraced in this grand family reunion; *fa·ràng* is the catch-all term for foreigner. It is mostly descriptive but can sometimes express cultural frustrations.

Saving Face

Interconnected with status is the concept of 'saving face,' a common consideration in Asian cultures. In a nutshell, 'face' means you strive for social harmony by avoiding firm or confrontational opinions and displays of anger. Thais regard outbursts of emotion and discourteous social interactions as shameful, whereas Westerners might shrug them off.

Social Conventions & Etiquette

Thais are generally tolerant of most social faux pas as they assume that foreign visitors know very little about their culture. Their graciousness should be returned with a concerted effort of respect.

Greetings

The traditional Thai greeting is with a prayer-like palms-together gesture known as a *wâi*. If someone shows you a *wâi,* you should return the gesture, unless the greeting comes from a child or a service person. A *wâi* can also express gratitude or an apology. Foreigners are continually baffled by when and how to use the *wâi* and such cultural confusion makes great conversation fodder. The all-purpose greeting is a cheery '*sà·wàt·dee kráp*' if you're male or '*sà·wàt·dee kâ*' if you're female. A smile usually accompanies this and goes a long way to diffuse a tense social situation. Also, Thais are great connoisseurs of beauty and a smile improves one's countenance.

Visiting Temples

When visiting a temple, it is important to dress modestly (cover yourself to the elbows and the ankles) and to take your shoes off when you enter any building that contains a Buddha image. Buddha images are sacred objects, so don't pose in front of them for pictures and definitely do not clamber on them. When visiting a religious building, act like a worshipper by finding a discreet place to sit in the 'mermaid' position (with your feet tucked behind you so that they point away from the Buddha images). Temples are maintained from the donations received and contributions from visitors are appreciated.

Touching

In the traditional parts of the country, it is not proper for members of the opposite sex to touch one another. Same-sex touching is quite common and is typically a sign of friendship, not sexual attraction. Older Thai men might grab a younger man's thigh in the same way that buddies slap each other on the back. Thai women are especially affectionate, often sitting close to female friends or linking arms. Women should not touch monks or their belongings; they should not sit next to them on public transport or accidentally brush against them on the street.

Novice Buddhist monks celebrate Songkran (p23)

JAKKREE THAMPITAKKULL/GETTY IMAGES ©

Religion

Religion is a fundamental component of Thai society, and colourful examples of worship can be found on every corner. Walk the streets early in the morning and you'll see the solemn progression of Buddhist monks engaged in bin·da·bàht, the daily house-to-house alms-food gathering. Household shrines decorate the humblest abodes, and protective amulets are common pieces of jewellery.

Buddhism

Approximately 95% of Thai people are Theravada Buddhists. This form of Buddhism is often called the Southern School because it travelled from the Indian subcontinent to Southeast Asia.

Religious Principles

Buddhism was born in India in the 6th century. A prince named Siddhartha Gautama left his life of privilege, seeking religious fulfillment. According to the practices of the time, he became an ascetic before he realised that this was not the way to reach the end of suffering.

Adopting a more measured Middle Way, his practice became more balanced until, on the night of the full moon of the fifth month (celebrated as Visakha Bucha), he became enlightened under the Bodhi tree. He became known as Buddha, 'the enlightened' or 'the awakened,' and spoke of four noble truths that had the power to liberate any human being who could realise them.

The four noble truths deal with the nature and origin of suffering and the path to the cessation of suffering. Loosely explained, this includes *dukkha* (all forms of existence are subject to suffering, disease, imperfection), *samudaya* (the origin of suffering is desire), *nirodha* (cessation of suffering is the giving up desire) and *magga* (the path to cessation of suffering is the eightfold path). The eightfold path is often described as the middle path: a route between extreme asceticism and indulgence. Following the path will lead to *nibbana* ('nirvana' in Sanskrit), which literally means the 'blowing out' or extinction of all grasping and thus of all suffering. Effectively, *nibbana* is also an end to the cycle of rebirths (both moment-to-moment and life-to-life) that is existence.

Religious Practice

In reality, most Thai Buddhists aim for rebirth in a 'better' existence rather than the supra-mundane goal of *nibbana*. By feeding monks, giving donations to temples and worshipping regularly at their local temple, they hope to improve their lot, acquiring enough merit (*bun* in Thai) to prevent rebirths (or at least reduce their number). The concept of rebirth is almost universally accepted in Thailand, even by non-Buddhists.

Thai Buddhists look to the Triple Gems for guidance in their faith: the Buddha, the dhamma and the sangha. The Buddha is usually the centrepiece of devotional activity inside a temple and many of the most famous Thai Buddha images have supernatural tales associated with them. The dhamma is chanted morning and evening in every temple and taught to every Thai citizen in primary school. There are two sangha (monastic) sects in Thailand: the Mahanikai and Thammayut. The former is more mainstream, while the latter is aligned with the monarchy and usually stricter in its practices.

Hinduism & Animism

There are many enduring legacies of Hinduism and animism in Thai culture and in the practice of Thai Buddhism today. Hinduism was the religious parent of Buddhism, imparting lasting components of mythology, cosmology and symbolism.

Thais recognise the contributions of Hinduism and treat its deities with reverence. Bangkok is especially rich in Hindu shrines. Many of the royally associated ceremonies stem from Brahmanism. Spirit worship and Buddhism have commingled to the point that it is difficult to filter the two. Monks often perform obviously animistic rituals, and Thais believe that merit-making (Buddhist religious rituals) benefits deceased relatives. Trees are wrapped in sacred cloth to honour the spirits of the natural world. Altars are erected on the dashboards of taxis to ensure immunity from traffic laws and accidents. Thais often wear amulets embossed with a Buddha figure or containing sacred soil from a revered temple to protect the wearer from misfortune. In fact, many of the religious rituals of Thai Buddhists, apart from meditation, appear to be deeply rooted in the spirit world.

Monks & Monasteries

Every Thai male is expected to become a monk (*prá* or *prá pík·sù* in Thai) for a short period, optimally between the time he finishes school and the time he starts a career or marries. A family earns great merit when one of its sons 'takes robe and bowl' and many young men enter the monastery to make merit for a deceased patriarch or matriarch.

Traditionally, Buddhist Lent (*pan·săh*), which begins in July and coincides with the three-month period of the rainy season, is when most temporary monks enter the monastery. Nowadays, though, men may spend as little as a week there. Historically the temple provided a necessary social safety net for families. The monastery was a de facto orphanage and also acted as a retirement home for older rural men. Though these charitable roles are not as sought after today, the temples still give refuge and sanctuary to all living creatures. This might mean that they help feed families in need, adopt orphaned or injured animals, and give shelter to overnight travellers (usually impoverished Thai university students).

In Thai Buddhism, women who seek a monastic life are given a minor role in the temple that is not equal to full monkhood.

🗨 Houses of the Holy

Many dwellings in Thailand have a 'spirit house' for the property's *prá poom* (guardian spirits). Based on pre-Buddhist animistic beliefs, guardian spirits live in rivers, trees and other natural features and need to be honoured (and placated) like a respected but sometimes troublesome family member. Elaborate doll-house-like structures, where the spirits can 'live' comfortably separated from human affairs, are consecrated by a Brahman priest and receive daily offerings of rice, fruit, flowers and water.

A Buddhist nun is known as *mâa chee* (mother priest) and lives as an *atthasila* nun (following eight precepts of Buddhism's code of ethics as opposed to the five for lay people and 227 for ordained monks), a position traditionally occupied by women who had no other place in society. Thai nuns shave their heads, wear white robes and take care of temple chores. Generally speaking, *mâa chee* aren't considered as prestigious as monks and don't have a function in the lay people's merit-making rituals, although there are *mâa chee* who have become revered teachers in their own right, with large followings.

Temple Visits

Thai Buddhism has no particular sabbath day when the faithful are supposed to congregate weekly. Instead, Thai Buddhists visit most often on *wan prá* (holy days), which occur every seventh or eighth day, depending on phases of the moon. A temple visit is usually a social affair involving groups of friends, families or office workers. Thais will also make special pilgrimages to famous temples in other regions as sightseeing and merit-making outings. Most merit-makers visit the *wí·hăhn* (the central sanctuary), which houses the primary Buddha figure. Worshippers will offer lotus buds (a symbol of enlightenment) or flower garlands, light three joss sticks and raise their hands to their forehead in a prayerlike gesture.

Other merit-making activities include offering food to the temple sangha (community), meditating (individually or in groups), listening to monks chanting *suttas* (Buddhist discourse) and attending a *têht* or dhamma (teachings) talk by the abbot or some other respected teacher.

Islam & Other Religions

Although Thailand is predominantly Buddhist, its minority religions often practise alongside one another. About 4.6% of the population are followers of Islam. The remainder are Christian, including missionary-converted hill tribes and Vietnamese immigrants, as well as Confucians, Taoists, Mahayana Buddhists and Hindus.

★ Buddhist Festivals

Monk carrying alms bowl

The majority of Muslims in Thailand live in the southern provinces, though there are pockets in Bangkok and central and northern Thailand. In the southernmost provinces the Muslims are ethnic Malays, while northern Thailand's Muslims are Yunnanese descendants. The form of Islam found in southern Thailand is mixed with elements of Malay culture and animism.

The southernmost provinces of Yala, Pattani and Narathiwat contain the country's largest Muslim majority and have long been geographically and culturally isolated to the mainstream society. These provinces were independent sultanates that were conquered by the Bangkok-based kings. During the ultra-nationalist era in the 1940s, this region responded with separatist resistance, later becoming a sanctuary for communist and insurgent activities in the 1980s. Violence flared again in the early 2000s and has persisted. Most observers classify the conflict as an ethno-nationalist struggle.

Thai Muslim women function in the society as actively as their Buddhist counterparts. Headscarves are prevalent but not mandatory: sometimes a visitor only realises that someone is a Muslim when they decline an offering of pork at the dinner table. Devout Thai Muslims often encounter spiritual incompatibilities with their Buddhist neighbours. The popular view of the Thai monarch as godlike is heresy for a monotheistic religion like Islam, though many Thai Muslims respect and even love the king and do not voice open criticism. Muslims also avoid alcohol and gambling (in varying degrees) – two pursuits that define much of rural life for Buddhist Thais. In this way, religion keeps the two cultures distinct.

Thai red chicken curry

ALEXPRO9500/GETTY IMAGES ©

Thai Cuisine

Thai food – one of the country's most famous exports – balances spicy, sweet, sour and salty flavours in complex combinations. Ingredients are fresh, flavours are assertive and the sting of the beloved chilli triggers an adrenalin rush.

Rice

In the morning Thais rise with two fundamental smells: rice being cooked and the burning joss sticks that are offered in household shrines. The start of the new day means another opportunity to eat, and eating in Thailand means eating rice (the Thai word 'to eat' is *gin kôw,* literally 'to eat rice').

Rice can be steamed, fried, boiled in a soup, formed into noodles or made into a dessert. In its steamed form it is eaten with a spoon or, in the case of *kôw nĕe·o* (sticky rice), eaten with the hands. The classic morning meal is a watery rice soup (either *jóhk* or *kôw dôm*) that is the ultimate comfort food, the equivalent of oatmeal on a cold day. The next meal of the day will probably be a stir-fry or curry, typically served over rice. In the evening in provincial towns, everyone heads to the night market to see and be seen and to eat more rice.

Street vendor, Bangkok

★ Street Stall Meals

○ *Kôw pàt* – fried rice

○ *Pàt gá·prow* – stir-fried chillies, holy basil and a choice of chicken or pork

○ *Pàt pàk ká·náh* –stir-fried Chinese kale and *mŏo gròrp* (fried pork belly)

Noodles

When rice just won't do there is another, albeit rice-derived, alternative: *gŏo·ay đĕe·o* (rice noodles). Day or night, city or village, *gŏo·ay đĕe·o* is the original Thai fast food, served by itinerant vendors or from humble shopfronts. It demonstrates Thais' penchant for micro-managing flavours. You choose the kind of noodle and the kind of meat and you flavour it yourself with a little fish sauce, sugar, vinegar and chillies; don't shy away from the sugar.

There are three basic kinds of rice noodles – *sên yài* (wide), *sên lék* (thin) and *sên mèe* (thinner than thin) – as well as *bà·mèe,* which is a curly noodle made from wheat flour and egg. Most of these only appear in noodle soups but a few are used in various stir-fries, such as *pàt tai* (thin rice noodles stir-fried with dried or fresh shrimp, tofu and egg).

Head to the morning market for a bowl of *kà·nŏm jeen* (rice noodles doused in a thin curry). This dish is piled high with strange pickled and fresh vegetables that will make you feel as if you've grazed on the savannah and swum through the swamp. *Kà·nŏm jeen* is usually served at rickety wooden tables shared with working-class women dressed in market clothes.

Curry

The overseas celebrity of Thai cuisine, *gaang* (curry) is a humble dish on home turf. At roadside stands, especially in southern Thailand, big metal pots contain various curry con-coctions of radioactive colours. When you ask vendors what they have, they'll lift the lids and name the type of meat in each: for example *gaang gài* (curry with chicken) or *gaang plah* (shorthand for sour fish curry). In Bangkok, street-side vendors and small shops will display their curry-in-a-hurry in buffet-style trays. In either case, you point to one and it will be ladled over rice. Use a spoon to scoop it up and push the lime leaves to the side – they aren't edible.

All curries start with a basic paste that includes ground coriander seed, cumin seed, garlic, lemongrass, kaffir lime, galangal, shrimp paste and chillies (either dried or fresh). Most visitors know their curries by their colour, mainly red (from dried red chillies) and green (from fresh green chillies). Green curry is a classic central Thailand dish.

Regional Cuisines

Over the past 20 years there has been so much migration within Thailand that many of the once region-specific dishes have been incorporated into the national cuisine.

Northern Thai

True to its Lanna character, northern Thai cuisine is more laid-back – the flavours are mellow and the influences have migrated over the mountains from Myanmar (Burma) and China. Thanks to the travelling Chinese caravans and settlers, northern cuisine is enamoured with pork, from *sâi òo·a* (local-style sausages) and *kâap mŏo* (crackling) to the popular street food *mŏo bîng* (grilled pork skewers). The Burmese influence has imparted the use of turmeric and ginger (though some could argue that northern Burmese food was influenced by Chinese) into the curry pastes used in *gaang hang·lair* (rich pork stew).

Northern flavours favour sour notes. Pickled vegetables are loaded on top of the signature noodle dishes of *kôw soy* (wheat-and-egg noodles with a thick coconut red curry) and *kà·nŏm jeen nám ngée·o* (rice noodles served with a curry broth made with pork and tomatoes); shallots and lime wedges are common seasoning garnishes. Northern Thailand shares Isan's love of *kôw nĕe·o*, which is often served in rounded wicker baskets and accompanies such dishes as *nám prík òrng* (a chilli paste made with ground pork and tomato).

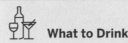

What to Drink

Thai beers, such as Singha (pronounced 'sing'), are hoppy lagers which are often mixed with ice to keep them cool and palatable. Fruit shakes are refreshing on a hot day and are served with a pinch of salt to help regulate body temperature. Sweet iced coffee and tea are popular street stall drinks. Thais get their drink on with rice whisky mixed with ice, soda water and a splash of Coke.

Southern Thai

Southern Thai food draws from the traditions of seafaring traders, many of whom were Muslims from India or ethnic Malays. Indian-style flat bread (known as roti) often competes with rice as a curry companion or is drizzled with sugar and sweetened condensed milk as a market dessert. Turmeric imparts its telltale yellow hue to *kôw mòk gài* (chicken biryani) and southern-style fried chicken.

The curries here are flamboyant, with dry-roasted spice bases prepared in the Indian fashion and featuring lots of locally produced coconut milk. Shaved, milked, strained and fresh, the coconut is a kitchen mainstay. Fresh seafood is plentiful. Plump squid is grilled and served on a stick with an accompanying sweet-and-spicy sauce. Whole fish are often stuffed with lemongrass and limes and barbecued over a coconut-husk fire.

Northeastern Thai

Northeasterners are known for their triumvirate dishes: *sôm·đam* (green papaya salad), *kôw nĕe·o* and *gài yâhng* (grilled chicken). In the morning, open-coal grills are loaded up with marinated chicken. Alongside the grill is a large mortar and pestle in which *sôm·đam* is prepared. In go strips of green papaya, sugar, chillies, fish sauce, green beans, tomatoes, dried shrimps and a few special requests: peanuts to make it *sôm·đam* Thai, or field crabs and *plah ráh* (fermented fish sauce) to make it *sôm·đam* Lao (referring to the ethnic Lao who live in northeastern Thailand). The vendor pounds the ingredients together with the pestle to make a musical 'pow-pow-pow' sound that is sometimes used as an onomato-poetic nickname. Isan girls are often told that they'll make good wives if they are adept at handling the pestle when making *sôm·đam* – the obvious sexual connotations are intended.

Grand Palace (p39), Bangkok

NECIP YANMAZ/GETTY IMAGES ©

Arts & Architecture

Thais' refined sense of beauty is reflected in their artistic traditions, from Buddhist sculpture to temple architecture. Monarchs were the country's great artistic patrons; their funeral monuments were ornate stupas, and handicrafts were developed specifically for royal use. Today religious artwork continues to dominate the artistic imagination but has been adapted to the modern context.

Religious Art

Temples are the country's artistic repositories, where you'll find ornate murals depicting Hindu-Buddhist mythology and Buddha sculptures. The country is most famous for its graceful and serene Buddhas that emerged during the Sukhothai era. Always instructional in intent, temple murals often depict the *jataka* (stories of the Buddha's past lives) and the Thai version of the Hindu epic *Ramayana*. Reading the murals requires both knowledge of these religious tales and an understanding of the murals' spatial relationship. Most murals are divided into scenes, in which the main theme is depicted in the centre with resulting events taking place above and below the central action. Usually in the corner of a dramatic tableau are independent scenes of Thai village life: women carrying bamboo baskets, men fishing or a festive get-together.

Thailand's Artistic Periods

The development of Thai religious art and architecture is broken into different periods defined by the patronage of the ruling capital. A period's characteristics are seen in the depiction of the Buddha's facial features, the top flourish on the head, the dress, and the position of the feet in meditation. Another signature is the size and shape of the temples' *chedi* (stupas) – telltale characteristics are shown in the pedestal and the central bell before it begins to taper into the uppermost tower.

Period	Temple & Chedi Styles	Buddha Styles	Examples
Dvaravati period (7th-11th centuries)	Rectangular-based *chedi* with stepped tiers	Indian-influenced with a thick torso, large hair curls, arched eyebrows to represent a flying bird, protruding eyes, thick lips and a flat nose	Phra Pathom Chedi, Nakhon Pathom; Lopburi Museum, Lopburi; Wat Chama Thawi, Lamphun
Srivijaya Period (7th-13th centuries)	Mahayana Buddhist-style temples; Javanese-style *chedi* with elaborate arches	Indian influenced: heavily ornamented, humanlike features and slightly twisted at the waist	Wat Phra Boromathat, Chaiya; Wat Phra Mahathat Woramahawihaan and National Museum, Nakhon Si Thammarat
Khmer period (9th-11th centuries)	Hindu-Buddhist temples; corn-cob-shaped *prang*	Buddha meditating under a canopy of the seven-headed *naga* and atop a lotus pedestal	Phimai, Nakhon Ratchasima; Phanom Rung, Surin
Chiang Saen-Lanna period (11th-13th centuries)	Teak temples; square-based *chedi* topped by gilded umbrella; also octagonal-base *chedi*	Burmese influences with plump figure, round, smiling face and footpads facing upwards in meditation pose	Wat Phra Singh, Chiang Mai; Chiang Saen National Museum
Sukhothai period (13th-15th centuries)	Khmer-inspired temples; slim-spired *chedi* topped by a lotus bud	Graceful poses, often depicted 'walking'; no anatomical human detail	Sukhothai Historical Park
Ayuthaya period (14th-18th centuries)	Classical Thai temple with three-tiered roof and gable flourishes; bell-shaped *chedi* with tapering spire	Ayuthaya-era king, wearing a gem-studded crown and royal regalia	Ayuthaya Historical Park
Bangkok-Ratanakosin period (19th century)	Colourful and gilded temple with Western-Thai styles; mosaic-covered *chedi*	Reviving Ayuthaya style	Wat Phra Kaew, Wat Pho and Wat Arun, Bangkok

Jim Thompson House (p48), Bangkok

COWARDLION/SHUTTERSTOCK ©

Contemporary Art

Adapting traditional themes and aesthetics to the secular canvas began around the turn of the 20th century, as Western influence surged in the region. In general, Thai painting favours abstraction over realism and continues to preserve the one-dimensional perspective of traditional mural paintings. Italian artist Corrado Feroci is often credited with being the father of modern Thai art. He was first invited to Thailand by Rama VI in 1924 and built Bangkok's Democracy Monument, among other European-style statues. Feroci founded the country's first fine arts institute in 1933, a school that eventually developed into Silpakorn University, Thailand's premier training ground for artists. In gratitude, the Thai government made Feroci a Thai citizen, with the Thai name Silpa Bhirasri.

The Modern Buddha

In the 1970s Thai artists began to tackle the modernisation of Buddhist themes through abstract expressionism. Leading works in this genre include the mystical pen-and-ink drawings of Thawan Duchanee. Montien Boonma used the ingredients of Buddhist merit-making, such as gold leaf, bells and candle wax, to create abstract temple spaces within museum galleries.

Protest & Satire

In Thailand's quickly industrialising society, many artists watched as rice fields became factories, forests became asphalt and the spoils went to the politically connected. During the student activist days of the 1970s, the Art for Life Movement was the banner under which creative discontents rallied against the military dictatorship and embraced certain aspects of communism and workers' rights. Sompote Upa-In and Chang Saetang are two important artists from that period. An anti-authority attitude continues today. Photographer Manit Sriwanichpoom is best known for his 'Pink Man on Tour' series, in which he depicted artist Sompong Thawee in a pink suit and with a pink shopping cart amid Thailand's most iconic attractions, suggesting that Thailand's cultural and natural spaces were for sale. He has since followed up this series with other socially evocative photographs poking fun at ideas of patriotism and nationalism.

During the political turmoil of the past decade, artists channelled first-person experiences into multimedia installations. Tanks, guns, violence, and protest imagery are woven together to express outrage, grief, anxiety and even apathy in the collective memory during the protest-coup-election era. Vasan Sitthiket created a collection of colourful but chaotic collages in the series descriptively called 'Hypocrisy'. Chulayarnnon Siriphol's short film *A Brief History of Memory* recounts one woman's experience of violent street protests.

Public Art

In this hierarchical society, artistic innovation is often stifled by the older generation who holds prestige and power. In the 1990s there was a push to move art out of the dead zones of the museums and into the public spaces, beyond the reach of the cultural authoritarians. An artist and art organiser, Navin Rawanchaikul, started his 'in-the-streets' collaborations in his home town of Chiang Mai and then moved his big ideas to Bangkok, where he filled the city's taxi cabs with art installations, a show that literally went on the road.

His other works have had a way with words, such as the mixed-media piece *We Are the Children of Rice (Wine)* in 2002 and his rage against the commercialisation of museums in his epic painting entitled *Super (M)art Bangkok Survivors* (2004), which depicts famous artists, curators and decision-makers in a crowded Paolo Veronese setting. The piece was inspired by the struggles the Thai art community had in getting the new contemporary Bangkok art museum to open without it becoming a shopping mall in disguise.

🛍 Handicrafts

Thailand's handicrafts live on for the tourist markets, and some have been updated by chic Bangkok designers.

o **Ceramics** The best-known ceramics are the greenish Thai-style celadon, and central Thailand's *ben·jà·rong* (five colour).

o **Lacquerware** Northern Thailand is known for this handicraft inherited from Burma.

o **Textiles** The northeast is famous for *mát·mèe* cloth – a thick cotton or silk fabric woven from tie-dyed threads. Each hill tribe has a tradition of embroidery; Chiang Mai and Chiang Rai are popular handicraft centres.

Pop Fun

True to the Thai nature, some art is just fun. The works of Thaweesak Srithongdee are pure pop. He paints flamboyantly cartoonish human figures woven with elements of traditional Thai handicrafts or imagery. In a similar vein, Jirapat Tasanasomboon depicts traditional Thai figures in comic-book-style fights or in sensual embraces with Western icons. In *Hanuman Is Upset!* the monkey king chews up the geometric lines of Mondrian's famous gridlike painting. Thai-Japanese artist Yuree Kensaku creates cartoon-like paintings with pop-culture references.

Sculpture

Although lacking in commercial attention, Thai sculpture is often considered to be the strongest of the contemporary arts: not surprising considering the country's relationship with Buddha figures. Moving into nonreligious arenas, Khien Yimsiri is the modern master creating elegant human and mythical forms out of bronze. Kamin Lertchaiprasert explores the subject of spirituality and daily life in his sculptural installations, which often include a small army of papier-mâché figures. His exhibit 'Ngern Nang' (Sitting Money) included a series of figures made of discarded paper bills from the national bank and embellished with poetic instructions on life and love.

ANDREW WATSON/GETTY IMAGES ©

Traditional Thai dancers

Theatre & Dance

Traditional Thai theatre consists of dance-dramas, in which stories are acted out by masked or costumed actors. Traditional theatre was reserved for royal or religious events but, with the modernisation of the monarchy, the once-cloistered art forms have lost their patrons and gone into decline. Classical Thai dance, on the other hand, has survived quite well in the modern era and is still widely taught in schools and universities.

Kŏhn & Lí·gair

Kŏhn is a masked dance-drama depicting scenes from the *Ramakian* (the Thai version of India's *Ramayana*). The central story revolves around Prince Rama's search for his beloved Princess Sita, who has been abducted by the evil 10-headed demon Ravana and taken to the island of Lanka.

Most often performed at Buddhist festivals by troupes of travelling performers, *lí·gair* is a gaudy, raucous theatrical art form thought to have descended from drama rituals brought to southern Thailand by Arab and Malay traders. It contains a colourful mixture of folk and classical music, outrageous costumes, melodrama, slapstick comedy, sexual innuendo and up-to-date commentary.

Classical & Folk Dance

Inherited from the Khmer, classical dance was a holy offering performed by the earthly version of *apsara* (heavenly maidens blessed with beauty and skilled in dance, who are depicted in graceful positions in temple murals and bas-reliefs). But traditional dancing enjoyed its own expressions in the villages and defined each region. In some cases the dances describe the rice-planting season, while others tell tales of flirtations. During local festivals and street parades, especially in the northeast, troupes of dancers, ranging from elementary-school age to college age, will be swathed in traditional costumes, ornate headdresses and white-powder make-up to perform synchronised steps accompanied by a marching band.

Music

Classical Thai music features a dazzling array of textures and subtleties, hair-raising tempos and pastoral melodies. The classical orchestra is called the *pèe pâht* and can include as few as five players or more than 20. Among the more common instruments is the *pèe*, a woodwind instrument that has a reed mouthpiece; it is heard prominently at Thai-boxing matches. The *rá·nâht èhk,* a bamboo-keyed percussion instrument resembling the xylophone, carries the main melodies. The slender *sor,* a bowed instrument with a coconut-shell soundbox, is sometimes played solo by street buskers.

If you take a cab in Bangkok, you're likely to hear Thailand's version of country music: *lôok tûng* (literally 'children of the fields'). Lust love, tragic early death and the plight of the hard-working farmers are popular themes sung plaintively over a melancholy accompaniment. More upbeat is *mŏr lam,* a folk tradition from the rural northeast that has been electrified with a fast-paced beat. Step into a shopping mall or a Thai disco and you'll hear the bouncy tunes of Thai pop (also dubbed 'T-pop'). The ageing hippies from the protest era of the 1970s and 1980s pioneered *pleng pêu·a chee·wít* (songs for life), which feature in the increasingly hard-to-find Thai country bars. The 1990s gave birth to an alternative pop scene – known as 'indie.'

Architecture

Traditional Homes

Traditional Thai homes were adapted to the weather, the family and artistic sensibilities. These antique specimens were humble dwellings consisting of a single-room wooden house raised on stilts. More elaborate homes, for the village chief or minor royalty for instance, might link a series of single rooms by elevated walkways. Since many Thai villages were built near rivers, the elevation provided protection from flooding during the annual monsoon. During the dry season the space beneath the house was used as a hideaway from the heat of the day, an outdoor kitchen or as a barn for farm animals. Later this all-purpose space would shelter bicycles and motorcycles.

Once plentiful in Thai forests, teak was always the material of choice for wooden structures and its use typically indicates that a house is at least 50 years old. Rooflines in central, northern and southern Thailand are steeply pitched and often decorated at the corners or along the gables with motifs related to the *naga,* mythical water serpent long believed to be a spiritual protector of Tai cultures throughout Asia.

In Thailand's southern provinces it's not unusual to come upon houses of Malay design, using high masonry pediments or foundations rather than wooden stilts. Residents of the south also sometimes use bamboo and palm thatch, which are more plentiful than wood. In the north, the homes of community leaders were often decorated with an ornate horn-shaped motif called *galare,* a decorative element that has become shorthand for old Lanna architecture. Roofs of tile or thatch tend to be less steeply pitched, and rounded gables – a feature inherited from Myanmar (Burma) – can also be found further north.

Temple Symbols

The architectural symbolism of Thai temples relies heavily on Hindu-Buddhist iconography. *Naga,* the mythical serpent that guarded Buddha during meditation, appears on handrails at temple entrances. A silhouette of the birdlike *chôr fáh* adorns the tip of the roof. Three-tiered roofs represent the triple gems of Buddhism: the Buddha, the dhamma and the sangha (the Buddhist community). The lotus, a reminder of religious perfection, decorates temple gates and posts, verandah columns and spires of Sukhothai-era *chedi,* and often forms the pedestal for images of the meditating Buddha. Lotus buds are used solely for merit-making.

Temples

The most striking examples of Thailand's architectural heritage are the Buddhist temples (wát), which dazzle in the tropical sun with wild colours and soaring rooflines. Thai temples are compounds of different buildings serving specific religious functions. The most important structures include the *uposatha* (*bòht* in central Thai, *sĭm* in northern and northeastern Thai), which is a consecrated chapel where monastic ordinations are held, and the *wí·hăhn,* where important Buddha images are housed.

A classic component of temple architecture is the presence of one or more *chedi* (stupas), a solid mountain-shaped monument that pays tribute to the enduring stability of Buddhism. *Chedi* come in myriad styles, from simple inverted bowl-shaped designs imported from Sri Lanka to the more elaborate octagonal shapes found in northern Thailand. Many are believed to contain relics (often pieces of bone) belonging to the historical Buddha. Some *chedi* also house the ashes of important kings and royalty. A variation of the stupa inherited from the Angkor kingdom is the corn-cob-shaped *prang,* a feature in the ancient Thai temples of Sukhothai and Ayuthaya.

Contemporary Architecture

Thais began mixing traditional architecture with European forms in the late 19th and early 20th centuries, as exemplified by Bangkok's Vimanmek Teak Mansion in Dusit Palace Park and certain buildings of the Grand Palace. The port cities of Thailand, including Bangkok and Phuket, acquired fine examples of Sino-Portuguese architecture – buildings of stuccoed brick decorated with an ornate facade – a style that followed the sea traders during the colonial era. In Bangkok this style is often referred to as 'old Bangkok' or Ratanakosin. In the 1960s and 1970s the European Bauhaus movement shifted contemporary architecture towards a stark functionalism. During the building boom of the mid-1980s, Thai architects used high-tech designs such as ML Sumet Jumsai's famous Robot Building on Th Sathon Tai in Bangkok. In the new millennium, shopping centres and hotels have reinterpreted the traditional Thai house through an industrial modernist perspective, creating geometric cubes defined by steel beams and glass curtains.

Village of Ko Panyi (p223), Ao Phang-Nga

YANN ARTHUS-BERTRAND/GETTY IMAGES ©

Environment

Thailand clings to a southern spur of the Himalayas in the north, cradles fertile river plains at its core and tapers between two shallow seas fringed by coral reefs. Its shape is likened to an elephant's head, with the Malay peninsula representing the trunk. Spanning 1650km and 16 latitudinal degrees from north to south, Thailand has the most diverse climate of any mainland Southeast Asia country.

Northern Thailand

Northern Thailand is fused to Myanmar (Burma), Laos and southern China through the southeast-trending extension of the Himalayan mountain range known as the Dawna-Tenasserim. The tallest peak is Doi Inthanon (measured heights vary from 2565m to 2576m), which is topped by a mixed forest of evergreen and swamp species, including a thick carpet of moss. Monsoon forests comprise the lower elevations and are made up of deciduous trees, which are green and lush during the rainy season but dusty and leafless during the dry season. Teak is one of the most highly valued monsoon forest trees but it now exists only in limited quantities and is illegal to harvest. The cool mountains of northern Thailand are considered to be some of the most accessible and rewarding birding

★ **National Parks**

Khao Sam Roi Yot National Park
(p178), near Hua Hin

Ang Thong Marine National Park
(p186), near Ko Samui

Ao Phang-Nga National Park (p222),
Phuket

Ang Thong Marine National Park (p186)

destinations in Asia and are populated by montane species and migrants with clear Himalayan affinities, such as flycatchers and thrushes.

Central Thailand

In the central region the topography mellows into a flat rice basket, fed by rivers that are as revered as the national monarchy. Thailand's most exalted river is the Chao Phraya, which is formed by the northern tributaries of the Ping, Wang, Yom and Nan – a lineage as notable as any aristocrat's. The river delta spends most of the year in cultivation, changing with the seasons from fields of emerald-green rice shoots to golden harvests. This region has been heavily sculpted by civilisation: roads, fields, cities and towns have transformed the landscape into a working core. In the western frontier, bumping into the mountainous border with Myanmar is a complex of forest preserves that cover 17,800 sq km – the largest protected area in Southeast Asia and a largely undisturbed habitat for endangered elephants and tigers. These parks have little in the way of tourist infrastructure or commercial development.

Northeastern Thailand

The landscape of Thailand's northeastern region is occupied by the arid Khorat Plateau rising some 300m above the central plain. This is a hardscrabble land where the rains are meagre, the soil is anaemic and the red dust stains as stubbornly as the betel nut chewed by the local grandmothers. The dominant forest is dry dipterocarp, which consists of deciduous trees that shed their leaves in the dry season to conserve water. The region's largest forest preserve is Khao Yai National Park, which, together with nearby parks, has been recognised as a Unesco World Heritage site. The park is mainly arid forest, a favourite of hornbills and more than 300 other bird species. There is a small population of wild elephants in the park but development around the perimeter has impacted important wildlife corridors.

Southern Thailand

The kingdom's eastern rivers dump their waters and sediment into the Gulf of Thailand, a shallow basin off the neighbouring South China Sea. In the joint of the fishhook-shaped gulf is Bangkok, surrounded by a thick industrial zone that has erased or polluted much of the natural environment. The extremities of the gulf, both to the east and to the south, are more characteristic of coastal environments: mangrove swamps form the transition between land and sea and act as the ocean's nursery, spawning and nurturing fish, bird and amphibian species. Thailand is home to nearly 75 species of these salt-tolerant trees that were once regarded as wastelands and were vulnerable to coastal development.

The long slender 'trunk' of land that runs between the Gulf of Thailand and the Andaman Sea is often referred to as the Malay Peninsula. This region is Thailand's most tropical: rainfall is plentiful, cultivating thick rainforests that stay green year-round. Malayan flora and fauna predominate and a scenic range of limestone mountains meanders from land to sea. On the west coast, the Andaman Sea is an outcropping of the larger Indian Ocean and home to astonishing coral reefs that feed and shelter thousands of varieties of fish and act as breakwaters against tidal surges. Many of the coral-fringed islands are designated marine national parks, limiting – to some degree – coastal development and boat traffic. The 2010 global coral bleaching phenomenon (in which El Niño weather conditions contributed to warmer sea temperatures) killed or damaged significant portions of Thailand's reefs.

National Parks & Protected Areas

With 15% of the kingdom's land and sea designated as park or sanctuary, Thailand has one of the highest percentages of protected areas of any Asian nation. There are more than 100 national parks, plus more than 1000 'nonhunting areas', wildlife sanctuaries, forest reserves, botanic gardens and arboretums. Thailand began its conservation efforts in 1960 with the creation of a national system of wildlife sanctuaries under the Wild Animals Reservation and Protection Act, followed by the National Parks Act of 1961. Khao Yai National Park was the first wild area to receive this new status. Despite promises, official designation as a national park or sanctuary does not guarantee protection from development or poaching. Local farmers, hunters and moneyed interests often circumvent conservation efforts. Enforcement of environmental regulations lacks political will and proper funding. Foreign visitors are often confused by resort development in national parks despite their protected status. In some cases private ownership of land pre-dated the islands' protected status, while in other cases rules are bent for powerful interests.

Ko Khao Phing Kan (p223), Ao Phang-Nga

IVANMATEEV/GETTY IMAGES ©

Environmental Trivia

○ Thailand is equivalent in area to the size of France.

○ Bangkok sits at about N14° latitude, level with Madras, Manila, Guatemala and Khartoum.

○ The Mekong rivals the Amazon River in terms of biodiversity.

○ Thailand is home to venomous snakes, including the pit viper and the king cobra.

○ Thailand's limestone formations are a soft sedimentary rock created by shells and coral from an ancient sea bed 250 to 300 million years ago.

Mekong River

Defining the contours of Thailand's border with Laos is the Mekong River, Southeast Asia's artery. The Mekong is a workhorse, having been dammed for hydroelectric power, and a mythmaker, featuring in local people's folktales and festivals. The river winds in and out of the steep mountain ranges to the northeastern plateau where it swells and contracts according to seasonal rainfall. In the dry season, riverside farmers plant vegetables in the muddy flood-plain, harvesting the crop before the river reclaims its territory. Scientists have identified the Mekong River as having impressive biodiversity. As many as 1000 previously unidentified species of flora and fauna have been discovered in the last decade in the Mekong region (which includes Vietnam, Laos and Cambodia).

Environmental Issues

Thailand has put enormous pressure on its ecosystems as it has industrialised. Natural forest cover now makes up about 28% of land area, compared to 70% some 50 years ago. Thailand's coastal region has experienced higher population and economic growth than the national average and these areas suffer from soil erosion, water pollution and degradation of coral reef systems. Seasonal flooding is a common natural occurrence in some parts of Thailand due to the nature of the monsoon rains. But high-level floods have increased in frequency and severity. The record-busting 2011 flooding was one of the world's costliest natural disasters. Of the country's 77 provinces, 65 were declared flood disaster zones; there were 815 deaths and an estimated US$45.7 billion worth of damage.

Fisheries continue to experience declining catches as fish stocks plummet, and an industry once dominated by small family fisherfolk has shifted to big commercial enterprises that can go into deeper waters.

In 2013 a pipeline unloading an oil tanker off the coast of Rayong spilled 50,000L of crude into the sea, coating the western side of Ko Samet. While the outward condition of beaches quickly recovered with the use of dispersants, experts say there may be considerable long-term effects of the spill on both human health and the marine ecosystem.

Hiking with a guide in Chiang Mai

Responsible Travel

Thais are a warm and friendly people who generally welcome foreign visitors and appreciate efforts to understand their culture and society. There are numerous volunteer organisations for travellers who are keen on contributing, and they can be a rewarding way to learn more about Thailand, its people and environment.

Cultural Etiquette

The monarchy and religion (which are interconnected) are treated with extreme deference in Thailand. Thais avoid criticising or disparaging the royal family for fear of offending someone or, worse, being charged with a violation of the country's very strict *lèse majesté* laws, which carry a jail sentence.

Buddha images are sacred objects. Thais consider it bad form to pull a silly pose in front of one for a photo, or to clamber upon them (in the case of temple ruins). Instead they would show respect by performing a *wâi* (a prayer-like gesture) to the figure no matter how humble it is. As part of their ascetic vows, monks are not supposed to touch or be touched by women. If a woman wants to hand something to a monk, the object is placed within reach of the monk or on the monk's 'receiving cloth'.

From a spiritual viewpoint, Thais regard the head as the highest and most sacred part of the body and the feet as the dirtiest and lowest. Many of the taboos associated with the feet have a practical derivation as well. Traditionally Thais ate, slept and entertained on the floor of their homes with little in the way of furniture. To keep their homes and eating surfaces clean, the feet (and shoes) contracted a variety of rules.

Shoes aren't worn inside private homes and temple buildings, as a sign of respect and for sanitary reasons. Thais can kick off their shoes in one fluid step and many lace-up shoes are modified by the wearer to become slip-ons. Thais also step over – not on – the threshold, which is where the spirit of the house is believed to reside. On some buses and 3rd-class trains, you'll see Thais prop their feet up on the adjacent bench, and while this isn't the height of propriety, do notice that they always remove their shoes before doing so. Thais also take off their shoes if they need to climb onto a chair or seat.

Thais don't touch each others' heads or ruffle hair as a sign of affection. Occasionally you'll see young people touching each others' heads, which is a teasing gesture, maybe even a slight insult, between friends.

Social Conventions & Gestures

The traditional Thai greeting is made with a prayer-like, palms-together gesture known as *wâi*. The depth of the bow and the placement of the fingers in relation to the face is dependent on the status of the person receiving the *wâi*. Adults don't *wâi* children and in most cases service people (when they are doing their jobs) aren't *wâi-ed,* though this is a matter of personal discretion.

In the more traditional parts of the country, it is not proper for members of the opposite sexes to touch one another, either as lovers or as friends. Hand-holding is not acceptable behaviour outside the major cities such as Bangkok. But same-sex touching is quite common and is typically a sign of friendship, not sexual attraction. Older Thai men might grab a younger man's thigh in the same way that buddies slap each other on the back. Thai women are especially affectionate with female friends, often sitting close to one another or linking arms.

Thais hold modesty in personal dress in high regard, though this is changing among the younger generation. The importance of modesty extends to the beach as well. Except for urbanites, most provincial Thais swim fully clothed. For this reason, sunbathing nude or topless is not acceptable and in some cases is even illegal. Remember that swimsuits are not proper attire off the beach; wear a cover-up in between the sand and your hotel.

Tourism

Most forms of tourism, despite the prevailing prejudices, have a positive economic effect on the local economy in Thailand, providing jobs for young workers and business opportunities for entrepreneurs. But in an effort to be more than just a consumer, many travellers look for opportunities to spend where their money might be needed, either on charitable causes or activities that preserve traditional ways of life. Thailand has done a surprisingly good job at adapting to this emerging trend by promoting village craft programs and homestays. Unfortunately, much of this is aimed at the domestic market rather than international visitors. But more and more, foreign tourists can engage in these small-scale tourism models that offer an insight into traditional ways.

Diving

The popularity of Thailand's diving industry places immense pressure on fragile coral sites. To help preserve the ecology, adhere to these simple rules.

o Avoid touching living marine organisms, standing on coral or dragging equipment (such as fins) across the reef. Coral polyps can be damaged by even the gentlest contact.

o When treading water in shallow reef areas, be careful not to kick up clouds of sand, which can easily smother the delicate reef organisms.

o Take great care in underwater caves where your air bubbles can be caught within the roof and leave previously submerged organisms high and dry.

o Join a coral clean-up campaign that's sponsored by dive shops.

o Don't feed the fish or allow your dive operator to dispose of excess food in the water. The fish become dependent on this food source and don't tend to the algae on the coral, causing harm to the reef.

Elephant Encounters

Throughout Thai history, elephants have been revered for their strength, endurance and intelligence, working alongside their mahouts harvesting teak, transporting goods through mountainous terrain or fighting ancient wars.

But many of the elephants' traditional roles have either been outsourced to machines or outlawed (logging was officially banned in 1989, although it still goes on along the Thai–Myanmar border), leaving the 'domesticated' animals and their mahouts without work. Some mahouts turned to begging on the streets in Bangkok and other tourist centres, but most elephants find work in Thailand's tourism industry. Their jobs vary from circus-like shows to elephant camps giving rides to tourists, to 'mahout-training' schools, while sanctuaries and rescue centres provide modest retirement homes to animals that are no longer financially profitable to their owners.

It costs about 30,000B (US$1000) a month to provide a comfortable living for an elephant, an amount equivalent to the salary of Thailand's upper middle class. Welfare standards within the tourism industry are not standardised or subject to government regulations, so it's up to the conscientious consumer to encourage the industry to ensure safe conditions for elephants.

With more evidence available than ever to support claims by animal welfare experts that elephant rides and shows are harmful to these gentle giants, who are often abused to force them to perform for humans, a small but growing number of sanctuaries offer more sustainable interactions, such as walking with and bathing retired and rescued elephants. If you're still bent on riding one, however, ask the right questions to ensure you choose a well-run operation.

o **Does the camp employ a veterinarian?** Good camps keep their elephants under regular medical supervision.

o **What is its policy on procuring new elephants?** Some camps buy illegally caught wild elephants with forged registration so they appear to have been born in captivity.

o **How many hours per day do the elephants work?** A brisk-paced walk for about four hours per day (with breaks for eating and drinking in between) is considered adequate exercise.

o **How many adults do the elephants carry?** An Asian elephant can carry a maximum of 150kg on its back, plus a mahout on its neck. Tally up the combined weight of you and your partner and request a separate elephant if you tip the scales.

Essential Etiquette
Do

Stand respectfully for the national anthem It is played on TV and radio stations as well as public and government places at 8am and 6pm.

Rise for the royal anthem It is played in movie theatres before every screening.

Smile a lot It makes everything easier.

Bring a gift if you're invited to a Thai home Fruit, drinks or snacks are acceptable; flowers are usually for merit-making purposes, not home decor.

Take off your shoes When you enter a home, temple building or wherever there are sandals piled up at the door.

Lower your head slightly When passing between two people having a conversation or when passing near a monk; it is a sign of respect.

Dress modestly for temple visits Cover to the elbows and ankles and always remove your shoes when entering any building containing a Buddha image.

Give and receive politely Extend the right hand out while the left hand gently grips the right elbow when handing an object to another person or receiving something – truly polite behaviour.

Respect all Buddha images and pictures of the monarchy Signs of disrespect can have serious consequences.

Sit in the 'mermaid' position inside temples Tuck your feet beside and behind you so that your feet aren't pointing at the Buddha image.

○ **Are the elephants kept in a shady spot near fresh water and a food source? What do they eat?** A balanced diet includes a mixture of fruit, grasses, bamboo and pineapple shoots.

○ **Do the elephants have noticeable wounds?** This is often a sign of mistreatment.

○ **What kind of a seat is used for elephant riding?** Wooden seats, custom-made to fit the elephant's back, cause less irritation and stress on the animal.

○ **What is the camp's birth/death rate?** Happy elephants have babies.

Hill-Tribe Hikes

Though marginalised within mainstream society, Thailand's hill-tribe minorities remain a strong tourism draw, with large and small businesses organising 'trekking' tours (these can range from proper hikes to leisurely walks) to villages for cultural displays and interactions. Economically it is unclear whether hill-tribe trekking helps alleviate the poverty of the hill-tribe groups, which in turn helps to maintain their separate ethnic identity. Most agree that a small percentage of the profits from trekking filters down to individual families within hill-tribe villages, giving them a small source of income that might help avoid urban migration.

In general, the trekking business has become more socially conscious than in past decades. Most companies now tend to limit the number of visits to a particular area to lessen the impact of outsiders on the daily lives of ordinary villagers. But the industry still has a long way to go. It should be noted that trekking companies are Thai owned and employ Thai guides, another bureaucratic impediment regarding citizenship for ethnic minorities. Without an identification card, guides from hill tribes do not qualify for a Tourist Authority of Thailand (TAT) tour guide licence and so are less than desirable job candidates.

Trekkers should also realise that the minority tribes maintain their own distinct cultural identity and many continue their animistic traditions, which define social taboos and conventions. If you're planning on visiting hill-tribe villages on an organised trek, talk to your guide about acceptable behaviour.

Here is a general prescription to get you started.

○ Always ask for permission before taking any photos of tribespeople, especially at private moments inside their dwellings. Many traditional belief systems regard photography with suspicion.

○ Show respect for religious symbols and rituals. Don't touch totems at village entrances or sacred items hanging from trees. Don't participate in ceremonies unless invited.

○ Avoid cultivating the practice of begging, especially among children. Talk to your guide about donating to a local school instead.

○ Avoid public nudity and be careful not to undress near an open window where village children might be able to peep in.

○ Don't flirt with members of the opposite sex unless you plan on marrying them.

○ Don't drink or do drugs with the villagers; altered states sometimes lead to culture clashes.

○ Smile at villagers even if they stare at you. Ask your guide how to say 'hello' in the tribal language.

○ Avoid public displays of affection, which in some traditional systems are viewed as offensive to the spirit world.

○ Don't interact with the villagers' livestock, even the free-roaming pigs; these creatures are valuable possessions, not entertainment. Also avoid interacting with jungle animals, which in some belief systems are viewed as visiting spirits.

○ Don't litter.

○ Adhere to the same feet taboos that apply to Thai culture. Don't step on the threshold of a house, prop your feet up against the fire or wear your shoes inside.

Essential Etiquette Don't

Get a tattoo of the Buddha It is considered sacrilegious.

Criticise the monarchy The monarchy is revered and protected by defamation laws.

Prop your feet on tables or chairs Feet are considered dirty and people have to sit on chairs.

Step on a dropped bill to prevent it from blowing away Thai money bears a picture of the king. Feet + monarchy – grave offence.

Step over someone or their personal belongings Aaah, attack of the feet.

Tie your shoes to the outside of your backpack They might accidentally brush against someone; gross.

Touch a Thai person on the head It is considered rude, not chummy.

Women cannot touch monks or their belongings Step out of the way when passing a monk on the footpath and do not sit next to them on public transport.

Homestays

A visit to a homestay is one of the best ways to experience Thailand's rural culture, not to mention a way to ensure that your baht are going directly to locals. More popular with domestic tourists, homestays differ from guesthouses in that visitors are welcomed into a family's home, typically in a small village that isn't on the tourist trail. Accommodation is basic: usually a mat or foldable mattress on the floor, or occasionally a family will have a private room. Rates include lodging, meals with the family and cultural activities that highlight the region's traditional way of life, from rice farming to silk weaving. English fluency varies, so homestays are also an excellent way to exercise your spoken Thai.

Volunteering

There are a myriad of volunteer organisations in Thailand to address both the needs of the locals and visitors' desires to help. A regularly updated resource for grassroots-level volunteer opportunities in Thailand is **Volunteer Work Thailand** (www.volunteer-workthailand. org). Be aware though that so-called 'voluntourism' has become a big business and that not every organisation fulfils its promise of meaningful experiences. Lonely Planet does not endorse any organisations we do not work with directly, so it is essential that you do your own thorough research before agreeing to volunteer with any organisation.

A number of NGOs undertake local conservation efforts and run rescue and sanctuary centres for wild animals that have been adopted as pets, or veterinarian clinics that tend to the domesticated population of dogs and cats. At centres and sanctuaries that rely on volunteer labour, your hard work is often rewarded with meaningful interactions with the animals.

Northern Thailand, especially Chiang Mai and Chiang Rai, has a number of volunteer opportunities working with disadvantaged hill-tribe groups. Chiang Mai, Mae Sot and Sangkhlaburi have distressed communities of Burmese refugees and migrants. There are also many volunteer teaching positions in northeastern Thailand, the country's agricultural heartland.

When looking for a volunteer placement, it is essential to investigate what your chosen organisation does and, more importantly, how it goes about it. If the focus is not primarily on your skills and how these can be applied to help local people, that should ring alarm bells. Any organisation that promises to let you do any kind of work, wherever you like, for as long as you like, is unlikely to be putting the needs of local people first.

For any organisation working with children, child protection is a serious concern, and organisations that do not conduct background checks on volunteers should be regarded with extreme caution. Experts recommend a three-month commitment for volunteering with children. Visit www.thinkchildsafe.org for more information.

ATLANTIDE PHOTOTRAVEL/GETTY IMAGES ©

Survival Guide

Directory A–Z

Accommodation

Thailand offers a wide variety of accommodation, from cheap and basic to pricey and luxurious. In places where spoken English might be limited, it is handy to know the following: *hôrng pát lom* (room with fan) and *hôrng aa* (room with air-con).

Costs

Accommodation costs tend to be higher in big cities (like Bangkok and Chiang Mai) and the islands. Small towns and less popular tourist towns have more reasonable rates, though the high-end options are limited. Prices fluctuate with the seasons and tourist demand.

Customs Regulations

The customs department (www.customs.go.th) maintains a helpful website with specific information about customs regulations for travellers.

Thailand allows the following items to enter duty free:

- o reasonable amount of personal effects (clothing and toiletries)
- o professional instruments
- o 200 cigarettes
- o 1L of wine or spirits

Thailand prohibits the import of the following items:

- o firearms and ammunition (unless registered in advance with the police department)
- o illegal drugs
- o pornographic media

When leaving Thailand, you must obtain an export licence for any antique reproductions or newly cast Buddha images (except personal amulets). Submit two front-view photos of the object(s), a photocopy of your passport, the purchase receipt and the object(s) in question, to the **Office of the National Museum** (Map p62; ☎02 224 1370, 02 224 7493; National Museum, 4 Th Na Phra That; ⊗9am-4pm Tue-Fri; ⛴Chang Pier, Maharaj Pier, Phra Chan Tai Pier). Allow four days for the application and inspection process to be completed.

Electricity

Thailand uses 220V AC electricity. Power outlets most commonly feature

two-prong round or flat sockets.

220V/50Hz

220V/50Hz

Food

The following price ranges indicate how much you

should expect to pay for a main dish in Thailand.

$ less than 150B
$$ 150–350B
$$$ more than 350B

Gay & Lesbian Travellers

Thai culture is relatively tolerant of both male and female homosexuality. There is a fairly prominent LGBT scene in Bangkok and Phuket. Public displays of affection – whether heterosexual or homosexual – are frowned upon.

Health

The majority of cities and provincial capitals have adequate, and even excellent, medical care. The exceptions include small islands like Ko Pha-Ngan and Ko Phi-Phi where serious medical conditions require transfer to the mainland.

Travellers tend to worry about contracting exotic infectious diseases, but these are far less common than problems with pre-existing medical conditions (such as heart disease) and accidental injury (especially as a result of traffic accidents).

Other common illnesses are respiratory infections, diarrhoea and dengue fever. Fortunately most common illnesses can be prevented or are easily treated.

Our advice is a general guide and does not replace the advice of a doctor trained in travel medicine.

Before You Go

Pack medications in clearly labelled original containers and obtain a signed and dated letter from your physician describing your medical conditions, medications and syringes or needles. If you have a heart condition, bring a copy of your electrocardiogram (ECG) taken just prior to travelling.

If you take any regular medication bring double your needs in case of loss or theft. In Thailand you can buy many medications over the counter without a doctor's prescription, but it can be difficult to find the exact medication you are taking.

Contact your home country's Department of Foreign Affairs or the equivalent and register your trip; this is a helpful precaution in the event of a natural disaster.

Insurance

Don't travel without health insurance – accidents *do* happen. You may require extra cover for adventure activities such as rock climbing or diving, as well as scooter or motorcycle riding. If your health insurance doesn't cover you for medical expenses abroad, ensure you get specific travel insurance. Most hospitals require an upfront guarantee of payment (from yourself

or your insurer) prior to admission. Enquire before your trip about payment of medical charges and retain all documentation (medical reports, invoices etc) for claim purposes.

Medical Checklist

Recommended items for a personal medical kit include the following, most of which are available in Thailand.

o antifungal cream, eg Clotrimazole

o antibacterial cream, eg Muciprocin

o antibiotic for skin infections, eg Amoxicillin/Clavulanate or Cephalexin

o antibiotics for diarrhoea include Norfloxacin, Ciprofloxacin or Azithromycin for bacterial diarrhoea; for giardiasis or amoebic dysentery, take Tinidazole

o antihistamine – there are many options, eg Cetrizine for daytime and Promethazine for night-time

o antiseptic, eg Betadine

Book Your Stay Online

For more accommodation reviews by Lonely Planet authors, check out http://hotels.lonely planet.com/thailand. You'll find independent reviews, as well as recommendations on the best places to stay. Best of all, you can book online.

Climate

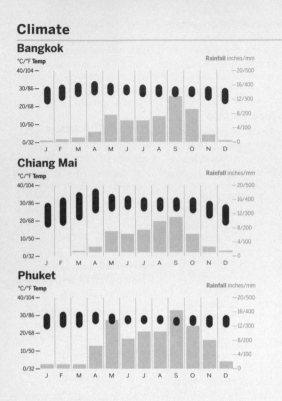

Bangkok

Chiang Mai

Phuket

- o antispasmodic for stomach cramps, eg Buscopan

- o contraceptives

- o decongestant

- o DEET-based insect repellent

- o oral rehydration solution for diarrhoea (eg Gastrolyte), diarrhoea 'stopper' (eg Loperamide) and anti-nausea medication

- o first-aid items such as scissors, Elastoplasts, bandages, gauze, thermometer (but not one with mercury), sterile needles and syringes (with a doctor's letter), safety pins and tweezers

- o alcohol-based hand gel or wipes

- o ibuprofen or another anti-inflammatory

- o indigestion medication, eg Quick-Eze or Mylanta

- o laxative, eg Coloxyl

- o migraine medicine – for migraine sufferers

- o paracetamol

- o permethrin to impregnate clothing and mosquito nets if at high risk

- o steroid cream for allergic/itchy rashes, eg 1% to 2% hydrocortisone

- o sunscreen, sunglasses and hat

- o throat lozenges

- o thrush (vaginal yeast infection) treatment, eg Clotrimazole pessaries or Diflucan tablet

- o Ural or equivalent if prone to urine infections

Recommended Vaccines

You should arrange your vaccines six to eight weeks prior to departure through a specialised travel-medicine clinic.

The Centers for Disease Control and Prevention (www.cdc.gov) has a traveller's health section that contains recommendations for vaccinations. The only vaccine required by international regulations is yellow fever. Proof of vaccination will only be required if you have visited a country in the yellow-fever zone within the six days prior to entering Thailand. If you are travelling to Thailand *from* Africa or South America you should check to see if you require proof of vaccination.

In Transit

Deep-vein thrombosis (DVT) occurs when blood clots form in the legs during long trips chiefly because of prolonged immobility. Though most blood clots are reabsorbed uneventfully, some may break off and travel through the blood vessels to the lungs, where they can cause life-threatening complications.

The chief symptom of DVT is swelling or pain of the foot, ankle or calf, usually but not always on one side. When a blood clot travels to the lungs, it may cause chest pain and difficulty in breathing. Travellers with any of these symptoms should immediately seek medical attention.

To prevent the development of DVT on long flights you should walk about the cabin, and drink plenty of fluids (nonalcoholic).

Jet lag is common when crossing more than five time zones. It results in insomnia, fatigue, malaise or nausea. To avoid jet lag, drink plenty of fluids (nonalcoholic) and eat light meals. Upon arrival, seek exposure to natural sunlight and readjust your schedule. Some people find melatonin helpful.

In Thailand

Infectious Diseases

Cuaneous Larva Migrans

This disease, caused by dog or cat hookworm, is particularly common on the beaches of Thailand. The rash starts as a small lump, and then slowly spreads like a winding line. It is intensely itchy, especially at night. It is easily treated with medicatios and should not be cut out or frozen.

Dengue Fever

This mosquito-borne disease is increasingly problematic in Thailand, especially in the cities.

As there is no vaccine, it can only be prevented by avoiding mosquito bites. The mosquito that carries dengue is a daytime biter, so use insect-avoidance measures at all times. Symptoms include high fever, severe headache (especially behind the eyes), nausea and body aches (dengue was previously known as 'breakbone fever'). Some people develop a rash (which can be very itchy) and experience diarrhoea.

There is no specific treatment, just rest and paracetamol – do not take aspirin or ibuprofen as they increase the risk of haemorrhaging. See a doctor to be diagnosed and monitored.

Dengue can progress to the more severe and life-threatening dengue haemorrhagic fever, but this is very uncommon in tourists. The risk of this increases substantially if you have previously been infected with dengue and are then infected with a different serotype.

Hepatitis A

The risk of hepatitis A in Bangkok is decreasing, but there is still significant risk in most of the country. This food- and waterborne virus infects the liver, causing jaundice (yellow skin and eyes), nausea and lethargy. There is no specific treatment for hepatitis A. All travellers to Thailand should be vaccinated against hepatitis A.

Hepatitis B

The only sexually transmitted disease (STD) that can be prevented by vaccination, hepatitis B is spread by body fluids, including sexual contact. In some parts of Thailand up to 20% of the population are carriers of hepatitis B, and usually are unaware of this. The long-term consequences can include liver cancer, cirrhosis and death.

Avoiding Mosquito Bites

Travellers are advised to prevent mosquito bites by taking these steps:

o use a DEET-containing insect repellent on exposed skin

o sleep under a mosquito net, ideally impregnated with permethrin

o choose accommodation with screens and fans

o impregnate clothing with permethrin in high-risk areas

o wear long sleeves and trousers in light colours

o use mosquito coils

o spray your room with insect repellent before going out

HIV

HIV is now one of the most common causes of death in people under the age of 50 in Thailand. Always practise safe sex, and avoid getting tattoos and using unclean syringes.

Influenza

Present year-round in the tropics, influenza (flu) symptoms include high fever, muscle aches, runny nose, cough and sore throat. Flu is the most common vaccine-preventable disease contracted by travellers and everyone should consider vaccination.

Leptospirosis

Leptospirosis is contracted from exposure to infected surface water – most commonly after river rafting. Early symptoms are very similar to flu and include headache and fever. It can vary from a very mild ailment to a fatal disease. Diagnosis is made through blood tests and it is easily treated with Doxycycline.

Malaria

Malaria is caused by a parasite transmitted by the bite of an infected mosquito. The most important symptom of malaria is fever, but general symptoms such as headache, diarrhoea, cough or chills may also occur – the same symptoms as many other infections. A diagnosis can only be made by taking a blood sample.

Most touristed parts of Thailand have minimal to no risk of malaria, and the risk of side effects from taking antimalarial tablets is likely to outweigh the risk of getting the disease itself.

Measles

This highly contagious viral infection is spread through coughing and sneezing. Most people born before 1966 are immune as they had the disease in childhood. Measles starts with a high fever and rash and can be complicated by pneumonia and brain disease. There is no specific treatment. Ensure you are fully vaccinated.

Rabies

This disease, fatal if left untreated, is spread by the bite or lick of an infected animal – most commonly a dog or monkey. You should seek medical advice immediately after any animal bite and commence post-exposure treatment. Having a pretravel vaccination means the postbite treatment is greatly simplified.

STDs

Sexually transmitted diseases most common in Thailand include herpes, warts, syphilis, gonorrhoea and chlamydia. People carrying these diseases often have no signs of infection. Condoms will prevent gonorrhoea and chlamydia, but not warts or herpes. If after a sexual encounter you develop any rash, lumps, discharge or pain when passing urine, seek immediate medical attention. If you have been sexually active during your travels, have an STD check on your return home.

Typhoid

This serious bacterial infection is spread through food and water. It gives a high and slowly progressive fever, severe headache and may be accompanied by a dry cough and stomach pain. It is diagnosed by blood tests and treated with antibiotics. Vaccination is recommended for all travellers spending more than a week in Thailand, or travelling outside of the major cities. Be aware that vaccination is not 100% effective, so you must still be careful with what you eat and drink.

Traveller's Diarrhoea

In over 80% of cases, traveller's diarrhoea is caused by a bacteria (there are numerous potential culprits) and responds promptly to treatment with antibiotics.

Here we define traveller's diarrhoea as the passage of more than three watery bowel movements within 24 hours, plus at least one other symptom such as vomiting, fever, cramps, nausea or feeling generally unwell.

Treatment consists of staying well hydrated; rehydration solutions such as Gastrolyte are the best for this. Antibiotics such as Norfloxacin, Ciprofloxacin or Azithromycin will kill the bacteria quickly. Seek med-

Rare But Be Aware

o **Avian Influenza** Most of those infected have had close contact with sick or dead birds.

o **Filariasis** A mosquito-borne disease that is common in the local population; practice mosquito-avoidance measures.

o **Hepatitis E** Transmitted through contaminated food and water and has similar symptoms to hepatitis A. Can be a severe problem in pregnant women. Follow safe eating and drinking guidelines.

o **Japanese B Encephalitis** Viral disease transmitted by mosquitoes, typically occurring in rural areas. Vaccination is recommended for travellers spending more than one month outside cities, or for long-term expats.

o **Meliodosis** Contracted by skin contact with soil. Affects up to 30% of the local population in northeastern Thailand. The symptoms are very similar to those experienced by tuberculosis (TB) sufferers. There is no vaccine, but it can be treated with medications.

o **Strongyloides** A parasite transmitted by skin contact with soil; common in the local population. It is characterised by an unusual skin rash – a linear rash on the trunk that comes and goes. An overwhelming infection can follow. It can be treated with medications.

o **Tuberculosis** Medical and aid workers and long-term travellers who have significant contact with the local population should take precautions. The main symptoms are fever, cough, weight loss, night sweats and tiredness. Treatment is available with long-term multidrug regimens.

o **Typhus** Murine typhus is spread by the bite of a flea; scrub typhus is spread via a mite. Symptoms include fever, muscle pains and a rash. Following general insect-avoidance measures; Doxycycline will also prevent it.

ical attention if you do not respond to an appropriate antibiotic.

Loperamide is just a 'stopper' that only treats the symptoms. It can be helpful, for example, if you have to go on a long bus ride. Don't take Loperamide if you have a fever, or blood in your stools.

Giardia lamblia is a parasite that is relatively common. Symptoms include nausea, bloating, excess gas, fatigue and intermittent diarrhoea. 'Eggy' burps are often attributed solely to giardiasis. The treatment of choice is Tinidazole,

with Metronidazole being a second-line option.

Amoebic dysentery is very rare in travellers, but may be misdiagnosed by poor-quality labs. Symptoms are similar to bacterial diarrhoea. You should always seek reliable medical care if you have blood in your diarrhoea.

Environmental Hazards

Jellyfish Stings

Box jellyfish stings are extremely painful and can even be fatal. There are two main types of box jelly-

fish – multitentacled and single-tentacled.

Multitentacled box jellyfish are present in Thai waters – these are the most dangerous and a severe envenomation can kill an adult within two minutes. They are generally found along sandy beaches near river mouths and mangroves during the warmer months.

There are many types of single-tentacled box jellyfish, some of which can cause severe symptoms known as the Irukandji syndrome. The initial sting can seem minor; however, severe symptoms such as back pain, nausea, vomiting, sweating, difficulty breathing and a feeling of impending doom can develop between five and 40 minutes later.

There are many other jellyfish in Thailand that cause irritating stings but no serious effects. The only way to prevent these stings is to wear protective clothing.

For severe, life-threatening envenomations, call for medical help and start immediate CPR if the victim is unconscious. If the victim is conscious, douse the stung area liberally with vinegar for 30 seconds.

Vinegar can also reduce irritation from minor stings. It is best to seek medical care quickly in case any other symptoms develop over the next 40 minutes.

Heat

For most people it takes at least two weeks to adapt to the hot climate. Prevent swelling of the feet and ankles as well as muscle cramps caused by excessive sweating by avoiding dehydration and excessive activity in the heat of the day.

Heat stroke requires immediate medical treatment. Symptoms come on suddenly and include weakness, nausea, a hot dry body with a body temperature of more than 41°C, dizziness, confusion, loss of coordination, fits and eventually collapse and loss of consciousness.

Insect Bites & Stings

Bedbugs live in the cracks of furniture and walls and then migrate to the bed at night to feed on humans. You can treat the itch with an antihistamine.

Ticks are contracted when walking in rural areas. They are commonly found behind the ears, on the belly and in armpits. If you've been bitten by a tick and a rash develops at the site of the bite or elsewhere, along with fever or muscle aches, see a doctor. Doxycycline prevents tick-borne diseases.

Leeches are found in humid rainforests. They do not transmit disease, but their bites are often itchy for weeks afterwards and can easily become infected. Apply an iodine-based antiseptic to the bite to help prevent infection.

Bee and wasp stings mainly cause problems for people who are allergic to them. Anyone with a serious allergy should carry an injection of adrenaline (eg an EpiPen) for emergencies. For others, pain is the main problem – apply ice to the sting and take painkillers.

Parasites

Numerous parasites are common in local populations in Thailand, but most of these are rare in travellers. To avoid parasitic infections, wear shoes and avoid eating raw food, especially fish, pork and vegetables.

Skin Problems

Prickly heat is a common skin rash in the tropics, caused by sweat being trapped under the skin. Treat by taking cool showers and using powders.

Two fungal rashes commonly affect travellers. The first occurs in the groin, armpits and between the toes. It starts as a red patch that slowly spreads and is usually itchy. Treatment involves keeping the skin dry, avoiding chafing and using an antifungal cream such as Clotrimazole or Lamisil. The fungus *Tinea versicolor* causes small and light-coloured patches, most commonly on the back, chest and shoulders.

Cuts and scratches become easily infected in humid climates. Immediately wash all wounds in clean water and apply antiseptic. If you develop signs of infection, see a doctor. Coral cuts can easily become infected.

Snakes

Though snake bites are rare for travellers, there are more than 85 species of venomous snakes in Thailand. Wear boots and long pants if walking in an area that may have snakes.

The Thai Red Cross produces antivenom for many of the poisonous snakes in Thailand.

Sunburn

Even on a cloudy day, sunburn can occur rapidly. Use a strong sunscreen (at least factor 30+), making sure to reapply after a swim, and always wear a wide-brimmed hat and sunglasses outdoors. If you become sunburnt stay out of the sun until you have recovered, apply cool compresses and take painkillers for the discomfort. One-percent hydrocortisone cream applied twice daily is also helpful.

Children's Health

Consult a doctor who specialises in travel medicine prior to travel to ensure your child is appropriately prepared. A medical kit designed specifically for children includes liquid medicines for children who cannot swallow tables. Azithromycin is an ideal paediatric formula used to treat bacterial diarrhoea, as well as ear, chest and throat infections.

Good resources include Lonely Planet's *Travel with Children* and, for those spending longer away, Jane Wilson-Howarth's *Your Child's Health Abroad*.

Women's Health

Pregnant women should receive specialised advice before travelling. The ideal time to travel is in the second trimester, when pregnancy-related risks are low. Ensure travel insurance covers all pregnancy-related possibilities, including premature labour.

Malaria is a high-risk disease in pregnancy. Pregnant women should *not* travel to those areas

with chloroquine-resistant malaria. None of the more effective antimalarial drugs are completely safe in pregnancy.

Traveller's diarrhoea can quickly lead to dehydration and result in inadequate blood flow to the placenta. Azithromycin is considered one of the safest anti-diarrhoea drugs in pregnancy.

In Thailand's urban areas, supplies of sanitary products are readily available. Bring adequate supplies of your personal birth-control option. Heat, humidity and antibiotics can all contribute to thrush, which can be treated with antifungal creams and Clotrimazole. A practical alternative is one tablet of fluconazole (Diflucan). Urinary-tract infections can be precipitated by dehydration or long bus journeys without toilet stops; bring suitable antibiotics for treatment.

Insurance

A travel-insurance policy to cover theft, loss and medical problems is a good idea. Policies offer differing medical-expense options. There is a wide variety of policies available, so check the small print. Be sure that the policy covers ambulances or an emergency flight home. Some policies specifically exclude 'dangerous activities,' which can

include diving, motorcycling and even trekking. A locally acquired motorcycle licence is not valid under some policies. You may prefer a policy that pays doctors or hospitals directly rather than you having to pay on the spot and claim later. If you have to claim later, make sure you keep all documentation.

Worldwide travel insurance is available at www.lonelyplanet.com/travel-insurance. You can buy, extend and claim online any time – even if you're already on the road.

Internet Access

As more and more people travel with mobile devices, internet cafes have begun to disappear, but wi-fi is almost standard in guesthouses and cafes. Signal strength deteriorates in the upper floors of a multi-storey building; you can always request a room near a router.

Legal Matters

In general Thai police don't hassle foreigners, especially tourists. They usually go out of their way to avoid having to speak English with a foreigner, especially regarding minor traffic issues.

One major exception is drugs, which most Thai

police view as either a social scourge against which it's their duty to enforce the letter of the law, or an opportunity to make untaxed income via bribes.

If you are arrested for any offence, the police will allow you the opportunity to make a phone call, either to your embassy or consulate in Thailand if you have one, or to a friend or relative if not. There's a whole set of legal codes governing the length of time and the manner in which you can be detained before being charged or put on trial, but a lot of discretion is left to the police. In the case of foreigners the police are more likely to bend these codes in your favour. However, if you don't show respect you will make matters worse.

Thai law does not presume an indicted detainee to be either 'guilty' or 'innocent' but rather a 'suspect,' whose guilt or innocence will be decided in court. Trials are usually speedy.

The **tourist police** (⊘1155) can be very helpful in cases of arrest. Although they typically have no jurisdiction over the kinds of cases handled by regular cops, they may be able to help with translations or with contacting your embassy. You can call the hotline number 24 hours a day to lodge complaints or to request assistance with regards to personal safety.

Maps

ThinkNet (www.thinknet.co.th) produces high-quality, bilingual city and country maps, including interactive-map CDs.

Money

The basic unit of Thai currency is the baht. There are 100 satang in one baht. Coins include 25-satang and 50-satang pieces and 1B, 2B, 5B and 10B coins. Paper currency is issued in 20B (green), 50B (blue), 100B (red), 500B (purple) and 1000B (beige) denominations.

ATM & Debit Cards

Debit and ATM cards issued by a bank in your own country can be used at ATMs around Thailand to withdraw cash (in Thai baht only) directly from your account back home. ATMs are widespread and can be relied on for the bulk of your spending cash.

The downside is that Thai ATMs charge a 150B to 180B foreign-transaction fee on top of whatever currency conversion and out-of-network fees your home bank charges. Before leaving home, shop around for a bank account that has free international ATM usage and reimburses fees incurred at other institutions' ATMs.

Aeon is the only bank we know of in Thailand that doesn't charge the 150B usage fee on foreign accounts, but its distribution of national ATMs is limited, largely relegated to Big C stores.

Credit cards as well as debit cards can be used for purchases at some shops, hotels and restaurants. The most commonly accepted cards are Visa and Master-Card. American Express is typically only accepted at high-end hotels and restaurants.

Contact your bank and your credit card provider before you leave home and notify them of your upcoming trip so that your accounts aren't suspended due to suspicious overseas activity.

Foreign Exchange

There is no limit on the amount of foreign currency that can be brought into Thailand, but people arriving or departing with amounts over US$20,000 need to declare this to the customs officer. The law also requires foreigners to demonstrate adequate funds for their visit. Usually this is only required when applying in advance for a tourist or other type of visa.

Tipping

Tipping is not generally expected in Thailand, though it is appreciated. The exception is loose change from a large restaurant bill – if a meal costs 488B and you pay with a 500B note, some Thais will leave the

12B change. It's not so much a tip as a way of saying 'I'm not so money grubbing as to grab every last baht'. At many hotel restaurants or other upmarket eateries, a 10% service charge will be added to your bill.

Opening Hours

All government offices and banks are closed on public holidays. See the Need to Know chapter for standard opening hours.

Photography

Be considerate when taking photographs of locals. Learn how to ask politely in Thai and wait for an embarrassed nod. In some of the regularly visited hill-tribe areas, be prepared for the photographed subject to ask for money in exchange for a picture. Other hill tribes will not allow you to point a camera at them.

Public Holidays

Government offices and banks close their doors on the following public holidays. For the precise dates of lunar holidays, see the Events & Festivals page of the Tourism Authority of Thailand (www.tourism

---

Practicalities

o **Newspapers** Bangkok Post (www.bangkokpost. com) and the business-heavy Nation (www.nation multimedia.com) are published daily in English.

o **Radio** There are more than 400 AM and FM radio stations; short-wave radios can pick up BBC, VOA, Radio Australia, Deutsche Welle and Radio France International.

o **TV** Six VHF TV networks carry Thai programming, plus TrueVision cable with international programming.

o **Weights & measures** Thailand follows the international metric system. Gold and silver are weighed in *bàat* (15g).

---

thailand.org/see-do/event-festival) website.

1 January New Year's Day

February (date varies) Makha Bucha Day, Buddhist holy day

6 April Chakri Day, commemorating the founder of the Chakri dynasty, Rama I

13–15 April Songkran Festival, traditional Thai New Year and water festival

1 May Labour Day

5 May Coronation Day, commemorating the 1950 coronation of HM the King and HM the Queen

May/June (date varies) Visakha Bucha, Buddhist holy day

July/August (date varies) Khao Phansaa, beginning of the Buddhist 'lent'

12 August Queen's Birthday

23 October Chulalongkorn Day

October/November (date varies) Ork Phansaa, the end of Buddhist 'lent'

5 December King's Birthday/ Father's Day

10 December Constitution Day

31 December New Year's Eve

Safe Travel

As Thailand has recently been the site of both violent political protest and military coups, it's wise to check the situation before planning your trip. The following government websites offer travel advisories and information on current hot spots.

Australian Department of Foreign Affairs (www.smart traveller.gov.au)

British Foreign Office (www. gov.uk/foreign-travel-advice)

US State Department (www. travel.state.gov/content/travel/en.html)

Telephone

The telephone country code for Thailand is 66 and is used when calling the

Important Phone Numbers

- Thailand country code ☎66
- Bangkok city code ☎02
- Mobile numbers ☎06, 08, 09
- Operator-assisted international calls ☎100
- Free local directory assistance ☎1133

country from abroad. All Thai telephone numbers are preceded by a '0' if you're dialling domestically (the '0' is omitted when calling from overseas).

International Calls

If you want to call an international number from a telephone in Thailand, you must first dial an international access code plus the country code followed by the subscriber number.

In Thailand there are various international access codes charging different rates per minute. Economy rates are available through different carriers – do an internet search to determine promotion codes.

Dial ☎100 for operator-assisted international calls or reverse-charge (collect) calls.

Mobile Phones

It is easy and affordable to buy a local mobile (cell) phone equipped with a local SIM card. Recharge cards are sold at the 7-Elevens. Domestic per-minute rates start at less than 50 satang.

Thailand is on the GSM network and mobile phone providers include AIS (1 2 Call), DTAC and True Move. Thailand finally has a 4G network. Coverage and quality of the different carriers varies from year to year based on network upgrades and capacity. Carriers usually sell talk-data packages based on usage amounts.

The main networks:
AIS (1 2 Call) (www.ais.co.th/12call/th)
DTAC (www.dtac.co.th)
TrueMove (www.truemove.com)

Time

Thailand's time zone is seven hours ahead of GMT/UTC (London). Times are often expressed according to the 24-hour clock.

The official year in Thailand is reckoned from the Western calendar year 543 BC, the beginning of the Buddhist Era (BE), so that AD 2016 is 2559 BE, AD 2017 is 2560 BE etc.

Toilets

Increasingly, the Asian-style squat toilet is less of the norm in Thailand. There are still specimens in rural places, provincial bus stations, older homes and modest restaurant.

If you encounter a squat, here's what you should know. Straddle the two foot pads and face the door. To flush use the plastic bowl to scoop water out of the adjacent basin and pour into the toilet bowl. Some places supply a small pack of toilet paper at the entrance (5B), otherwise bring your own stash or wipe the old-fashioned way with water.

Even in places where sit-down toilets are installed, the septic system may not be designed to take toilet paper. In such cases there will be a waste basket where you place used toilet paper and feminine hygiene products. Some toilets also come with a small spray hose – Thailand's version of the bidet.

Tourist Information

The government-operated tourist information and promotion service, **Tourism Authority of Thailand** (TAT; ☎1672; www.travelthailand. tourismthailand.org), was founded in 1960 and produces excellent pamphlets on sightseeing. TAT's head office is in Bangkok and there are 35 regional offices throughout the country; check the website for contact information.

Travellers with Disabilities

Thailand presents one large, ongoing obstacle course for the mobility impaired. With its high kerbs, uneven footpaths and nonstop traffic, Thai cities can be particularly difficult. In Bangkok many streets must be crossed on pedestrian bridges flanked with steep stairways, while buses and boats don't stop long enough even for the able-bodied. Rarely are there any ramps or other access points for wheelchairs.

A number of more expensive top-end hotels make consistent design efforts to provide disabled access to their properties. Other deluxe hotels with high employee-to-guest ratios are usually good about accommodating the mobility impaired by providing staff help where building design fails. For the rest, you're pretty much left to your own resources.

Some organisations and publications that offer tips on international travel include the following:

Accessible Journeys (www.disabilitytravel.com)

Asia Pacific Development Centre on Disability (www.apcdfoundation.org)

Mobility International USA (www.miusa.org)

Society for Accessible Travel & Hospitality (www.sath.org)

Wheelchair Holidays @ Thailand (www.wheelchairtours.com)

Visas

Citizens of 62 countries (including most European countries, Australia, New Zealand and the US) can enter Thailand at no charge. Depending on nationality, these citizens are issued a 14- to 90-day visa exemption if they arrive by air (most nationalities receive 30 days), or 15 to 30 days by land.

Without proof of an onward ticket and sufficient funds for your projected stay, you can be denied entry, but in practice this is a formality that is rarely checked.

Women Travellers

Women face relatively few problems in Thailand. Dress modestly if you're going to a temple or rural villages and don't wear beach attire off the beach.

Attacks and rapes are not common in Thailand, but incidents do occur, especially when an attacker observes a vulnerable target: a drunk or solo woman. If you return home from a bar alone, be sure to have your wits about you. Avoid accepting rides from strangers late at night or travelling around in isolated areas by yourself – common-sense stuff that might escape your notice in a new environment filled with hospitable people.

Frivolous flirting can unintentionally cause a Thai man to feel a loss of face if attention is then diverted to another person and, in some cases where alcohol is involved, the spurned man may become violent. In cases when foreigners have been senselessly attacked or killed, there is usually a correlation of alcohol and jealousy.

Transport

Getting There & Away

Flights and tours can be booked online at www.lonelyplanet.com/bookings.

Air

Suvarnabhumi International Airport (☑02 132 1888;

www.suvarnabhumiairport.com)
Thailand's main air international
terminal is located 30km east of
Bangkok. The airport's name is
pronounced *su·wan·na·poom*.

**Don Mueang International
Airport** (☎02 535 1253; www.
donmueangairportthai.com)
Located 25km north of central
Bangkok, Don Mueang serves
budget and domestic airlines.
When flying domestically verify
which Bangkok airport is being
used.

Phuket International Airport
(Map p213; ☎076 327230; www.
phuketairportthai.com) Several
domestic and international
destinations.

Chiang Mai International Airport (Map p113; ☎053 270222;
www.chiangmaiairport
thai.com) International destinations include major cities in
some Asian countries.

**Chiang Rai International
Airport** (Mae Fah Luang International Airport; ☎053 798000;
www.chiangraiairportonline.
com) International destinations
include Kunming, Macau and
Singapore.

Air Tickets

Travel agents in Thailand
can help arrange last-
minute travel or travel
changes. The amount of
commission an agent will
charge varies so shop
around to gauge the discrepancy in prices. Paying
by credit card generally offers purchasing protection,
because most card issuers
provide refunds if you can
prove you didn't get what
you paid for. Agents who accept only cash should hand
over the tickets straight
away and not tell you to
'come back tomorrow'. After
you've made a booking or
paid your deposit, call the
airline and confirm that the
booking was made.

Air fares during the
high season (December to
March) can be expensive.

Land

Thailand shares land
borders with Laos, Malaysia,
Cambodia and Myanmar
(Burma). Land travel between all of these countries
can be done at sanctioned
border crossings. With
improved highways and
new bridges, it is also easier
to travel from Thailand to
China via Laos.

Getting Around

Air

Hopping around the country
by air continues to be
affordable. Most routes originate from Bangkok (both
Don Mueang and Suvarnabhumi International Airports),
but Chiang Mai, Ko Samui
and Phuket all have a few
routes to other Thai towns.

Bicycle

Bicycles are a great way to
get around small towns and
historic sites.

Boat

The true Thai water transport is the *reu·a hǎhng yow*
(long-tail boat), so-called
because the propeller is
mounted at the end of a
long driveshaft extending from the engine. The
long-tail boats are a staple
of transport on rivers and
canals in Bangkok and
neighbouring provinces, and
between islands.

Between the mainland
and small, less-touristed
islands, the standard craft
is a wooden boat, 8m to
10m long, with an inboard
engine, a wheelhouse and a

Climate Change & Travel

Every form of transport that relies on carbon-based
fuel generates CO2, the main cause of human-induced
climate change. Modern travel is dependent on aeroplanes, which might use less fuel per kilometre per
person than most cars but travel much greater distances.
The altitude at which aircraft emit gases (including
CO2) and particles also contributes to their climate
change impact. Many websites offer 'carbon calculators'
that allow people to estimate the carbon emissions
generated by their journey and, for those who wish to do
so, to offset the impact of the greenhouse gases emitted
with contributions to portfolios of climate-friendly initiatives throughout the world. Lonely Planet offsets the
carbon footprint of all staff and author travel.

simple roof to shelter passengers and cargo. To more popular destinations, faster hovercraft (jetfoils) and speedboats are the norm.

Bus

The bus network in Thailand is prolific and reliable. The Thai government subsidises the Transport Company (*bò·rí·sàt kǒn sòng*), usually abbreviated to Baw Khaw Saw (BKS).

By far the most reliable bus companies in Thailand are the ones that operate out of the BKS stations. In some cases the companies are entirely state owned; in others they are private concessions. Bring a jacket for long-distance bus trips as air-con keeps the cabin at arctic temperatures.

We do not recommend using bus companies that operate directly out of tourist centres, such as Bangkok's Th Khao San, because of repeated instances of theft and commission-seeking stops. Be sure to be aware of bus scams and other common problems.

For some destinations, minivans are superseding buses. Minivans are run by private companies and because their vehicles are smaller, they can depart from the market (instead of the out-of-town bus stations) and will sometimes deliver guests directly to their hotel. Just don't sit in the front – that way you can avoid having to watch the driver's daredevil techniques!

Car & Motorcycle

In theory short-term visitors who wish to drive vehicles (including motorcycles) in Thailand need an International Driving Permit. In reality this is rarely enforced.

Fuel

Modern petrol (gasoline) stations are plentiful. In more rural areas *ben·sin/ nám·man rót yon* (petrol containing benzene) is usually available at small roadside or village stands. All fuel in Thailand is unleaded, and diesel is used by trucks and some passenger cars. Thailand also uses several alternative fuels, including gasohol (a blend of petrol and ethanol that comes in either 91% or 95% octane levels) and compressed natural gas, used by taxis with bi-fuel capabilities.

Hire

Cars, 4WDs and vans can be hired in most major cities and airports from local companies as well as all the international chains. Local companies tend to have cheaper rates, but the quality of their fleets vary. Check the tyre tread and general upkeep of the vehicle before committing. And do an inspection with the agent beforehand to take note of any existing damage to the vehicle.

Motorcycles can be hired in major towns and tourist centres from guesthouses and small mum-and-dad businesses. Hiring a motorcycle in Thailand is relatively easy and a great way to independently tour the countryside. For daily hires most businesses will ask that you leave your passport as a deposit. Before hiring a motorcycle, check the vehicle's condition and ask for a helmet (which is required by law).

Road Rules & Safety

Thais drive on the left-hand side of the road (most of the time!). Other than that, just about anything goes, in spite of road signs and speed limits.

The main rule to be aware of is that right of way goes to the bigger vehicle – this is not what it says in the Thai traffic laws, but it's the reality. Maximum speed limits are 50km/h on urban roads and 80km/h to 100km/h on most highways – but on any given stretch of highway you'll see various vehicles travelling as slowly as 30km/h and as fast as 150km/h.

Indicators are often used to warn passing drivers about oncoming traffic. A flashing left indicator means it's OK to pass, while a right indicator means that someone's approaching from the other direction. Horns are used to tell other vehicles that the driver plans to pass. When drivers flash their lights, they're telling you not to pass.

In Bangkok traffic is chaotic, roads are poorly signposted and motorcycles and random contraflows mean you can suddenly find yourself facing a wall of cars coming the other way.

Outside of the capital, the principal hazard when driving in Thailand, besides the general disregard for traffic laws, is having to contend with so many different types of vehicles on the same road – trucks, bicycles, túk-túk (pronounced đúk dúk) and motorcycles. This danger is often compounded by the lack of working lights. In village areas the vehicular traffic is lighter but you have to contend with stray chickens, dogs and water buffaloes.

Insurance

Thailand requires a minimum of liability insurance for all registered vehicles on the road. The better hire companies include comprehensive coverage for their vehicles. Always verify that a vehicle is insured for liability before signing a rental contract; you should also ask to see the dated insurance documents. If you have an accident while driving an uninsured vehicle, you're in for some major hassles.

Local Transport

Bus & Public Transport

Bangkok has the largest city-bus system in the country. The etiquette for riding public buses is to wait at a bus stop and hail the vehicle by waving your hand palm-side downward. You typically pay the fare once you've taken a seat or, in some cases, when you disembark.

Elsewhere, public transport is provided by *sŏrng·tăa·ou* ('two rows'; a small pick-up truck outfitted with two facing benches for passengers). They sometimes operate on fixed routes, just like buses, but they may also run a share-taxi service where they pick up passengers going in the same general direction. You can usually hail a *sŏrng·tăa·ou* anywhere along its route and pay the fare when you disembark. There is usually a buzzer inside the passenger area that informs the driver of an intended stop.

Rail

Bangkok is the only city in Thailand to have an above-ground (BTS) and underground light-rail (MRT) public transport system.

Taxi & Chartered Vehicles

Bangkok has the most formal system of metered taxis, although other cities have growing 'taxi meter' networks. In some cases, fares are set in advance or require negotiation. In bigger cities, traditional taxi alternatives and app-based taxi hailing initiatives are also available – sort of.

Uber (www.uber.com/cities/bangkok) was introduced to Thailand in 2014. It quickly gained popularity among those looking to avoid the usual Bangkok taxi headaches: communication issues, lack of change and reckless drivers. Yet in late 2014 Thailand's Department of Land Transport deemed the app-based outfit illegal, declaring that its vehicles weren't properly registered, its fares unregulated and its drivers unlicenced. At the time of writing, the situation seemed to have reached a stalemate, with Uber still operating in Bangkok, albeit less conspicuously.

The good news is that other outfits such as **GrabTaxi** (www.grabtaxi.com/bangkok-thailand) and **Easy Taxi** (www.easytaxi.com/th), both of which operate via already-registered taxis, haven't been affected by the ruling. And in 2015, a domestic alternative, **All Thai Taxi** (www.allthaitaxi.com), had even been introduced.

Motorcycle Taxi

Many cities in Thailand have motorcycle taxis that can be hired for short distances. If you're empty-handed or travelling with a small bag, they can't be beaten for transport in a pinch. In most cities, you'll find motorcycle taxis clustered near street intersections. Usually they wear numbered jerseys. You'll need to establish the price beforehand.

In tourist centres, *sŏrng·tăa·ou* can be chartered just like a regular taxi, but you'll need to negotiate the fare beforehand.

Săhm·lór & Túk-túk

Săhm·lór are three-wheeled pedicabs that are typically found in small towns where traffic is light and old-fashioned ways persist.

The modern era's version of the human-powered *săhm·lór* is the motorised túk-túk. They're small utility vehicles, powered by screaming engines (usually LPG-powered) with a lot of flash and sparkle.

With either form of transport the fare must be established by bargaining before departure. In tourist centres, túk-túk drivers often grossly overcharge foreigners, so have a sense of how much the fare should be before soliciting a ride. Hotel staff are helpful in providing reasonable fare suggestions.

Readers interested in pedicab lore and design may want to have a look at Lonely Planet's hardcover pictorial book, *Chasing Rickshaws* by Lonely Planet founder Tony Wheeler.

Train

Thailand's train system connects the four corners of the country and is a convenient and scenic, if slow, alternative to buses for the long journey north to Chiang Mai or south to Surat Thani. The train is also ideal for short trips to Ayuthaya from Bangkok, where traffic is a consideration.

The 4500km rail network is operated by the **State Railway of Thailand** (⟲1690; www.railway.co.th)

Dangerous Roads

Thailand's roads are dangerous: in 2014 the University of Michigan's Transportation Research Institute declared the country's roads the second deadliest in the world, with 44 road deaths per 100,000 people – more than double the world average. Several high-profile bus accidents involving foreign tourists have prompted some Western nations to issue travel advisories for highway safety due to disregard for speed limits, reckless driving and long-distance bus drivers using stimulants.

Fatal bus crashes make headlines, but nearly 75% of vehicle accidents in Thailand involve motorcycles. Less than half of the motorcyclists in the country wear helmets and many tourists are injured riding motorcycles because they don't know how to handle the vehicles and are unfamiliar with local driving conventions. British consular offices cited Thailand as a primary destination for UK citizens experiencing road-traffic accidents, often involving motorcyclists.

If you are a novice motorcyclist, familiarise yourself with the vehicle in an uncongested area of town and stick to the smaller 100cc automatic bikes. Drive slowly, especially when roads are slick or when there is loose gravel. Remember to distribute weight as evenly as possible across the frame of the bike to improve handling. And don't expect that other vehicles will look out for you: motorcycles are low on the traffic totem pole.

---

and covers four main lines: northern, southern, northeastern and eastern. All long-distance trains originate from Bangkok's Hualamphong station.

Fares

Fares are determined on a base price with surcharges added for distance, class and train type (special express, express, rapid, ordinary). Extra charges are added if the carriage has air-con and for sleeping berths (either upper or lower).

Classes

The SRT operates passenger trains in three classes – 1st, 2nd and 3rd – but each class varies considerably depending on whether you're on an ordinary, rapid or express train.

1st Class Private, two-bunk cabins define the 1st-class carriages, which are available only on rapid, express and special-express trains.

2nd Class The seating arrangements in a 2nd-class, non-sleeper carriage are similar to those on a bus, with pairs of padded seats, usually recliners, all facing towards the front of the train. On 2nd-class sleeper cars, pairs of seats face one another and convert into two fold-down berths. The lower berth has more headroom than the upper berth and this is reflected in a higher fare. Children are always assigned a lower berth. Second-class carriages are found only on rapid and express trains. There are air-con and fan 2nd-class carriages.

3rd Class A typical 3rd-class carriage consists of two rows of bench seats divided into facing pairs. Each bench seat is designed to seat two or three passengers, but on a crowded rural line nobody seems to care. Express trains do not carry 3rd-class carriages at all. Commuter trains in the Bangkok area are all 3rd class.

Bookings

Advance bookings can be made from one to 60 days before your intended date of departure. You can make bookings in person from any train station. Train tickets can also be purchased at travel agencies, which usually add a service charge to the ticket price. If you are planning long-distance train travel from outside the country, you should email SRT (passenger-ser@railway.co.th) at least two weeks before your journey. You will receive an email confirming the booking. Pick up and pay for tickets an hour before leaving at the scheduled departure train station.

It is advisable to make advanced bookings for long-distance sleeper trains between Bangkok and Chiang Mai, or from Bangkok to Surat Thani, as seats fill up quickly.

For short-distance trips you should purchase your ticket at least a day in advance for seats (rather than sleepers).

Partial refunds on tickets are available depending on the number of days prior to your departure that you arrange a cancellation. These arrangements can be handled at the train station booking office.

Language

There are different ways of writing Thai in the Roman alphabet – we have chosen one method below. The hyphens indicate syllable breaks within words, and some syllables are further divided with a dot to help you pronounce them. Thai is a tonal language – the accent marks on vowels represent these low, mild, falling, high and rising tones.

Note that after every sentence, men add the polite particle *káp*, and women *ká*.

To enhance your trip with a phrasebook, visit **lonelyplanet.com**. Lonely Planet iPhone phrasebooks are available through the Apple App store.

Basics

Hello.
สวัสดี · sà-wàt-dee

How are you?
สบายดีไหม · sà-bai dee măi

I'm fine.
สบายดีครับ/ค่ะ · sà-bai dee kráp/kâ (m/f)

Excuse me.
ขออภัย · kŏr à-pai

Yes./No.
ใช่/ไม่ · châi/mâi

Thank you.
ขอบคุณ · kòrp kun

You're welcome.
ยินดี · yin dee

Do you speak English?
คุณพูดภาษา · kun pôot pah-săh
อังกฤษได้ไหม · ang-grìt dâi măi

I don't understand.
ผม/ดิฉัน ไม่เข้าใจ · pŏm/dì-chăn mâi kôw jai (m/f)

How much is this?
เท่าไร · tôw-rai

Can you lower the price?
ลดราคาได้ไหม · lót rah-kah dâi măi

Accommodation

Where's a hotel?
โรงแรมอยู่ที่ไหน · rohng raam yòo têe năi

Do you have a single/double room?
มีห้องเดี่ยว/ · mee hôrng dèe·o/
เตียงคู่ไหม · đee·ang kôo măi

Eating & Drinking

I'd like (the menu), please.
ขอ (รายการ · kŏr (rai gahn
อาหาร) หน่อย · ah-hăhn) nòy

What would you recommend?
คุณแนะนำอะไรบ้าง · kun náa-nam à-rai bâhng

That was delicious.
อร่อยมาก · à-ròy mâhk

Cheers!
ไชโย · chai-yoh

Please bring the bill/check.
ขอบิลหน่อย · kŏr bin nòy

I don't eat ...
ผม/ดิฉัน ไม่กิน ... · pŏm/dì-chăn mâi gin . . .
(m/f)

eggs	ไข่	kài
fish	ปลา	þlah
nuts	ถั่ว	tòo·a
red meat	เนื้อแดง	néu·a daang

Emergencies

I'm ill.
ผม/ดิฉันป่วย · pŏm/dì-chăn þòo·ay (m/f)

Help!
ช่วยด้วย · chôo·ay dôo·ay

Call a doctor!
เรียกหมอหน่อย · rêe·ak mŏr nòy

Call the police!
เรียกตำรวจหน่อย · rêe·ak đam·ròo·at nòy

Where are the toilets?
ห้องน้ำอยู่ที่ไหน · hôrng nám yòo têe năi

Directions

Where's (a market/restaurant)?
(ตลาด/ร้านอาหาร) · (đà-làht/ráhn ah-hăhn)
อยู่ที่ไหน · yòo têe năi

What's the address?
ที่อยู่คืออะไร · têe yòo keu à-rai

Could you please write it down?
เขียนลงให้ได้ไหม · kĕe·an long hâi dâi măi

Can you show me (on the map)?
ให้ดู (ในแผนที่) · hâi doo (nai păn têe)
ได้ไหม · dâi măi

Behind the Scenes

Acknowledgements

Climate map data adapted from Peel MC, Finlayson BL & McMahon TA (2007) 'Updated World Map of the Koppen-Geiger Climate Classification', *Hydrology and Earth System Sciences*, 11, pp1633–44.

This Book

This book was curated by China Williams and researched and written by Mark Beales, Tim Bewer, Joe Bindloss, Austin Bush, David Eimer, Bruce Evans, Damian Harper and Isabella Noble. This guidebook was produced by the following:

Destination Editor Sarah Reid

Product Editors Carolyn Boicos, Kate Kiely

Cartographers Gabriel Lindquist, Wayne Murphy, Diana Von Holdt

Book Designer Mazzy Prinsep

Assisting Editors Bruce Evans, Gabrielle Innes, Victoria Smith

Cover Researcher Naomi Parker

Thanks to Victoria Harrison, Liz Heynes, Indra Kilfoyle, Kate Mathews, Campbell McKenzie, Kirsten Rawlings, Dianne Schallmeiner, John Taufa, Juan Winata

Send Us Your Feedback

We love to hear from travellers – your comments keep us on our toes and help make our books better. Our well-travelled team reads every word on what you loved or loathed about this book. Although we cannot reply individually to postal submissions, we always guarantee that your feedback goes straight to the appropriate authors, in time for the next edition. Each person who sends us information is thanked in the next edition, the most useful submissions are rewarded with a selection of digital PDF chapters.

Visit lonelyplanet.com/contact to submit your updates and suggestions or to ask for help. Our award-winning website also features inspirational travel stories, news and discussions.

Note: We may edit, reproduce and incorporate your comments in Lonely Planet products such as guidebooks, websites and digital products, so let us know if you don't want your comments reproduced or your name acknowledged. For a copy of our privacy policy visit lonelyplanet.com/privacy.

A–Z
Index

Symbols & Map Key

Look for these symbols to quickly identify listings:

- ◉ Sights
- ✪ Activities
- ☯ Courses
- ◎ Tours
- ✪ Festivals & Events
- ✖ Eating
- ⊖ Drinking
- ✪ Entertainment
- 🅐 Shopping
- ❶ Information & Transport

These symbols and abbreviations give vital information for each listing:

🌿 Sustainable or green recommendation

FREE No payment required

- ☎ Telephone number
- ☾ Opening hours
- 🅿 Parking
- ⊘ Nonsmoking
- ❆ Air-conditioning
- @ Internet access
- 🛜 Wi-fi access
- 🏊 Swimming pool
- 🚌 Bus
- ⛴ Ferry
- 🚋 Tram
- 🚆 Train
- 🍴 English-language menu
- 🥗 Vegetarian selection
- 👪 Family-friendly

Find your best experiences with these Great For... icons.

- 💳 Budget
- 🍽 Food & Drink
- 🍷 Drinking
- 🚲 Cycling
- 🛍 Shopping
- 🏀 Sport
- 🖼 Art & Culture
- 🎆 Events
- 📷 Photo Op
- 🔭 Scenery
- 👨‍👩‍👧 Family Travel
- 🗺 Short Trip
- 🧭 Detour
- 🥾 Walking
- 💬 Local Life
- 📖 History
- 🎟 Entertainment
- 🏖 Beaches
- ❄ Winter Travel
- ☕ Cafe/Coffee
- 🦊 Nature & Wildlife

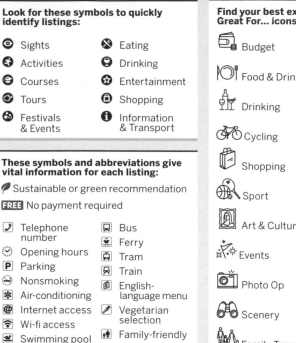

Sights
- 🐚 Beach
- 🐦 Bird Sanctuary
- ☸ Buddhist
- ♜ Castle/Palace
- ✝ Christian
- ☯ Confucian
- 🕉 Hindu
- ☪ Islamic
- 🕉 Jain
- ✡ Jewish
- ❶ Monument
- 🏛 Museum/Gallery/ Historic Building
- 🏚 Ruin
- ⛩ Shinto
- ☬ Sikh
- ☯ Taoist
- 🍷 Winery/Vineyard
- 🦓 Zoo/Wildlife Sanctuary
- ◉ Other Sight

Points of Interest
- 🏄 Bodysurfing
- ⛺ Camping
- ☕ Cafe
- 🛶 Canoeing/Kayaking
- • Course/Tour
- 🤿 Diving
- 🍷 Drinking & Nightlife
- ✖ Eating
- ✪ Entertainment
- ♨ Sento Hot Baths/ Onsen
- 🅐 Shopping
- ⛷ Skiing
- 🛏 Sleeping
- 🤿 Snorkelling
- 🏄 Surfing
- 🏊 Swimming/Pool
- 🚶 Walking
- 🏄 Windsurfing
- ✪ Other Activity

Information
- 🅢 Bank
- 🕌 Embassy/Consulate
- ➕ Hospital/Medical
- @ Internet
- 👮 Police
- 📮 Post Office
- ☎ Telephone
- 🚻 Toilet
- ❶ Tourist Information
- • Other Information

Geographic
- 🐚 Beach
- ⊢⊣ Gate
- 🏠 Hut/Shelter
- 🚨 Lighthouse
- 🔭 Lookout
- ▲ Mountain/Volcano
- 🌴 Oasis
- 🌳 Park
-)(Pass
- 🧺 Picnic Area
- 💧 Waterfall

Transport
- ✈ Airport
- Ⓑ BART station
- ⊗ Border crossing
- Ⓣ Boston T station
- 🚌 Bus
- +Ⓒ+ Cable car/Funicular
- —🚲— Cycling
- —⊖— Ferry
- Ⓜ Metro/MRT station
- ═Ⓜ═ Monorail
- 🅿 Parking
- ⛽ Petrol station
- 🅢 Subway/S-Bahn/ Skytrain station
- 🚕 Taxi
- +Ⓡ+ Train station/Railway
- ⨯⨯⨯⨯ Tram
- ⊖ Tube Station
- Ⓤ Underground/ U-Bahn station
- • Other Transport

Joe Bindloss

Joe was first smitten with Thailand while travelling overland through Asia in the early 1990s, and he has returned more times than he can count over the intervening years to climb, dive, trek and. shop for cooking paraphernalia so he can make Thailand's fantastic food at home. Joe has written for more than 50 Lonely Planet titles, from *Thailand* and *Myanmar* to *India* and *Nepal*. When not on the road, Joe is Lonely Planet's Destination Editor for the Indian Subcontinent.

Austin Bush

Austin came to Thailand in 1999 as part of a language-study program hosted by Chiang Mai University. The lure of city life, employment and spicy food eventually led him to Bangkok. City life, employment and spicy food have managed to keep him there since. Austin is a native of Oregon and a writer and photographer who often focuses on food; samples of his work can be seen at www.austinbushphotography.com.

David Eimer

A decade of visiting Thailand in search of beaches and fine food prompted David to relocate to Bangkok in 2012. Since then, his work as a journalist for a variety of newspapers and magazines has taken him from the far south of Thailand to its northernmost extremities, with many stops in between. Originally from London, David spent seven years living in Beijing, and another five in LA, prior to moving to Bangkok.

Bruce Evans

Bruce first visited Thailand in 1973 and it was love at first sight. He was back there in 1975 as part of a spiritual quest that ended in a Buddhist monastery in Northeast Thailand with the famous meditation teacher Venerable Ajahn Chah. He became a monk and stayed in various monasteries, mostly in Isan. After 17 years, he left the monkhood and worked as an editor and translator in Bangkok before moving to Australia in 1999, where he worked as an editor and managing editor at Lonely Planet until 2013. He now works as a freelance editor, translator and interpreter, and lives in Melbourne with his wife, Lek, and two children, Emilie and Richard. He is stoked to have had the chance to go back to his familiar haunts while researching this book.

Damian Harper

Damian traded a career in bookselling for a four-year degree in Chinese, a decision that propelled him towards the Far East and a sharp change of tack into travel journalism and guidebook writing. Since the late 1990s, Damian has worked on Lonely Planet guides as diverse as *China, Malaysia, Singapore & Brunei, Vietnam, Hong Kong, London* and *Ireland.*

Isabella Noble

English-Australian-Spanish Isabella writes about Thailand, India, Spain and beyond for Lonely Planet, Telegraph Travel and others. A big fan of Phuket despite its touristy reputation (she also penned Lonely Planet's *Pocket Phuket*), Isabella first fell for the Andaman on a 2008 backpacking extravaganza. She lives in London and blogs at www.isabellanoble.blog spot.com. Find her on Twitter and Instagram (@isabellamnoble).

Our Story

A beat-up old car, a few dollars in the pocket and a sense of adventure. In 1972 that's all Tony and Maureen Wheeler needed for the trip of a lifetime – across Europe and Asia overland to Australia. It took several months, and at the end – broke but inspired – they sat at their kitchen table writing and stapling together their first travel guide, *Across Asia on the Cheap*. Within a week they'd sold 1500 copies. Lonely Planet was born. Today, Lonely Planet has offices in Melbourne, Franklin, London, Oakland, Dublin, Beijing and Delhi, with more than 600 staff and writers. We share Tony's belief that 'a great guidebook should do three things: inform, educate and amuse'.

Our Writers

China Williams

China Williams first travelled to Thailand in 1997 to teach English in the rural northeast. Since then she has filled two passport books and has inaugurated both of her children's passports with Thai entry and exit stamps. Before children she wandered all over the US but is now firmly planted in the suburbs of Baltimore, MD, USA.

Mark Beales

After working as a journalist for 13 years, Mark swapped the chilly shores of England for the sunnier coasts of Thailand. Since 2004 Mark has lived in Thailand, where he has contributed to around a dozen books for Lonely Planet, been a TV presenter and dragged his backpack to every country in Southeast Asia. He is currently Head of English at an international school on the eastern seaboard. Mark lives with his wife, Ann, and their son, Daniel. For more on Mark's work, visit www.markbeales.com.

Tim Bewer

While growing up, Tim didn't travel much. He's spent most of his adult life making up for this, and has since visited more than 80 countries, including most in Southeast Asia. After university he worked briefly as a legislative assistant before quitting capitol life to backpack around West Africa. It was during this trip that the idea of becoming a freelance travel writer and photographer was hatched, and he's been at it ever since. He now lives in Khon Kaen, Thailand. Find him at www.timbewer.com.

3 1170 01023 8438

STAY IN TOUCH LONELYPLANET.COM/CONTACT

EUROPE Unit E, Digital Court, The Digital Hub, Rainsford St, Dublin 8, Ireland

AUSTRALIA Levels 2 & 3 551 Swanston St, Carlton, Victoria 3053 ☎ 03 8379 8000, fax 03 8379 8111

USA 150 Linden Street, Oakland, CA 94607 ☎ 510 250 6400, toll free 800 275 8555, fax 510 893 8572

UK 240 Blackfriars Road, London SE1 8NW ☎ 020 3771 5100, fax 020 3771 5101

 twitter.com/ lonelyplanet

facebook.com/ lonelyplanet

instagram.com/ lonelyplanet

youtube.com/ lonelyplanet

lonelyplanet.com/ newsletter